BIG BUNCHES AT
THE JAM FACTORY

We are Only Dead If We are Forgotten

KEITH PAULUSSE

ARPress
ILLUMINATED IDEAS.
EMPOWERING VOICES

ARPress
45 Dan Road Suite 36
Canton MA 02021

Hotline: 1(800) 220-7660
Fax: 1(855) 752-6001

Ordering Information:
Quantity Sales. Special discounts are available on quantity purchases by corporations, associations, and others. For details, contact the publisher at the address above.

Printed in the United States of America.
Library of Congress Control Number
ISBN-13   Paperback   979-8-89389-265-9
               eBook   979-8-89389-266-6
Library of Congress Control Number: 2024907382

Dedicated to unlimited love

To the thousands of friends that died of HIV-AIDS complications. They were gifted with beauty, imagination and creativity and much talent as they stood against societies' dominant and often oppressive forces. They were not only fighting for our rights and their own lives but simultaneously waging a war against ignorance injustice and indifference. These men and women are heroes never to be forgotten.

Acknowledgements

In this age of social media I want to thank my many Face Book friends, who motivated and encouraged me to complete this memoir about our many friends, lovers, partners who died on the battlefield that was AIDS.

I am grateful to the Australian Lesbian and Gay Archives for finding the Big Bunches advertisements and Phil Carswell OAM for reading chapter 13 about the formation of The Victorian AIDS Council and becoming its first inaugural President. To Don Baxter former President of ACON for his eulogy to Arjen Broekhuizen Dutch Journalist specialising in the reporting of HIV-AIDS treatments.

Friends Layne Ramon Shoebridge - Harris, for his photographs of his late partner Ian Harris and their wedding, (commitment service) and our mutual friend the late Robert Brown, Gary Whitelaw former owner of *Soda Sisters* for extra information and photographs. Miklos Ladopoulos for urgently spurring me on to begin writing after viewing pictures of Big Bunches.

Friends who engaged in affirming discussions, Joyce Wong, John Saluni, Daniel Reichard and Cassidy Poon, Leah Devries, Peta Hay, Dr John Wallace, Monique Edwards, DrHelen Driscoll, fellow authors Walter Hes and Peter McKinnon. Not forgetting the enlightening conversations with long term HIV survivors Laurens Hutchins and Ewen my bromance. My Indian friend Vishal Bhagad for keeping me fit and motivated through physical exercise and a vegetarian/vegan lifestyle and meditation.

The AIDS memorials were an enormous resource of checking up on friends passed. I am indebted to the individuals who maintain these sites in a voluntary capacity such as: aidsmemorial.nlstichting NAMENproject Nederland. The Australian AIDS Quilt Project disappeared but I am appreciative to; red-jos.net for displaying most of the Australian AIDS Quilts of our friends who died. In America I used the aidsmemorial@yahoo and in particular Ash Jones' AIDS memorial on Face Book .

Then there was the valiant Dutch Community and tulip flower growers in Australia who stood alongside during Big Bunches' AIDS years supporting the boys who were dying of AIDS and dissipating fears through bringing so much enlightenment comforts and understanding. Several of these Dutchies read selected paragraphs of draft readings of *Big Bunches at The Jam factory* and commented as only the Dutch can do without subtlety but in a nice yet direct tone and manner. I' m pleased to have cogitated with, Hetty Schellenbach, Tineke van Kooten, Tineke Uwland, Adriana Cafra –Wanders, Henk Van Loon, Pieter Den Heten, Evi van der Niet, Jeannette Johanson, Elly Hes, Marianne Verhagen.

Not forgetting my Ghanaian friend Osei Owusu Banahene for producing the Big Bunches trailer and future filming. Kai Jiang for photographic and drawing services.

I'd especially thank my American – Australian friend Dean R P Edwards residing in NYC for being editorial advisor and fixing up my Dunglish into a semblance of reasonable English. Without his pointed questions and editorial skills this book may not have happened. Thank you Dean for the challenge.

Contents

Dutch connections, Dolf, Robbie and Bill.

Meeting openly gay men was a revolutionary act.

There was only two bad things in this world: having AIDS and not being talked about.

Despite the ravages of the virus he still possessed a strong, rugged face with the body of Adonis.

Gay men frequently introduced us to their parents.

There was a certain *je ne sais quoi* around the flower shop.

On Australia Day 1994, Joan was awarded the Order of Australia Medal for her work.

This loneliness caused by AIDS unfortunately occurs when all of one's friends fade way.

Her pastor's son, Dale, had been diagnosed with HIV/AIDS the day prior.

Dale was gay, a fact his doctor impulsively divulged without a smidgen of discretion.

Gordon Archer, the director of the Sydney Blood Bank, had publicly announced that men who had sex with other men should refrain from donating blood.

Many friends with AIDS could not verbalise their anxiety and were often paralysed by it.

It was not always easy to look after people in the early days of AIDS.

Deterioration of the mental and physical states happened so quickly.

Frivolity became an important ally against despondency.

The AIDS crisis had opened my eyes to the cruelty of many churches.

The subject of the talk: Jesus's wet dreams! I couldn't help but chortle.

Organising a memorial service for the tenth anniversary of the firebombing of a Gay MCC church, thirty two parishioners died.

The assault on gay men by Nile and other Christian leaders coincided with the ongoing exposure, from 1983 onwards, of sexual abuse and paedophilia in the Christian churches, across all denominations.

Ian feared he had not much longer to live. I wasn't surprised, as I knew other gay men living with AIDS who wished to marry their partners.

The flower shop was stocked with five hundred hot pink tulips ready for Gay Day at Olympic Park.

Exposing several serious-looking dark blue blotches.

Suddenly, he asked whether I still found him physically desirable.

Umberto compared going to Steam Works or Pokey's on a Sunday night to therapy or having a holiday.

A hormone called oxytocin, without which there was no romantic desire or appetite to bond with another (or, for the men, have erections).

Exploring ways to make safe sex erotic

On 16 June 1983, the Alternative Lifestyle Organisation held its major community-wide public meeting on the unfolding AIDS crisis.

It was practically a family affair, albeit a family under siege, coming together in a time of grave crisis.

Admiring the political acumen of young activists, some with links to socialist and trade union movements.

Many volunteers were facing their own mortality because of the disease and had not yet learnt how to discuss it openly.

There was also an influx of straight women volunteers, which challenged some of the gay men.

All these spices improved the aroma and flavour of the food and, more importantly, awakened our friends' struggling appetites.

Dorothy called out amid the crowd, "Russell wants to know if we have a hazing or initiation test"

A gentle smile or a slight caressing silent touch or hug usually soothed the disillusionment of the moment.

Everyone enjoyed the rich, creamy black forest cake, which was baked and donated by Mordecai, a Jewish baker who ran a cake shop on St Kilda's famous Acland Street.

Our newly unified tribe was no pack of cowards, either: we were fearless fighters up against a mainstream society.

Diverse subcultures within the gay community presented a steep learning curve for me as well: Bears, Chubs, Drag Queens, Leather, S&M, Androgynous, Pansexual, Bisexuals, Queer.

Being driven to the Première AIDS Charity performance of *La Cage aux Folles*.

He bowed and did a quick tap dance as Tante/ Aunt Dolly emerged from the limousine, the group started singing: *"Hello, Dolly, it's so nice to see you again.*

As more gay men fell ill, the Big Bunches bunch joined with other VAC friends seeking alternative therapies.

Tablets, powders, potions and lotions, with little in the way of assurances given by medical doctors.

He concocted a mixture of dried goods: mushrooms, ginseng, grasshoppers, seaweed, and some other pungent herbs.

They all walked on hot coal cinders, and did not get burnt.

"Fire walking, Jack explained, revealed that our state of mind reflected a preconceived set of thoughts and beliefs.

Many people now legitimised their prejudice against homosexuality with spurious beliefs about how the disease operated.

Some referred to us as "the poofter AIDS flower shop"

Police officers arrived at the Jam Factory, along with an anxious, barking police dog, and headed straight to the male toilets.

The question seemed to bother Jason, who brushed away the question with his sharp tongue. "Only if you fuck him without a condom.

Suddenly, Umberto began to sing softly, a tune called "All by

Myself," written and sung originally by John Carmen in 1975, and set to the *Adagio sostenuto* second movement of classical composer Sergei Rachmaninoff's *Piano Concerto No. 2 in C Minor.*

Valentine's Day was a high energy day, filled with emotions and pregnant with romantic hopes.

1985 was not an insignificant year for gay men. AIDS was at its most destructive since the beginning of the crisis.

It took three hours to create a spectacular Valentine's Day display, and with around $10,000 worth of fresh flowers!

Umberto was spoilt by many secret lovers and received no less then eleven bunches of flowers and a kilogram of handmade Belgian chocolates,

We helped write the Valentine messages poems, prose and sayings; "*come my dear friend, my fair and beautiful lover, come to me! Come, you shy and modest hunk*".

Another of our regulars was Jeremiah, a handsome 29-year-old and a Mormon, giving us the biggest order of the day.

The Jam Factory attracted many younger gay people who didn't know much about the broader gay community (or where to even begin looking for one).

Almost everyone was invited to the Big Bunches gatherings that we held on Friday nights after nine o'clock, where we talked in a social setting about issues that concerned the LGBTI community.

Romance or bromance - going on dinner dates, emotionally investing in each other is what they yearned for.

Mindful that some of the potential influences at the clubs were not always in gay peoples best interests; the overuse of recreational drugs and alcohol, and the frequency of anonymous sex with multiple partners.

Former South Australian Labor premier Don Dunstan joined our group several times. Another famous guest joining our discussions was the centenarian Monte Punshon, who was 103 years-old.

We learned, for instance, that Zeus, the mightiest of the Greek gods, fell in love young, Ganymede, and brought him to Mount Olympus as the gods' wine-bearer.

And then there were relationships formed or divorces at these social gatherings.

My late friend and psychologist Bruce McNicol had asked me to assist him with arranging 'personal growth weekends' at Porto Bello near Mount Dandenong.

Attendees at the weekend retreats were challenged about their views on sex and intimacy, family, spirituality, assertiveness.

Her grey hair hung formless over her cheeks and neck, looking like a mess of spider webs, which she continually swiped away from her face with her hand.

In Australian schools Personal emotional development was not usually encouraged; rather, the education system emphasized group conformity and team loyalty.

Perhaps we had not quite got fully around the complex issues of love, eroticism, or attraction, but we all knew that we all wanted to be loved.

Our Big Bunches crew came down to Melbourne International Airport to welcome our dear American friend, the Jewish Polish princess Gloria Jaworski, all the way from San Francisco, with her entourage of friends.

Umberto was not only excited to see Gloria, but also Anthony, the English dancer from Bristol who had trained with me in San Francisco.

Anthony brought another dancer with him from London, his friend Callum.

Why are gay men and women so interested in noting people's idiosyncrasies, their dress and body language?

Often quirky and whimsical she adored glitter and Polka Dots.

The crisis was not limited to the disease itself, but was worsened by the evils of misinformation and fear mongering, most of which came from fundamentalist and conservative forces.

Sitting on the veranda, John glanced at Terry and then me, looking perplexed. "How come people fall so quickly in and out of love?"

Gloria confided in me that nearly all the boys she had brought were exhibiting symptoms of HIV/AIDS.

I knew that meat eaters gravitated to the herbivorous offerings: they'd tuck into it till there was nothing left for the vegetarians, and then they'd move on to their carnivores' banquet!

Death is a part of life but when you are 23 and diagnosed with HIV-AIDS its inevitably looming large; despite this we collectively raised to practice unlimited love.

"There is too much rubbish in my brain at times," Umberto blurted out in frustration at his partner Angelo, who had recently lost his mind to an AIDS-related dementia.

I had called his estranged father Mario, who lived in Italy, to inform him of Umberto's condition.

I won't refer to Maria as the ex-nun, as Umberto had described her. She was no longer a woman of the cloth.

Before I drove to Fairfield hospital I called Abby, a close friend of Angelo's, who himself was not yet diagnosed with AIDS although he showed all the symptoms; the debate as to whether to be tested or not was still raging.

The nurse had said we could dab the coffee on his lips as he could not swallow. Dabbing, holding hands, gently he faded.

The handsome Singapore Airlines crew were welcome money spending customers at the Fashionable Jam Factory.

They frequently sauntered or may be cruised, sipped coffee, people watched, making eye contacts, smiling delightfully.

Eight bright red Banksias sold to him by Jason 30 minutes earlier stuck out of his backpack.

His charm was even further enhanced when a discreetly placed on his firm neck showed a little devil tattoo. Homosexuality remained a criminal offence on the statute book in Singapore and people with HIV/AIDS were stigmatised badly.

Robert started the conversation about some conservative Moslem families in Brunswick practicing female circumcision.

Young Asians studying in Australia, especially students, experienced an entirely new freedom for which they were ill prepared.

Now they could publicly hold hands, even cuddle and wear sexy clothes on Aussie streets, they did not know anything about bodily fluids.

Joanne added that he became very sick unexpectedly after catching a cold in Singapore. He was brought to an isolated ward for infectious diseases and fell asleep.

Umberto suggested that I take him and Robert to Sydney, as it would probably be their last Mardi Gras.

We boarded the plane on what was a very hot day together with wheelchairs, morphine pumps and oxygen tanks.

Mardi Gras from deviancy to moral excellence.

Luke asked if I would carry his photograph the following year.

The Mardri Gras theme was *"Fighting for our lives"*

We focused on Jason because it was his Dutch ex-boyfriend, Wim, whose funeral we had been attending.

He was one of the first people with AIDS who moved into the palliative care unit made available by the Good Shepherd Sisters.

Death brought many emotions and experiences to bear: the awkwardness, the mystery, the deep spiritual psyche that helped extraordinary people to comprehend death, to help humble and often nameless helpers rise above ordinariness.

This time Yetty's *vlaai* had colourful fruits arranged to look like circular rainbow pride flags, which was, even as a small touch, uplifting for us.

Yes, you're leaving, dear," Gloria said, while cupping his handsome face in her soft red finger nailed hands.

We had to challenge the status quo, and its rules and regulations that were discriminatory and inhumane, racist xenophobic and sexist, all at once.

The magnitude of this catastrophic epidemic revealed not only the world of love, peace and serenity, but also the world of force, solidarity and power.

A popular twenty-four-year-old gay man one of our customers , drove to Melbourne's Westgate Bridge, parked his car alongside the bridge's rail guard and;

Umberto had called our dried flower suppliers in Western Australia to order thirty six-red banksias: not red roses, but banksias.

Dirk explained that he was thinking about doctor-assisted suicide, or what is called euthanasia.

I had felt uncomfortable with this sudden snuffing life out by choice and wondered what would drive a person to take such a drastic measure.

It was no ordinary house; it was a large villa surrounded by old elm trees that had survived the cataclysm of World War Two.

I heard her sing *Panis Angelicus*, "Bread for the Angels,".

Toby innocently asked me if I would also like to try "a farmer's boy." I blushed, which he noticed.

There was no safe sex education at any school conservatives would not allow it as they are fighting it now.

Would it have been different if penises and vaginas and sexuality were openly discussed?

Sadness engulfed me as I learned that my Dutch friend, who wanted to join my VAC support group and with whom we had morning tea that day, had been mercilessly shot dead.

We seriously asked ourselves repeatedly if Frank Vitkovic had the opportunity to attend sex education classes at his Catholic school would it have made a difference to his relationship with women later on in life.

Their mother was 73, her 89-year-old father had died the previous year, their mother did not cope well with that bad news.

I barely recognised him, he had gone from a highly confident computer executive, with the world at his disposal, to a frightened man.

Monty was suffering badly from AIDS-related complications until we obtained cannabis oil, which is extracted from marijuana and was illegal.

Our first chat was about Dame Edna Everage, the famous Australian straight drag queen comedian Barry Humphreys'.

I, with 120,000 other readers, eagerly read his popular serial columns about a man called Rick,

His final resting place was alongside a forest the mist moved in at four pm in the late afternoon, out in the forest a lone saxophonist played "Baker Street".

My partner Rob and I have an attic built into the roof-space of our house. Arjen named it – of course – the "Anne Frank Room".

It is a tragedy to think your time is almost over and assuming that your life did not make any difference to anyone that is an even greater tragedy.

HIV-AIDS it had almost psychologically consumed me, I had started to act and think as though I myself was dying of HIV -AIDS.

My involvement with HIV-AIDS had fogged up some of the clear mirrors of my life.

I decided that it would be heaven to visit my "bromance" Ewen who lived in the hills between Byron Bay and Nimbin the famous Australian Hippy town.

People living with HIV are experiencing a range of non aids related co morbidities (co morbidity, the presence of two diseases) are at a higher risk as they age for developing chronic non HIV- AIDS conditions.

Bill's suicide note said he was lonely felt isolated and lost meaning he felt that people like him had faded from public consciousness and he believed that he no longer had a useful function in life and that society had side lined him.

I am eager to capture as much as possible of Laurence's memory because both of us are of the generation that lived through and still lives with the AIDS experience. Each time we meet up it's like performing the past, a replay of the theatre of the memory.

He used to make me coffees at Café *Paradiso*; the cool humidity positively affected my temperament and with coffee it would even get better.

I could hardly believe my eyes what beauty they saw, everything instantly felt romantic even more so when I got out of the 'ute' I was delightfully confronted with a magnificent paradise

Chapter 30 *Eugenella a Gay Household of seven wiped out by HIV-AIDS*

Ewen and Bradley had earlier been part of what could be called a Gay self sustainable farm named Eungella after a nearby town. The farm was created by seven gay urban boys from Melbourne.

I want to touch, kiss and hug it thoughts and more thoughts of peace and calm, overcome with tranquil beauty, this continued as we chugged along in Ewen's FJ Holden ute.

Jeffrey put on some old 75 Bakelite records featuring Al Bowlly then to my surprise he showed me his *Alice B Toklas Cookbook* containing her superb but robust Lesbian recipes.

The Lesbian recipes intrigued us immensely as we had never eaten Lesbian food yes and I have to admit that the food served that afternoon by the boys was a kind of extended orgasm of taste, art and style.

Rodney with his tranquil honest eyes would tell me that he would plant a tree for Julian I asked him if there were other trees in memory of friends that have passed away.

Ewen and Bradley had earlier been part of what could be called a Gay self sustainable farm named Eungella after a nearby town. The farm was created by seven gay urban boys from Melbourne yet I still have to meet a gay man with absolutely no pretences, I mostly see pretentiousness as a sign of a curious mind, a driving force in the art because it entails risks to be different,

Chapter 31 *Their legacy*

To the boys who died as though they were still alive today. I am telling them that they did not die for nothing, their deaths and struggles cumulated in a "legacy of good things".

Preface

Big Bunches at the Jamfactory is the result of a promise fulfilled to my many friends who died or are still struggling with permanent HIV complications that they would not become a faded memory lost in the public consciousness or in an academic reference work.

This memoir is a slice of life that focuses on one seminal event that changed everything; Big Bunches at a micro level reflected on what was happening on a global scale, the repercussions would forever change the way we communicated about our destinies, opening up taboo subjects such as alternative healing and medicine, assisted suicide, homosexuality, safe sex, and cervical cancer caused by the Human Papilloma Virus in women, stopping the sexual revolution dead in its track and accelerating the development of new medical technologies and drugs.

Only at Big Bunches it was personal; confronting HIV AIDS head on young men and their families, touched the deepest recesses of the human soul in a display of raw emotions of joy, sadness happiness or sorrow all capturing the mood of the time. This memoir gives them names and characters forging a symbiotic relationship with these heartwarming touching characters and their personalities.

It is confounding to realise that the friends and lovers we lost during the 80s, 90s are comparable with those young boy soldiers who fought and died in the First World War. Their vibrant voices of memoir are recorded in the Big Bunches journals and are as factual as my mind permitted, bringing with me the pieces of shared memories of friends who lost their lives. They were judged by society because they were different. The media rarely gave a good reflection of homosexuals forgetting that not everyone is a ' shallow scene queen or a salacious party boy or girl' many of us are writers, musicians, cardiologists, cancer specialist, florist, High Court Judges, Presidents and Prime Ministers, Kings and Queens, cake makers, bankers, spies and scientists.

I have underplayed the chronological dates but each chapter is a move forward in time from the before chapter: each a turning point of a new experience, covering themes of the metaphysical, gay romance, friendships, physical attraction, heroism, survival, relationships, death and dying, activism, social justice and fighting for our lives, equality and same sex marriage.

Names and some locations of characters have been changed because some of their families are still alive and continue to suffer from shame stigma and ostracition especially those belonging to conservative religious circles. Real names are used of those friends who have an AIDS quilt made after them.

In writing this memoir I became aware that the human mind is a delightful place of recall as we enter into other peoples intimate lives displaying human truths that make sense of all our lives, writers can do this they often see details other people cannot see. My aim is also to initiate a form of reminiscence therapy for those who lived and loved through those early, dark years of the HIV/AIDS crisis. The poignancy of it all evokes much regret and sadness yet the irony is that it equally evokes hope; in times of stress these memories being relived give reassurance. I realised that dying is not the end of their story but a new beginning as we merge symbiotically with their eternal spirits and expand our own consciousness feeling at one with the universe.

Keith Paulusse

Leopold Victoria Australia June 2018

Chapter 1

Your invitation to a Big Bunches Soirée

T he year is 1985, you dear reader, are invited to a Sunday soirée at the Big Bunches Flower Shop, located at the trendy, chic and popular Jam Factory on Melbourne's famed commercial avenue, Chapel Street in South Yarra. There had been many soirees over the years, this soiree you're invited to is an imaginative gathering of all the soirees joined together for the purpose of this invitation.

I am charmed to be your host, and grateful to have the opportunity to introduce you to some fascinating, creative, and, above all, lovable characters. Many of them are fighting for their very lives. Once you enter their world and get to know them, they will become like family to you. They will leave all of us less fearful of life's problems, and much more joyful. After meeting them, they will be forever etched in your mind. Of that I am confident, for they are forever with me, too.

I have employed pseudonyms where I believe appropriate and as a legal necessity. You will understand that there are limits to free speech, and as a young writer, I don't want a legal brawl. Not that I would defame any of these lovely personalities, but discretion and legal niceties, especially when others are involved, have their time and place.

Let's go have a drink at the bar first. In fact, it's just an ordinary flower trestle, temporarily converted to look like a bar, just for one night. This special night at Big Bunches like all our soirées, we aim to impress in every way. I often call it "the Way of Beauty".

I can see that you are already enchanted. One of our barmen has caught your eye—the young, handsome one sporting a glowing Queensland tan, punctuated by brilliant blue eyes and a gleaming smile of perfectly straight, white teeth. What a beautiful sight to behold!

He smiles at you and holds out his hand, saying, "Hi, I am Robert, Keith's friend." He asks what you would like to drink: a Martini or—for those inclined to sample Dutch favorites—a Bols Genever gin, or some Dutch-style punch. Robert is happy to show you the range of exotic fruit juices we have on offer today, too. He refers to the juices by their French name, I suppose to sound sophisticated. So, will it be a glass of *jus d'orange* instead?

Robert knew I was keeping a daily chronicle of the HIV/AIDS situation in 1980s Melbourne. I remember one day, he spoke to me while wearing a sad, puppy-like expression; a look I have never forgotten, even after all these years. That face lingers in the back of my mind. "How will you remember me and all my friends who are in the same perishing boat as me?" he asked. "As they say, out of sight, out of mind. Everybody will forget us after we have transitioned." By transitioned, Robert meant the almost inevitable, terminal fate met by any person living with HIV- AIDS in those early years.

Despite his worries, I promised Robert that, one day, I would write a book, and not just any lifeless history of those dark days but one with courageous resilient personalities. It would not be a sanitised or merely academic version of events. Nor would it be politically correct. Instead, the idea for a book that Robert and I hatched those nearly four decades ago would be sensitive, respectful, and comprehensive. It would not reflect the politics of the major AIDS organisations, as good as those organisations were and are, or any cooperating governments or officials. We wanted this book to be, above all, a transcription of an oral history of the AIDS crisis, to share knowledge and insights not available elsewhere. We did not want a dry catalogue of names and places and events.

Robert would bring up the subject of the book often, usually over a few strong drinks. He called it "our book". Our exchanges would be humorous, sometimes catty repartees, yet they usually also had a serious edge; they were always warm, emotional, affirming.

"All the boys and girls that will perish over the next few years will leave a legacy of hope, so it will not be a sad book," Robert told me adding, "I don't want to die in vain and be forgotten." Many others expressed similar sentiments to me. I would write about these extraordinary Australians and their families and friends, and those with neither, all of who were affected by HIV- AIDS in some way.

This book is written for everyone, and to open minds to the fact that gay sexuality is not just about sex. These are complex individuals, with stories of their own and some common themes, too: family, love, creativity, finding one's purpose in life. This book also provides a form of reminiscence therapy for those who lived and loved through those early, dark years of the AIDS crisis.

Most of the historical content here—such as the history of Sydney's celebrated Mardi Gras festival, Gilbert Baker and the designing of the rainbow pride flag, the Shanti volunteers in San Francisco—has been pulled directly from my daily diaries, which I kept studiously during those years. But you don't have to take my recollection as gospel, it is only as good as my mind permits. I encourage you to explore the rich histories of gay activism and pride.

Ah, here is Umberto, Big Bunches' chief floral designer and personality extraordinaire. You will get the instant feeling that he is genuinely glad to meet you, and he is. Umberto counts every new waking day as a bonus for him. His charming blue eyes and tulip lips give him an almost devilish look. They melt everybody's heart. Umberto's healthy looks and magnetic personality are both key to Big Bunches' success, yet they belie the reality of his deteriorating condition.

You will notice that everybody at the soirée is attractive and dressed well, remembering that beauty is in the eye of the beholder. You can also see that some well-known people are in attendance, so don't be too disconcerted if some of my artist friends, like Mary Bodkins, are looking for handsome faces to photograph, draw, or paint amid the exotic floral diversity for which Big Bunches became famous. Mary's tasteful nudes are on display. They are being auctioned later for an AIDS charity.

Although I admit that some of our guests look slightly haggard, judging from their slumped posture on the benches scattered around the Jam Factory. I am *almost* sorry for having introduced the popular *Jonge Jenever*—Young Dutch Gin—to them! "Have a Young One!" as the Aussies called it, a cheeky double entendre.

Here comes a cheery personality her eyes lighting up joyfully, "Oh hallo, Love! My name is Dorothy. What's yours?" Dorothy is our wedding and funeral specialist, born in tiny Natimuk in country Victoria to Melbourne's northwest. "Doesn't she look smashing today in her yellow and black polka dot outfit?" asks Ian Harris, a close friend from the Metropolitan Community Church, also known as the Gay Church. Ian heads up a group called WOGS, which stands for Wrath of God Syndrome—a tongue-in-cheek reference to the slur used by homophobic Christians in the 1980s. Yes, Ian, Dorothy is a real gem. Slightly naïve when it came to gay issues, which is not unusual for her generation of country women, and religious of sorts, but not obnoxiously so. She adores all and embraces and loves her gay boys, and they love her in return.

Serving Coffee and tea with homemade pumpkin scones, strawberry jam, and cream are Susan and Pearl. The couple are dressed in their stylishly trimmed Harley Davidson jeans and T-shirts, both wearing studded "real" pearl earrings and bright red lipstick, surely the best of Lesbian chic. These sweet ladies deliver homemade frozen healthy meals on their Harleys during the week to young men too sick to care for themselves and whose families have deserted them.

A young man turns around to say "cheers!" It's Dale: a smiling, blond Aussie Rules footballer and son of a Fundamentalist Christian pastor. His typical Aussie "no worries" demeanor is, sadly, a façade. Those with empathy and intuition can see that underneath, there's a smoldering cauldron of sadness, guilt and anxiety waiting to boil over. I am glad to see that Dale is helping Gloria Jaworski, our colourful Polish Jewish Princess, together with Anthony, a popular salsa and ballet dancer with whom I shared a room (no, *not* a bed!) in San Francisco. They have come over from San Francisco especially for the occasion. Gloria was my landlady and "cultural coach," as it were, which I so needed, when I volunteered with Shanti in San Francisco. Shanti was (and still is) a major, volunteer-driven organisation that looked after the boys and girls living with HIV/AIDS. They were crucial allies in those early dark days. Anthony, by the appearance of things is finding the time for more than a few minutes of flirtation with Dale, while both helping Gloria serve her infamous Polish hash-infused potato cakes to a coterie of adoring young men and women surrounding her. She is making a fuss of everybody and all are easily taken in by her charm, her quaint Polish-American accent, and her stunning head gear. "You're all my *darlinks*," she says with her usual, genuine warmth.

Before we continue, I must introduce you to my dad, Piet, and mum, Bets. They are surely the most down-to-earth and warm-hearted people you will have ever met. I must forewarn you, though: they are typical Dutch liberals, open-minded, frank and honest. The drawback is that they are not always "subtle," a word I am sure is not in the Dutch vocabulary. I know I am biased as their son, but I am confident that you will find them very tolerant, years ahead in their thinking, and good company. They are sort of fearless, a product of Dutch intellectual culture and the generation that survived the Nazi occupation during the Second World War. As you may know, my family essentially bought Big Bunches so that Umberto and his partner could pay for their funerals and other business debts. If you and I are recent friends, I tell that story here in this book. Umberto and his partner were diagnosed in 1982 with a serious condition that later, in 1983, became known as HIV/AIDS. My parents took that initiative well before the gay community was fully organised around the Victorian AIDS Council (VAC) in 1984.

Oh, wait a moment! Mum Bets is talking to Terry and both seem to be enjoying their *Jonge Jenever* (perhaps a bit too much!). Mum likes Terry, a respected and popular legislator from South Australia, where his Party decriminalised homosexuality in 1975. Terry introduces you to his partner, Brian, a lawyer and colleague of mine at Australia Post. But Brian should have been a fashion model, given his good looks and a habit of spending his cash on clothes, haircuts, and his body. By the way, meeting Brian transformed my life, a story you will here read in some detail. It suffices for now to say he invited me to an after-work function at what was called the "Melbourne University Club," a scene unbeknownst to me, a gay social club located in one of the major commercial buildings along Melbourne's tree-lined Collins Street.

If you don't mind, I want you to meet Dennis, our friend from the U.S. Air Force. He will do the honours of introducing you to more guests. He is real eye-candy, as you can tell from the women flocking around him. They are wasting their time, I tell them laughingly, but they won't believe me. Denis is on secondment to the Royal Australian Air Force, inspecting and certifying the new F115 fighter planes. Right now, he is talking to fellow countryman Vito Russo, whose book *The Celluloid Closet*, a study of Hollywood's portrayal of homosexuality in film, had recently been released in Australia. Vito was here in Australia to promote his book and we are having dinner with him tomorrow night.

In the distance, towards the entrance of the Jam Factory, we hear singing. *"Oranje boven, Oranje boven…"* That's Dutch for "Orange above, Orange above…", customarily sung in praise of the Dutch Queen, as Sheila and Kees Tesselaar arrive with the biggest bunch of orange tulips you have ever seen. Kees had told me recently that one of his friends was diagnosed with HIV/AIDS, and he and Sheila wanted to do something positive to help. Other Dutch growers also arrive, including our friend Bill Schreurs, famed for growing celery that was sold across Australia, and his partner, Robbie. We are so glad to have the support of Dutch farmers and flower growers.

We also hear the soft, yet crystal clear voice of Ethel May "Monte" Punshon, the famous 103-year-old lesbian and true Melbourne icon. Later, in 1988, Monte became an honorary ambassador for the World Expo held in Brisbane. She is in attendance with her carer and longtime partner, Margaret. They are enjoying the live Palm Court Orchestra, playing a selection of ragtime music, hits from the 1930s and 40s, and Cole Porter tunes standing next to her is her friend David Kelly music aficionado and manager of the Mighty Music a record and CD boutique across the road from Big Bunches. Monty has much delight in telling us that she met Cole Porter once and that he was a Gay man and that is why we are playing his music today.

Look who is standing at the bar! Our friends from Australia's very own Follies Bergère (well, in my opinion, anyhow!) the cabaret crew from

Pokey's at the Prince of Wales Hotel in St Kilda. Allow me to point them out to you: the gorgeous Douglas Lucas; the one with the fantastic eyelashes, Jan, looking stunning in her tux; Terry; Michelle; the young dancers, Alex and Simon, all in their *American Dream* costumes, ready for a musical night in a couple of hours. I should tell you that before the VAC came along, the cabaret and entertainment venues, such as Pokey's, with their drag queens and loyal gay patrons, were already hard at work, raising funds for the cause, paying for people's rent, food and electricity bills, not to mention that Jan Hillier paid for and installed a colour TV set in every room at Fairfield Infectious Diseases Hospital so that the boys would not have to pay TV rental. We owe them so much.

The Pokey's crew breaks out with a performance of "Boogie Woogie Bugle Boy," a dance routine à la the Andrews Sisters. They are joined by the boys from Soda Sisters, a 1950s-themed American milk bar just along the road at 380 Chapel Street. The handsome Soda Sisters boys serve their customers on their rollerblades and body-hugging uniforms.

It is thrilling to see so many of our new VAC Support Group friends here, too. They are all volunteers. They cluster around Peter Knight's mum, who had just arrived from England. I notice Keith Harbour, who later went on to mentor me in volunteer leadership, and Jim Nagle. Jim had shocked many at his work by announcing to all that he was gay and had HIV/AIDS. His announcement was even more difficult for him having been brought up a Mormon. He was admired because of his courage. It was rare to be so honest and authentic. Jim was a kind and genuine person, as was Keith.

One could not ignore Dirk van Sant, a young Dutch diplomat who had a rollicking, sardonic sense of humour. He gets away with it probably because he is tall, blond, and blue-eyed. He was already enjoying some Dutch punch with Monty van Doren and his mother, Irene. They call out to us, wanting to introduce us to Joep Lange, a Dutch AIDS specialist and researcher. (As a side note, the tragedy of Joep's life is that he was aboard the Malaysian Airlines plane MH17, which was shot down over the Ukraine on 17 July 2014. Joep was on his way to the World AIDS Conference in Melbourne that year.)

What where the afterglows of these soirees? It raised moods and spirits, usually creating a desire for a new experience. Giving straight people and those still in the closet a snippet of what 'Gay Happiness' might look like, imparting a desire for a vicarious experience with the bodies and personalities in the chapters to follow. In the end we too become aware that our individual worlds are made up of dreams. The Soirees were exhilarating, discovering a new world beyond their own daily slog of ordinariness, who doesn't want to experience joyous exhilaration? Often eyes were opened beyond ordinariness seeing a very rich trove of Gay artistic expression and culture, many not aware that such a world existed. Yet the catastrophe of t HIV-AIDS hovered over us continually, nothing in this life seemed like it was supposed to be, there was no end of the beauty of the world and its cruelty, still many did not fear death they seemed to feel a oneness with the universe, we journeyed on.

Ethel May "Monte" Punshon, the famous 103-year-old lesbian and true Melbourne icon. She is in attendance with her carer and longtime partner, Margaret. They are enjoying the live Palm Court Orchestra, playing a selection of ragtime music, hits from the 1930s and 40s, and Cole Porter tunes.

Chapter 2

Smashing Gay stereotypes

Brian was different. He made me feel at ease and said to me, "You're the human relations expert; I am the legal expert". The irony was that he had impeccable manners and a somewhat sweet nature, and a politeness that was not humdrum. Yet as I continued to work with him over the weeks, he could be vulgar, wildly funny and mercilessly wicked.

Life is full of coincidences, some happy, some sad, many somewhere in between. My story at Big Bunches, and more broadly in the gay community, starts north of the Yarra River, that fabled dividing line between north and south Melbourne. In the span of a day, beautiful personalities were to enter my life that not only changed the course of my own identity as a gay man, but also the fight against HIV/AIDS in those waning days of the 1970s. As many young gay men may sympathise, it all began with a trip to the gym.

It was to be a long, hot evening after a tortuous day at Australia Post's national headquarters in Carlton. It was November 1979 and thank goodness it was Friday! My colleagues and I had been drafting an equal opportunity policy proposal for Australia Post's women employees. Not very long ago, they had finally received equal pay, and it was only eight years before that women could retain their government jobs once they married. My boss, Mary Yacovsen, had a degree in psychology and political science from Melbourne University. Sharp as a tack, she could smell and taste the bulldust coming from the old boys' club. She was a no-nonsense woman and could be assertive using few, choice words thrown like a dart straight to the bullseye. Mary proved difficult for some of the misogynists around the office. They were intimidated by smart women, particularly ones with the ambition to take on roles typically filled by men, such as in management. The men around Mary were different and followed her loyally.

Mary sported short blonde hair and stood around five foot four, slim and fit. Most striking was the glow of her bijou, an exquisitely crafted, solid gold bracelet inlaid with blue gemstones. She also wore a small diamond ring on her right little finger. Yet none of her jewellery was ostentatious. Mary once told me that they were a gift from her Jewish grandmother. She also said I was a *"quel beau juif,"* and looked away with a smile, adding under her breath, "such a waste." My French was not all that good and I was too flushed to ask her. Later, I looked the phrase up; it meant "what a beautiful Jew." I smiled. Unbeknown to me at the time, Mary knew that I would go to Sabbath services with a then Jewish boyfriend, as she had seen us at the Cathedral Synagogue on St Kilda Road inMelbourne. The synagogue was particularly popular then with Jewish gay men. I had felt Mary always treated me differently than other men. We seemed to enjoy a mutual affinity for each other's company.

Mary was somewhat of a fitness fanatic as well, and worked out with me at the City Baths. She often asked me to spot her. I think she liked the attention of younger men. She reckoned that a fit body equals a fit mind and, in the work context, must have viewed me as a good balance for her Equal Opportunity Team. She complimented the "Dutch critical thinking into any situation" that I could provide, by which she meant that I spoke my mind plainly and openly, something she may not have easily obtained from a typical Australian male.

Earlier in the day, I had gone to the gym at the Melbourne City Baths for a quick swim and time in the sauna, all in two hours. That was fine as far as work was concerned. Australia Post had just introduced flexible work hours, so I made my way to the gym three times a week. I enjoyed everything that goes on at a gym, especially meeting new people, who, like me, were interested in health and fitness. I even liked the infamous attitude of some of the regular gym bodies. I, too, had some attitude—a good attitude, an attitude of someone who took pride in his youthful looks and strong frame. Nothing wrong, I thought, with a little narcissism, though just enough to build a confident ego. Who doesn't take a gander at themselves in large shop windows? Even the self-deprecating surely steal a stealthy glance. I compared my progress and my body with other young men my age, as we all do at that age. But my self-interest was not some mere inversion of others' self-denial. I believed that to love myself, not in an arrogant manner, I needed to embrace style and elegance, to live a rich cultural life.

Most of my gym mates were health-conscious and positively self-aware. Their gym clothes complemented their bodies with tight T-shirts and short football shorts contouring the aesthetic shapes of the male body. Everyone seemed to be wearing the classic white Adidas runners. I also made many friends and acquaintances who enjoyed dressing quite fashionably outside the gym; fine Italian suits were quite popular then. Serious gym goers were often called "gym junkies," but we saw that as a superficial title. My friends and I at the iconic Melbourne City Baths in the 1970s were no mere gym junkies. We had many other interests—hobbies, sports and cultural pursuits—which we discovered in conversation while relaxing at the all-male sauna. Nowadays, it may sound sexually charged to say one had good conversations in the sauna, but it was a simpler culture back in those days. In some ways, men were not as guarded as they are today. Although, of course, in many different, more critical ways, men back then were more confined by what society expected of their behaviour. The sauna was a good place to listen to men talking about their lives. One might overhear someone say they liked reading Charles Dickens, Stephen King or Armistead Maupin. Another would hook into the conversation and a friendship began based upon common interests. In hindsight, it is odd that footy was rarely talked about. I suppose your footy-following Aussie blokes would not sit half-naked in an all-male sauna. The women, of course, had their own saunas, as there were no mixed gender saunas in those days.

Back at the office, the air conditioning had broken down at the 171

Rathdowne Street office. The temperature outside was well over 36 degrees Celsius and it was humid. At around six o'clock that evening, we finished up work and Mary suggested that we to should have a few cold beers at a nearby Carlton beer garden, where she also would introduce me to the legal team. Well, there is nothing better, they say, than a chilled beer on a stinking hot day. Not that I was a beer drinker, and besides, at 27, I was overly concerned with maintaining my six-pack and did not like the thought of a beer gut.

At drinks, I met Brian. Brian worked for Australia Post's Legal Department and was also a friend of Mary's. He was six years my senior. We had briefly met at the City Baths, where we exchanged hellos and the usual kind of superficial, obvious niceties. "Isn't it a sunny day?" when the sun was shining brightly overhead. Or, at the gym, to say either of us was looking good today. Well, to be honest, most of the people at the gym were looking good quite well all the time!

Brian was the quintessence of looking smart. He wore a well-fitted, black Italian suit (as I would discover, he always wore stylish and expensive designer clothing), which contrasted with the baggier suits his blokey mates would sport, with their beer guts. Brian had on a whiff of some signature scent, a cologne, perhaps English Leather or something like it. His glasses were fashionable, his hair coiffed and coloured by a South Yarra salon. I had heard of the salon before; it was renowned among the trendy set in those swansong days of the 1970s. It must have cost a small fortune. In other words, pocket change for an up and coming lawyer! I, on the other hand, wore smart clothes as best I could, but I never sported the expensive brands. Better yet, my mother, Bets, would sew my shirts according to the latest fashions, and I still went to my usual, unremarkable barber. I suppose my parents had taught me from childhood to live within my means, yet also to look smart. There was a line between just right and ostentation. It was what you would probably have expected from a good Dutch Calvinist family.

I don't know why exactly but I could never quite trust lawyers. I thought they were a bit like used car salesmen, and besides, they twisted people's words for a living (like a number of politicians I knew!) The stereotypical lawyer made me apprehensive about working alongside any, and certainly about forming any meaningful friendship with a lawyer. Besides, I considered that the sort of justice lawyers offered was for the rich and privileged. For working-class types like me, that justice was just too expensive. I also noted that many students studying law came from the upper middle classes. The well-to-do, a spoilt lot, I thought, when compared with me. I had started my first full-time job as a teenager, working at a butter factory in Kiewa.

Consequently, I was guarded when Mary said I would have to discuss the equal opportunity policy with Brian. Inwardly, I felt intimidated. The best thing for me then, I thought, was to be quiet and listen, smile and nod, and above all else, come across as intelligent. I quickly made use of my strengths where I perceived his weaknesses; there seemed to be a competitive edge whenever males start working together. Brian, however, was different. Upon our meeting, he made me feel at ease, and during our conversation, said, "You're the human relations experts. I am the legal expert." I was disarmed by his impeccable manners, coupled with his somewhat sweet nature. Yet, as I continued to work with him over the weeks, he could be alternately vulgar, wildly funny and mercilessly wicked. He said after cold beers that he would shout me at the Empress of China Restaurant. I knew it well, as my mum, Bets, and I would have a meal and a glass or two of the red wines she enjoyed when she would come to the city to shop.

At the Empress, Brian and I joined a few of his other lawyer friends and enjoyed a superb meal with far too much Merlot—a weakness of mine. They invited me to come along to a social gathering called "the Melbourne University Club," which met on the tenth floor at 110 Collins Street. They said I would enjoy the group, and that it was air-conditioned to boot. In my mind, I visualised students and alumni from Melbourne University. Yet the balmy night was still young and I felt relaxed. The Moon hung in the warm twilight sky and added to the intrigue and my curiosity. What would the social world of lawyers be like? I wondered. I agreed to join Brian and his friends later that evening at the Melbourne University Club.

The plain 1950s foyer impressed me. For a moment, I half-expected Marilyn Monroe to sweep through the doors of the lift. 110 Collins Street was a designated National Trust building and Australia's first totally glass exterior building, situated next to the elegant former German Embassy on Alfred Place. As we entered the lift the attendant smiled and handed me a pink nipple-coloured rose. He introduced himself as Umberto and said that he had opened a florist shop at the newly converted Jam Factory along Chapel Street in South Yarra. Umberto was handing roses to the arriving clientele to advertise his new shop. He took us in to the ageing lift as it crept up to the tenth floor, speaking to us in his charming Milanese accent, enthusiastically retelling his entire life story for all to hear—and none to avoid! His mother was an Italian opera singer and his father had eloped with a young nun… The stories continued. All I could do was smile in amazement, whereupon I received another rose. Little did I realise then that my whole life was about to change, to be thrust in a new direction. They say serendipity just happens; a happy coincidence.

Upon arriving at the club, Brian introduced me to many of his acquaintances, nearly all of them being white-collar professionals. But there was a mixture of styles on display: Boy George types, alongside cowboys sporting tight T-shirts and blue jeans, and some Village People as well. Everyone came across as creative and expressive, not insular or typical of the suburban Melbourne I had been used to, and there was an energy there that I had never experienced elsewhere. The disco music so popular then was not thumping loud, and it seemed that conversation was more important than dancing. Perhaps we had simply got there too early; the time was around 9:30 pm. I was not so naïve, however, to fail noticing several drag queens. I even counted at least a dozen or so Dame Edna Everage lookalikes! I had been to clubs like this in Antwerp, back in my native Netherlands, where there were many such clubs. Another notable thing about the University Club was the absence of women. In all, there was a bar, a disco floor, a coffee room for quiet chats, and many of Melbourne's prominent gay men.

I asked Brian if the University Club were a gay club. He hushed me, winking, and said that while it was not a gay club, it just might as well have been one. "This is one of the few places where gay men can be authentic without discrimination or unpleasant repercussions," he told me. Men having sex with other men was still illegal in Victoria in 1979. Brian introduced me to Joe, who came from Portland in Southwest Victoria. Joe and I had first met several years prior, at an antiwar demonstration while the Vietnam War was still ravaging Southeast Asia. Joe was then known as Ken and he had been jailed as a conscientious objector, making headlines across the nation. He was a notorious figure to the average Australian, but for me he was a hero with moral convictions. Here I was privileged enough to meet again the first publicly gay Australian conscientious objector. Joe said he remembered me, too. We hugged and he introduced me to his partner, Angelo, another Italian Roman Catholic, I surmised, given his name and the small gold chain crucifix he wore around his neck. There was Sean, a young Irish-Australian lawyer, softly spoken with penetrating eyes, who enjoyed a Bloody Mary. Sean in turn introduced me to his friend, Vincent Visser, a fellow Dutchman, and a portrait painter who did not look unlike his namesake, Vincent Van Gogh, with his light skin and red hair. (I noticed, however, that he had kept both his ears.) Vincent, incidentally, came over on the same ship as my family and I had, the *MV Johan Van Oldenbarnevelt*, boarding on 9 November 1961 to sail our respective families to Australia.

My new gaggle of friends asked how I felt being in a gay club. Was I shocked? Dryly I answered no, I was not shocked. I am Dutch, I explained, and besides I had no difficulty with any sexuality including my own; one is what one is. I said that I was rather shocked and disgusted by a society that was still so perverse as to criminalise an integral part of the human condition. After being offered several Bloody Marys in the coffee lounge, we were joined by more people around a large coffee table. I recognised some of them from my gym. They were surprised to see me here, as I was straight-acting and always friendly with the women. They seemed apprehensive as to what to make of it all. Perhaps they thought I was an undercover agent, as the Victorian Police frequently raided the club, as so many LGBT venues were back then. I asked them what straight-acting meant, but I thought their answers were skewed by perhaps a lack of knowledge or exposure. Some men, I said, are more feminine, others more masculine, with many in between, and some are what we call transgender today. I was intrigued by the intensity and authenticity of the conversations. These men appeared to display no pretensions. I especially enjoyed their sharp, camp humor, delighting in impertinence and wit to challenge social conventions. This was a different class of people from the crew that I normally associated with, and I liked their honesty and genuine interest in engaging with me. As I was listening I wondered what Australian society feared from such intelligent, literate and down-to-earth men; a wrongly persecuted and misunderstood minority.

After declining any more Bloody Marys I requested a coffee, and I continued to explain to my new friends how I had begun crafting my own identity and had never felt repressed about sexuality. I supposed that had something to do with the longer history of Dutch social enlightenment. The Netherlands decriminalised homosexuality in 1811, under the Napoleonic Code, and Dutch society had long been far more generally tolerant of gay sexuality. I explained that I was a liberated Christian and had the same moral identity as Christ's. Brian, Angelo and Vincent and several others took umbrage with my statement, as they viewed Christianity (or any religion for that matter) as a source of oppression against gay men. Normally I would not have expressed myself with such candour, but these people whom I had just met that evening were interested in my feelings as I was interested in theirs. Much more so then the blokes at the pub or at the footy. There we would rarely talk about the real issues of life.

I realised that it was nearing midnight and had missed my train to Geelong. I thought that I would need to use my new bankcard to stay somewhere nearby, perhaps at the Hilton on the edge of Fitzroy Gardens in East Melbourne. Despite the late hour, some of Angelo's friends arrived only then and he introduced all of them. They seemed to be in a party mood and quite happy. I excused myself and said I would have to get going. There was no shortage of offers to stay at peoples' places. Some joked, saying there were no spare beds in their homes but I could share theirs. As it turned out, Brian offered a spare bed at his place in East Melbourne, just across from Treasury Gardens near St. Peter's on Eastern Hill, one of Melbourne's oldest Anglican Churches. Brian and his partner occasionally attended the church because, he said, it was a safe church for gay men to attend. We walked to Brian's home ten minutes down the road from Collins Street, with two of Umberto's roses in a clean Coca-Cola bottle to keep them fresh.

Brian's apartment was built in the 1930s Art Deco style, designed by the Australian architect Marcus Barlow. Barlow had also designed the iconic Manchester Unity Building, located opposite the Melbourne Town Hall on Swanston Street. Barlow was also the architect behind the equally renowned Century Building, diagonally placed opposite Melbourne Town Hall. I could not have predicted at that time that, in twenty years, I would purchase and live in an Art Deco apartment in the Manchester Unity building. Another of life's happy coincidences. Architecture was my hobby and therefore part of my emotional makeup. I was stimulated by all things beautiful and was certainly enamoured by the aesthetics of Brian's apartment. I felt at home instantly; I imagined in a past life I must have been Frank Lloyd Wright, a world renowned American Architect.

Brian's partner was a well-known, retired Australian politician. I will call him Terry (not his real name). I happened to respect Terry's political colours, yet I was intrigued by his situation. I knew from public coverage that Terry had a wife and I wondered how one's conscience allowed him to live a double life. I figured that, in practice, the ends could justify the means. At the time, I decided that it was best to keep my thoughts to myself, as it was really none of my business. Years later, as our relationship deepened, Terry told me that his then wife was, in fact, a lesbian. For appearance sake and due to his high political office, the happy marriage was a necessary pretence. Their marriage lasted until 1978, when his wife tragically succumbed to lung cancer in her mid-forties, even then a young age.

Mentally exhausted, I was restored after some calming herbal tea and the more laidback conversations with Terry and Brian. All the while I was absorbed by the gripping aesthetics of the surrounding Art Deco abode; the original paintings hanging on its walls, and the many books on the teak wood bookshelves. I loved looking at the contents of peoples' libraries, as it gave me a good idea as to what kind of people they might be.

Following the tea and late-night chat, Terry led me to their guest bedroom with an ensuite bathroom and a peculiar circular bed placed in the middle of the room, with its carrousel frame and blue and white soft woolen blankets and silken sheets. Despite its shape the bed looked inviting. In the distance, I could hear the noise of twilight traffic and the squeaking of Melbourne's trams, a reassuring and comforting sound in a strange bed and place.

The next morning, Terry knocked on the bedroom door, gently opening it a smidge. Smiling, he invited me down to breakfast, where they had prepared an array of freshly baked plain and almond croissants, poached eggs, brewed coffee and squeezed orange juice. He handed me a fresh towel, a clean white T-shirt, new socks, and underwear still in unwrapped packaging, and a new toothbrush. It was so considerate of them, as I had not planned an overnight stay in Melbourne. Apparently, Terry had been up for two hours that morning, shopping for fish and fresh vegetables at Queen Victoria Market, as they were having a dinner party that evening. He said that his friends from the art world would be attending and invited me, too. I declined, not because I did not want to join, but at the time, I felt slightly intimidated by this new and different world. I had already enjoyed one busy evening of meeting artists, authors, playwrights, sculptors, and Terry himself, a well-regarded politician. I was more familiar with the straight Australian crowd, some of whom viewed sophistication, art, literature and style with derision.

Breakfast was served in a separate lounge and art gallery. It must have been obvious that I was greatly enchanted by all the artwork. Brian asked what I thought of Jeffrey Smart, the Australian artist. Not that I was too familiar with Jeffrey's work, but I knew he painted road signs and surf clubs, and considered himself European with an Australian passport. I knew as well that he preferred to paint men rather than women. "Precisely," Brian said, as he showed me an original Smart. I tried to act cool and sophisticated in replying but the reality was that I was overcome by awe. It nearly knocked me off my breakfast stool! Next to the Smart painting hung original nudes by another famous Australia painter, Donald Friend—now that really made an impression on me.

At times in my life, albeit fleetingly, I felt that I was on a different planet in Australia. I thought I did not really belong here, although I was happy. And now, with my newfound friends at the University Club, I was surrounded by people with similar cultural interests to mine, whose emotions and expressions were informed by beauty and culture. Suddenly, it dawned on me that morning why scores of Australians who loved culture moved overseas in those days, who felt compelled to leave. They lived in America or Britain, there to fully discover themselves, to seek out opportunities and earn recognition for their talents.

"The best Australians always leave for overseas," Terry told me. "Think Olivia Newton John, the Bee Gees, Germaine Greer, Peter Allen, to name a few. All sought their fame and recognition overseas first before they were recognised by the Australian public." I agreed and added several more to the list: Joan Sutherland, the opera singer; Sidney Nolan, the painter; Barry Humphries, the comedian best known at home and internationally as his cross-dressing personality, Dame Edna Everage; the author Clive James; art critic and author Robert Hughes, whose world-acclaimed history, *The Fatal Shore*, remains a definitive account of early Australian colonisation. The exception to the exodus was, of course, the renowned Australian author Patrick White, who won Australia's first Nobel Prize for Literature in 1973. To think that, in the 1940s, no Australian publisher would publish White's work, even though his writing was excellent. Was it because he was gay, or because he was not already well-established overseas? Up until that time, not many Aussies knew who he was, except that White was a highbrow homosexual living openly with his partner, Manoly Lascaris, in Sydney. White, like Humphries, satirised Australian suburban life savagely. He was only lifted from obscurity after winning the Nobel Prize.

The breakfast chat was invigorating. It was surreal to be surrounded by original paintings and plenty of books—by White, Wilde, Maugham, Waugh, and my personal favourite, E. M Forster. On a side table lay a well-read copy of Christopher Isherwood's *A Single Man*. The book was dear to me; I purchased my copy in 1968, when I was still a young teenager! Terry was delighted that I was knowledgeable about literature and said he was looking forward to many future dinners where we could talk about books and films. In passing, I mentioned to Terry that, a fortnight prior, I had seen the film *Cruising*, starring Al Pacino. As a leather man, it upset me. Worse yet, until I met Terry and the others, I had nobody to discuss my criticism with. I disliked the dishonesty and the violent sex and gay killings in the film. I contrasted this with *Boys in The Band*, which I had seen in 1971. That film at least portrayed a range of gay stereotypes. Brian and Terry were elated to have an eager conversationalist, and we began plotting future dinners.

Our conversation moved onto the people whom I had only just met at the University Club the previous night. Brian was especially keen to hear my analysis of the characters there, many of who were creative people. I noted how I hadn't met any "stereotypical" gay men at the club. No exaggerated performances or pretences. All the men I met that night had smashed through those stereotypes, perniciously, if unthinkingly, trotted out by Australian television and the tabloids (and perpetuated *very* purposely by the Christian fundamentalists).

Our conversation around that breakfast table must have lasted at least four hours. (I had begun keeping a daily diary since the age of nine, and I made sure to record the many highlights of my conversation with Terry and Brian, and the events covered in this book that were to follow.) We discussed at length the great contributions made by gay men and women to the arts. Imagine a world without, say, Michelangelo's *David*. In fact, it had not been too long ago that a major Melbourne department store had displayed a plaster copy of *David* in its storefront window. The churches and their conservative political allies had demanded that the sculpted penis be covered—so promptly went on a pair of undies to cover the offending material! That should give one sufficient insight into the cultural zeitgeist of mid-century Australia, reeling as it was from the stifling morality of centuries past.

Terry also mentioned D.H. Lawrence's controversial book, *Lady Chatterley's Lover*, which had been censored by the Australian Government for its sexually charged content, until a firestorm ignited in 1965 that led to the easing of the earlier, draconian censorship. The abuse bestowed upon Lawrence's work was similar, Terry said, to the abuse heaped upon gays and lesbians in Australia. He warned that darker times might still lie ahead.

As I noted earlier, Terry was instrumental in bringing about the decriminalisation of male homosexuality in South Australia in 1975—the first Australian jurisdiction to do so. I told Terry that I had remembered the decriminalization vividly, as I was a member of a fundamentalist Christian church at the time. My pastor and fellow parishioners were appalled. Surely it was a sign of the end times, they said! The moment was a clarifying one for me personally, as an issue of faith and social values.

My gracious hosts asked me again to join them that night for dinner as their special guest. Apparently in attendance would be the nonagenarian Ethel May "Monte" Punshon, the first woman to hold a motorcycle licence in Victoria, a great conversationalist (even at the age of 97), artist, and, infamously, an open lesbian. I was tempted to say yes, but relented. I did not want to wear out my welcome. It seemed, however, that at Brian and Terry's place new careers and connections were launched. No wonder, I thought, that their lives were the epitome of living productively. They were both successful in their careers and promoted the arts through their social life and activism. I was humbled to be in their company and to be considered a friend, and I was inspired. I was desirous of their *gezelligheid*, a Dutch term best approximated in English as "cosiness," and was eager to continue the journey started amid these brave gay men.

On the 7ᵗʰ floor 100 Collins Street the first true multi-story commercial "glass box" building in Australia, the first building in Australia to express the new international Modern aesthetic as opitomised by New York's Lever House. It certainly befitted to have a Gay Club, "The University Club" in this smart building situated on the "Paris end of Collins Street.

*I don't make a habit of interrupting this story with footnotes, but I believe one is in order here. I employ the term "gay community" here and throughout *Big Bunches*. While much of what is discussed here affected lesbians, bisexuals, transgender and other non-heterosexual sexualities, I use "gay community" because of the particular effect of the HIV/AIDS crisis on gay men, and my involvement in the gay community in the fight against the disease and social injustice

Chapter 3

Work hard and be nice to people

"Life is often like this: it offers us unexpected things every day, yet many don't see it when their lives are in a rut. We are all connected, and there is no such thing as being alone. Loneliness is a state of mind. The solution lies in the willingness to let go and to take up the gifts that life is offering."

Mary had just returned from her lunchtime gym session. She was still sporting a post-exercise blush when she announced some pleasant news. She invited me to join a summer program in Social Psychology, to be held at the University of California's famed Berkeley campus. She asked whether I were interested. Just to think: I would be within stone's throw of San Francisco, one of the gay meccas of the Western world! I was instantly excited. I was about to jump out of my skin when Mary added some caveats: I would be responsible for my own travel and accommodation, and the time spent away would come out of my annual leave. The decision was still an easy one for me. The thought of encountering a different culture and new social environments, to explore a new horizon of humanity discovering what it means to be authentically and fully human. I said yes.

Within the hour, I was with Maarten Dorp, a travel agent whom I met at the University Club on my first night. Maarten promised me a very good deal with Pan Am and I booked my tickets with my brand new Bankcard. I was going to be on my way to San Francisco.

The summer school theme was "Discovery of the Changing Self." The idea of changing one's life had always intrigued me. I grew up as a migrant, after all, and much of my childhood was spent adjusting to new cultural norms, from Dutch origins to our new Australian reality. I remember looking out at the open sea as an eleven year-old, sitting on the sun deck of the *MV Johan van Oldenbarnevelt*, en route to Australia. The endless horizon awakened my consciousness, and I realised then that I was different than other boys. I was thinking about creating my own identity.

My life had greatly changed since my first visit to the University Club. I was busy weaving a network of new friends and discovering a refined culture of music, literature and tight-knit relationships, consisting of sensitive, intelligent and, above all, authentic people. New Renaissance types. My father, Piet, had encouraged me from an early age to be a Renaissance man: someone who possesses a range of skills and interests. For example, Leonardo Da Vinci, a gay man, was the epitome of a Renaissance man. Leonardo was a highly accomplished painter, scientist, engineer and mathematician—and with social skills to boot. I was now meeting these sorts of people. I knew such a world existed somewhere, but up till that time, I had not found it anywhere in Australia. Now I could explore this world, or at least our little corner of it in Oceania. How poles apart my new friends were from the fundamentalist Christians I had known in childhood! Of course, I had always realised that the fundamentalists were lying about homosexuality, but now I could call home a new community, one free from that malice and false love. I regularly received invitations from my new friends, to dinner, coffees, outings to the opera and art galleries. I also increasingly held dinner parties at my house. My vegetarian cooking and knowledge of wines improved as a welcome result.

I had been staying with my parents in Leopold, a suburb of Geelong, when it was time for me to travel to the United States. I was recuperating from the flu at the time, and my mother, Bets, had been nursing me back to health. The night before my departure, she made me rub my feet with a layer of Vicks Vapour Rub. As though a miracle, the symptoms abated and I felt renewed by the next morning. In the early hours of the morning, on a balmy and sunny winter day in August 1982, we drove to Melbourne's Tullamarine International Airport.

Umberto surprised me by coming all the way from the Jam Factory to the airport, carting a huge bunch of various native Australian dried flowers. Just as well they were dried, I said, as I could not take the flowers with me on the plane! Umberto laughed and said his mind was not working as well as it should and that he had been sick of late. Terry, Ken, Angelo and other friends also joined Umberto and my family to wish me safe travels. Our family always made it a big deal to farewell loved ones at the airport. At times, we would travel with two full cars to say our goodbyes or welcome relatives and friends from the Netherlands. I could not help but think of my uncle Bram, who died in a KLM Constellation passenger plane crash in 1957, on the island of Biak, then part of Dutch New Guinea. The crash killed 76 passengers and crew; there were no survivors. I remembered my father, Piet, regretting that he did not say his proper goodbyes to Bram.

My mum had a fairly long chat with Umberto and liked his personality immediately. She later described Umberto to me as warm, authentic, intelligent, creative and loveable, just the sort of person the world needs more of. My mother took Umberto's gift of the dried flowers home with her. Those flowers were to last for years in her home, becoming a cherished souvenir of those happy times.

I hugged everybody before parting ways for Customs. I showed my passport to the officer, who, stamping it, noted that the first stop was Hawaii. "Don't forget to visit Queen's Surf beach," he said. "You will meet lots of friends there," he added, giving me a wicked wink as he handed back my passport. I smiled back and told him not to be cheeky.

As I made my way onto the plane, I was greeted by the friendly crew. Terry had introduced me to several of them prior to boarding. He probably was not aware but I had actually met one of them earlier at the University Club. The air stewards wore their smart uniforms, gossamer hair and white sparkling smiles, and welcomed us aboard the new Jumbo Jet, a Boeing 747. I was happy to be escorted by one of the stewardesses, who must have been in her fifties, wearing little makeup but sporting the most sincere smile. A wave of the hand pointed to my window seat that I had requested months ago. I didn't want to be packed in the middle of a four-seat row, much like sheep on an Australian transport bound for the Middle East!

It was not long before another person sat next to me. A young man listening to his Sony Walkman, so loud in fact that I could hear Freddy Mercury's "Bohemian Rhapsody" exploding from his trendy earphones. At least he had a romantic streak about him, I thought to myself then. I looked up to find a tall, slender man. I flashed a quick smile. He casually unplugged his earphones and returned a disarming smile, introducing himself as Jason. I was impressed by his confidence, something I didn't lack myself. I replied that I also enjoyed Freddy Mercury, in the hope that would spur on further conversation on common interests. It was refreshing to have someone to chat to on what was, and remains, an interminable flight from Australia to the United States.

Jason's voice was unique; it was mannered yet not affected. The rhythm of his speech belied his Australian origins. He said that he liked my accent and Dutchmen all in one breath, and he wondered why I retained a slightly Dutch accent after so many years in Australia. I replied that it was because of my education. People asking about my accent is a minor annoyance for me, yet it also amuses me. Not a day seemed to go by where I had to explain my accent and origin story. I liked to reassure myself that at least I was not being ignored. However, I knew instinctively that Jason was interested in me. (Sometimes you can just tell, can't you?) Jason was a medical researcher who was also attending a summer school in the U.S., not far from where I was going to be based. We were engrossed in conversation when we realised that we were high up in the sky, with Lake Eldon in Gippsland already far beneath us.

Jason happened to not only live in one of the Art Deco apartments near my house on St Kilda Road, but he also knew Umberto. He had noticed Umberto at the airport with the large bouquet of dried Australian natives, but he hadn't made the connection between Umberto and me. My mind flashed to the theory of "six degrees of separation." My family would often play a game around the theory in the Netherlands; back there, in densely packed Europe, it seemed one had a connection to everyone! It was a comfort to know that so many of us are close, but with Jason I had reached just two degrees of separation. He knew so many of my acquaintances, even though we moved in different circles. Then again, he was a sort of Renaissance man and we had much in common. My first impression was that Jason came across as arrogant, but on further reflection, I fear I might have been projecting my own insecurities onto him. As it was, we were destined to become lifelong friends.

Jason explained that he was doing research into blood cancers, such as leukemia, and that he had a research paper on lymphoma being reviewed in the U.S. He found the review process daunting but he was confident in his research. We shared notes about our respective studies, but kept mentioning several times that he had heard there was some sort of "gay disease" in the U.S. and that it appeared to be spreading fast. He didn't know much about the disease or the situation, except that several hundred gay men appeared to have already perished from the disease. He wasn't aware of the symptoms but warned me to be on guard. "No sex in the States," he advised, adding that that proposition would be difficult for him, too. He confessed that he was always looking for love in a handsome face and intelligent mind. "Maybe like I am experiencing with you right now," he said coyly. I couldn't help but smile an embarrassing smile and managed to mumble a "thank you."

The news about the "gay disease" caused me to reflect on recent events concerning people I knew. Several acquaintances—two in Melbourne returning from the U.S., and one in Amsterdam—had suddenly fallen ill with a form of opportunistic pneumonia. It was a rare disease for healthy young men and indicated a weakened immune system. Antibiotics battled hard to bring the nasty bug to heel.

Jason's first concrete advice to me was to avoid San Francisco's saunas. That puzzled me initially, as I had always gone to the Melbourne City Bath's saunas. When I explained that to Jason, he laughed and said the Californian saunas were a different sort. I was embarrassed at my naivety. Jason went on to explain that the saunas were places for recreational sex among gay men, but that they were also popular social haunts, safe havens for gay men to congregate and experience cultural life together. Apparently straight men would attend saunas, too, perhaps to escape their mundane suburban lives and girlfriends. I was awestruck by this information and we continued to discuss U.S. bathhouse culture, all of which was new to me. I learned that many famous artists launched their careers in the American bathhouses: the Andrews sisters, Shelly Ackerman, Chubby Checker, Natalie Cole, Connie Francis, even the Australian songwriter Peter Allen. Nearly all of them being my father's favourite singers! "Wait till I tell him," I chuckled. Bette Midler had come to prominence singing in New York City's Continental Bathhouse cabaret lounge, giving rise to her nickname "Bathhouse Betty." Barry Manilow was her pianist. The gays had made all these people famous, including the famous opera star Barbara Cook. I knew her music well, but was astounded to learn she sang opera at bathhouses. My gay cultural information was appallingly lacking, but Jason told me not to worry too much.

We discussed our mutual love for reading as well. I had my copy of Marcus Clarke's *For the term of his natural life*, an unofficial biography of Rufus Dawes, a British convict transported to Australia for a murder he didn't commit. It was a semi-fictionalised account that left its mark on Australia's colonial history. I enjoyed reading histories and about social justice. I told Jason this was my fourth copy of the book, as I read it on every long-distance flight and my occasional journeys to the Netherlands, clocking in at 28 hours total, were indeed very long. I would always hand off my copy at the time to friends living overseas; at the very least, they would gain some understanding of Australia's history and national character. Jason had removed a copy of Armistead Maupin's gay novel *Tales of the City* from his stylish brown leather backpack. He shared some passages with me, to see whether I found them funny or interesting. The excerpts were raunchy and clever, filled with innuendo, and involved affairs and plenty of penises and vaginas. I admitted I didn't find them particularly interesting, as far as my tastes in literature were concerned. Wasn't there more to life than one's escapades in the bedroom? I offered. Relationships needn't involve sex and could be as simple as what we had enjoyed on that flight. Jason smiled at my reply and brushed my cheek with his warm hand. "You're sweet," he said.

Nineteen hours was a long time to sit next to a virtual stranger, sharing all manner of thoughts. It was refreshing therefore that I was seated next to Jason, a critical thinker willing to express his own informed opinions. Sweet man that he was, Jason put one of his earpieces into my left ear, as he wanted to share his music with me. "Listen to some Ella Fitzgerald," he said. What a sensitive and attentive man, I thought, sharing what an average Aussie bloke from the footy or pub would never do. They'd think it would be kind of queer, wouldn't they? I had said earlier that I liked 1930s and 40s jazz singing, and here was Ella singing "It's De-Lovely."

"Hopefully, you'll remember me every time you hear that song," Jason said. "It will be our song. I told you in the first minute I met you that I liked Dutchmen because they are straightforward, honest, well-presented, tall and handsome"—he was full of praise—"you seemed to be all of that except you are much more subtle than most Dutchmen I know." I was blushing but managed to thank him graciously. He gave me his contact details in the U.S. and exhorted me to read Maupin. The plane landed in Hawaii, where I would stay for four days relaxing on Waikiki Beach—at least that was the plan. Jason was continuing his travel and said he was sad to leave me in Hawaii. He added that this was the most enchanted flight he had ever been on. We promised to meet again in San Francisco in several weeks' time.

My first thoughts on arriving in Hawaii were that I felt transported back in time and space to the 1950s. I half-expected to see Elvis riding in one of those big, colourful American convertibles coasting down the highway from Honolulu Airport to Waikiki Beach. Terry had booked me a hotel room overlooking the ocean, and after checking in, I made my way to the beach to relax and swim. I found the beauty of the islands enchanting and the Hawaiian Americans polite and personable. They were a world away from the casual aloofness of Australians. Americans, on the other hand, would actually stop to talk, and take their time! In Australia, I found most Aussies very friendly but reserved when it came to talking to strangers. Consequently, the Americans won me over on personality stakes.

At Waikiki Beach, two attractive young women invited me to join them. They complimented my accent. "It's Australian, isn't it?" one asked, which made me smile. We walked over to another Australian, who they wanted to introduce me to. It turned out to be none other than the renowned Australian singer-songwriter Peter Allen, who had co-written "Arthur's Theme (Best that you can do)", from the film *Arthur*, which won the Academy Award for Best Original Song in 1981. Peter said it was refreshing to hear another Australian accent. I was lapping up the recognition as an Australian. Back home, I was always singled out for the Dutch twinge to my accent. Here, I was practically a full-blooded Aussie. Peter wished me well during my time in the U.S. and said he hoped that I fell in love in New York City or San Francisco, giving me a cheeky Australian grin. After all, wasn't his music often about falling in love? He also invited me to stay at his place in San Diego, should I ever visit. I was over the Moon. Peter delighted me even more when, surprisingly, he asked whether I knew Umberto from Big Bunches in Melbourne. My jaw must have dropped; I was speechless for what seemed like minutes. A small world, indeed.

The young women introduced me to several others during our time at the beach. A friend of Peter's, a handsome Japanese-Hawaiian named Derrick, who was around my age. He studied American History at Honolulu University. I would spend the next four days with Derrick as my guide around Hawaii. We would fly to the island of Maui, where we explored the old state capital and climbed the island's impressive volcanic mountains. We happened to come across American astronauts practising their lunar walks over the lava-strewn mountains, and ate at places with funny names like Hamburger Mary and Joe's Greasy Spoon, and numerous salad bars. There were plenty of options for vegetarians. No wonder everybody looked so healthy in Hawaii!

Friendships are valuable things and I was grateful that I could form instant bonds with people like Jason and Derrick, generous souls who were also fellow travellers in life. I count myself fortunate in that regard. Life throws a lot of unexpected things at us daily—from personal woes to crises with family and friends. Meeting new faces was important for my own formation, and a way to experience life more fully. Loneliness is a state of mind, I found, and a solution lay in my willingness to let go of things out of my control, and to embrace the gifts that life offered. These early friendships, made in my first days away from home and Australia, encouraged me as I prepared for what awaited me in San Francisco and, in some ways, the challenges that still lay ahead.

Sensuous Instincts

"Human beauty, in its simplest natural form, is physical attraction and our central motivation to find beauty is enjoyment; the main obstacle seems to be attachment."

The weather was very mild in California, even in late September, which is not uncommon for the Bay Area. I had settled into my accommodations at the University of California at Berkeley, not far from the hub of San Francisco across the bay. I attended the customary student orientation and welcoming parties, but I chose, for the most part, to be quiet so as to observe more intently my new surroundings. There was a mix of people: male and female, of different ages and ethnic backgrounds, from Europe, Brazil, Australia, Indonesia, South Africa. The majority, however, were Americans.

My group mostly consisted of Social Psychology majors. We were very similar in personality type, too, even down to the food we ate. Most of us were vegetarians and interested in maintaining a healthy and harmonious lifestyle. I estimated there were about eleven gay men in our group of 50. I hazarded that guess based on my interactions with the others. In my experience, gay men, as opposed to straight men, seemed to be more socially responsive and not as self-centred. We had come out of some sort of suffering, even those like me, who had enjoyed an easy-going childhood. We still fought for our place in society. Straight men, on the other hand, had it relatively easy: They were already equal before the law and experienced no discrimination, insofar as it came to their sexuality, in employment and housing, as many gay people faced regularly.

The first three days were largely spent getting to know each other. I shared a room with Pieter Botha from South Africa, a Clinical Psychology lecturer at Witwatersrand University in Johannesburg. When we first met, I remarked that everybody in South Africa seemed to be called Botha. As it were, Pieter turned out to be related to the then prime minister of South Africa, also called Pieter Botha. Pieter was a good-natured man and married to the love of his life, Betsie. He considered the Dutch as cousins, given the Afrikaners' historical ties to the Netherlands, so we got along swimmingly.

Several of us picnicked on the Berkeley campus lawns on the second day of being there. I was primarily conversing with Anthony, a young dancer and actor, who also travelled a great distance to attend the summer school. Anthony hailed from Bristol in the United Kingdom—almost as far from Berkeley as Melbourne was. Anthony wanted to talk to me about "the way of beauty," as he had heard me mention it several times during our tutorials. There was a ring to the phrase "the way of beauty" that obviously appealed to him, especially when there were so many negative attitudes surrounding queer sexuality. Of course, I was not talking about new ideas myself. Plato had beat me to it by a couple thousand years, when he spoke about "the way of beauty" as the height of aesthetic experiences. The idea went something like this: Our first interaction with beauty is involuntary, an emotional response to the physical attractiveness of others, usually in the form of sexuality and its promised pleasures. As we move further into our appreciation of beauty, we begin to value things such as intelligence. The summit of beauty is that of the intellect, of its lucid harmony, its truth and power, such as the beauty of mathematics, philosophy and science. I paraphrased Plato's words for the 20th century. It was in our minds, he said, that we appreciate beauty or ugliness; the choice is ours. "Absolutely everything is rooted in attitudes!" Anthony exclaimed, whereupon he gave me a kiss on the cheek and said, "I agree so much with you, thank you."

Anthony had been invited to dance at the forthcoming San Francisco Lesbian and Gay Freedom Day Parade, the forerunner of what became Gay Pride. He was chosen not only because he was eye-candy; but a professional salsa dancer. It did not surprise me that Anthony was chosen to grace one of the parade's truck platforms. He had such a positive disposition, with an athletic body. I knew that salsa dancing is sensual, which would appeal to the spectators, who would doubtlessly desire Anthony's body. Perhaps it would encourage them to take up healthy living and fitness, to gain confidence by looking desirable themselves. Nobody looked good from consuming destructive foods or too much alcohol and recreational drugs. There was little tolerance in our training group for swelled heads, know-it-alls, or self-deceivers. There were a few Evangelicals in our group; they were, of course, sure of everything because they spoke to God and God answered them.

Good looks don't usually come naturally: the whole human package—body and mind—needs to be exercised and the mind cultivated towards the way of beauty. Anthony stood up to stretch and performed a few salsa moves. The others watched and clapped. As he finished Anthony bowed and curtsied to more clapping, although the second round of applause was perhaps not so much for the dancing but rather for his delightful character and English accent. His was the consummate beauty of body and mind. I could have fallen in love with Anthony, but there were so many pleasing boys like him around San Francisco. Falling for any one of them was out of the question: I needed to apply myself not to romance but to disciplined study. Most of the time I succeeded, but not always. Jason had contacted me already. He wanted to take me out to a bathhouse where Bette Midler was performing. I told my roommate, Pieter, about my intended visit to the bathhouse with Jason. He promptly asked me if he could join. That was no problem, I replied, but what about Betsie?

Several more friends joined the picnic as the hours stretched on. While there was no food left to share, the others joined just the same for convivial bonding. Remember that, at that time, the counterculture had not run its course, of all places certainly not in San Francisco. The hippy movement was still in its afterglow in the Bay Area; some San Franciscans, in fact, still wore flowers in their hair.

Making friends paid off; the way of beauty always pays its dividends. My new friends invited me to interesting personal growth events. One of the events was hosted by a Christian Gay support group named, Seventh Day Adventists Kinship, they were having their annual retreat called a "Kampmeeting" in Julian a small town, about 100 kilometers east of San Diego. It was an exciting adventure to hire and drive a car on my own from Los Angeles down to Julian, especially given the Americans drove on the wrong side of the road! The route was packed with tourist attractions along the way, including the renowned ocean liner, the decommissioned RMS Queen Mary (heaven for an Art Deco freak like me). Nearby was Howard Hughes' infamous Spruce Goose. Both had been long since retired from service, but each was a testament to their creators' sense of beauty in form and function. I was transfixed by the natural beauty en route, and the people I encountered along the way were interesting, too. I stopped at rest stops, diners, petrol stations. To me, it seemed like the U.S. was one large smiling face; everyone in California seemed to have perfect white teeth and a Hollywood smile.

Alongside the road there were many hitchhikers thumbing for a lift. Some held up cardboard signs on which they had scribbled where they wanted to go. There were pretty women, young men with very short hair, and I am sure, if I remember correctly, they all wore clip-on sunglasses with tortoise frames. But I realised that I was amidst a gun-toting culture, so I was not going to be beguiled by pretty smiles and sharp looks. I had enough street smarts to know that much. My father Piet had long ago taught me not to trust anyone freely but always to be trustworthy myself. However, I had to stop for one of these clip-on tortoise shell sunglasses types—a young man sporting a white, tight T-shirt. I thought some company would be good, plus he was attractive and, well, it would be good to have a local tour guide. It is interesting how one can rationalise something one would otherwise never do, particularly when a handsome face is involved.

His name was Sandy. I learned Sandy was a sailor in the U.S. Navy, hence his tight white shirt. He would be a safe passenger, I thought, as I knew there was a large U.S. Naval Base near San Diego. And while he had a smile as wide as the South Pacific, he was smaller than me, so I calculated quickly that in an altercation I could fight him off. I needn't have worried, however, as Sandy proved to be delightful company and a chatterbox, too. He was so trusting that in about ten minutes flat, he had practically recounted his whole life to me. I figured that these quick self-revelations are a cultural trait of Americans, who were self-centred in many ways, some good, some bad. Sandy also said he was gay (not that I could half tell), but that was a secret to his straight counterparts or an unperceptive mind. Sandy kept his sexuality a secret, as, in those days, openly gay men could not serve in the U.S. military. If the U.S. Navy discovered his sexuality, he would be dismissed, like any queer soldier or sailor, including his girlfriend, a lesbian who also served in the Navy as a first lieutenant. He said the whole pretence of a fake relationship and living a constant lie worried him, but as he said, that is what American society wanted and it was easier that way, at the time. Unauthentic, dishonest lives don't live as long, I feared; worry wears down the human immune system, and can lead to rash decisions.

My intrigue got the better of me; I queried him why he so readily exposed his intimate personal life to a stranger like me. Quick off the mark, he replied, "Well, you're Dutch." He could tell from my accent and had worked alongside plenty of Dutch sailors in the Navy. Sandy found the Dutch to be open and tolerant, and never heard them judge people because of their being different. I was honoured that he was inclined towards the Dutch because of our reputation as humanitarians. "Yes," he repeated cheekily, "I love the Dutch." "Sandy" I said, "are you just saying this, as well as being so friendly, because you want me to like you?" He chuckled, as did I.

It was lunchtime. Time to visit a diner with a salad bar and Sandy had had one in mind. It seemed as though half the Navy were there, as Sandy seemed to know everyone in the joint. I was taken aback by the vivaciousness of Americans and kept quiet, preferring to observe my company for a while.

Sandy later invited me to stay at his parents' place overnight so I would be refreshed the next morning to recommence my trip to Julian. I agreed and we drove to his family home nearby. Americans are incredibly friendly and polite, as well as, in cases like this proud Navy family, fervently nationalistic. I figured that I was on their turf and could cope with their high energy patriotism. I managed just fine. The American war in Vietnam had finished less than a decade prior, but the remnant psychological scars left from the U.S. defeat probably accounted in part for the enthusiastic flag-waving. Later in my journey, back in Berkeley, I would meet and witness plenty of Vietnam veterans living it tough on the street. As a matter of fact, I had never seen so many people living destitute as I saw in California. On a sardonic note, it was just as well that they lived in California, since the weather was always fine. But I began to question America as being the land of the free: it seemed like an oxymoron to me. How could one be free if you lived in dire material poverty? With no shelter or personal safety, living from hand to mouth with the constant worry of survival in the land of the free?

But these are questions for another time. Sandy and I would remain the best of friends. Later on, he would visit me at my place in Australia, until.

Picture : One of the events was hosted by a Christian Gay support group named, Seventh Day Adventists Kinship, they were having their annual retreat called a "Kampmeeting" in Julian a small town, about 100 kilometers east of San Diego, the camp site was abuzz with worrying discussions about an awful disease, first called GRID, for Gay-Related Immune Deficiency. It was here I met Shanti Volenteers who invited me to their training courses about GRID.

Chapter 5

Distorting Mirrors of Life

"I found accommodation in a wooden, three-story apartment complex on Mission Street. The large home was built in the 1930s and housed a fascinating mix of residents, rich in culture, language and the arts — all the good things that remained from San Francisco's countercultural renaissance."

The warm welcome provided by the Kinship family at the Julian Kamp meeting raised my spirits. Seventh-Day Adventist Kinship International (a support group not recognized by The Seventh Day Adventist Church) was, and remains to this day, a network providing a range of psychological, spiritual and educational support for ostracised gay people and same sex families within the Adventist community. For the many thousands of gay men and woman marginalised and discriminated against by the Church, Kinship has been a vital resource, one that is inclusive and welcoming to all.

The Seventh Day Adventist Church, despite its many good works, especially in public health, has sanctioned and preached prejudice and exclusion against gay men, lesbians, and transgender and intersex persons and same sex families. That was true in the early 1980s as it remains today. In 2014, for instance, Pastor Ted Wilson, the Church's General Conference President, stated that "it is inconsistent with the Church's understanding of scriptural teaching to admit into or maintain in membership persons practicing homosexuality." Such authoritarian diktats undergirded a homophobic ideology that has caused many Adventists to become religious refugees; hence the urgent need for groups like Kinship. People from all walks of life were present at this Kinship event, of diverse sexualities, nationalities and forms of spirituality, including some having a plurality of beliefs. In attendance were also several Adventist professional psychologists and supporting pastors, who would be part of the group's discussions. I hasten to add that, notwithstanding the official line toed by the Church, many Adventists are highly educated, enlightened people fighting for socially just causes. These Adventists were repulsed by the Church's homophobic stances. They, who are too many to be named, and their actions in support of vulnerable Church members and their families, are to be commended.

Besides socialising at the Kampmeeting, the camp site was abuzz with worrying discussions about an awful disease, first called GRID, for Gay-Related Immune Deficiency. Most concerning about GRID, especially in 1982, was the fact that the disease predominantly affected gay men. Indeed, at the time, the disease seemed to strike exclusively gay men. Today, of course, we now know GRID as AIDS.

Some friends at Kinship introduced me to Ricardo, a 23-year-old man from San Diego. Ricardo had once been handsome but was now terribly afflicted by lesions (*Kaposi sarcoma*) on his face. He was the first person I met who had been visibly affected by AIDS. Ricardo was coping with the disease, but was more concerned about the deterioration of his looks, as he knew he was no longer desirable. It hurt when he looked in the mirror, so much so that he would smash the glass. He felt ostracised, purposely excluded from social contact by people whom he had thought to be friends. Kinshippers, however, had become his new steadfast friends. Too many young men like Ricardo were suffering from *Kaposi sarcoma*. No one knew at first what was causing the disease or lesions (complicating the matter, *Kaposi sarcoma* lesions were not uncommon in older men of Mediterranean origin). I visited Ricardo for a second time later during my stay in America. By that point, he had had operations to remove some of the lesions on his face and hands, and his body had responded well to treatment. Ricardo was consequently much happier, and had the benefit of company of his new Kinship friends, who had also kindly gifted him a puppy to look after.

Many Kinship members had themselves been persecuted and ostracised by what they called their "church family." Through this suffering they developed compassion and empathy worthy of a Good Samaritan for their fellow gay men and women. Unloved and abandoned by their church and oftentimes actual families, they involved themselves in artistic communities, gay churches such as the Metropolitan Community Church, and other accepting fellowships. These were places to utilise their amazing talents and capacity to love unconditionally. Others, unfortunately, found relief in the wrong places, drowning their sorrows with alcohol and other drugs. I still believe that fundamentalist churches, which shamefully chased out their gay sons and daughters, are largely responsible for exacerbating the spread of HIV, not unlike how the Catholic Church forbade condoms for birth control and safer sex. Both policies, blind to human reality and needs, have led to the plight of millions worldwide.

At Kampmeeting I also became friends with Shanti volunteers operating in San Francisco. The Shanti organisation cared for people with serious life-threatening illnesses and those who were underserved because of lack of finance or medical cover. It was through these friendships that I learned the U.S. had no universal health care like they did in The Netherlands and practically any other western democracy (Australia would only guarantee free and universal health care in 1984, after initial attempts in the late 70s were stymied by a change of government). Poor and disenfranchised Americans depended on volunteer organisations like Shanti, whose motto said it all: "Embracing Compassion, Care and Community."

I drove my hire car back to Los Angeles. I did not ride alone on the return trip, as this time I was joined by three new friends whose presence was spiritually and psychologically invigorating. They were educated Americans—articulate, energetic and committed to doing something about this frightening disease. They told me that several of their friends had symptoms of AIDS, such as pneumocystic pneumonia and toxoplasmosis, a parasite that causes brain damage, among other terrible effects.

Upon returning to San Francisco, Shanti invited me to participate in their volunteer induction course, which comprised safe sex education and assertive training in schools, and dealing with needle exchanges like they have in Amsterdam. After completing the course, Shanti was to match me with a compatible client. I would visit him at his home, assisting with tasks such as going shopping, house cleaning, baking and cooking, as well as being a friend—perhaps the most critical role.

Shanti's volunteer office was on Folsom Street in San Francisco's storied Mission District, near the famous gay precinct on Castro Street. Being in the neighbourhood allowed me to understand some history of the area, especially gay history, and to develop a deeper feeling for the place and the people who lived there. I later discovered that it was here, in the Castro District, where Harvey Milk, the first openly gay city supervisor of San Francisco was assassinated in 1978, together with Mayor George Moscone, by another supervisor, Dan White. On the day Harvey Milk was assassinated, over 40,000 people rallied around the City Hall on Van Ness Avenue. Harvey Milk was called the "Mayor of Castro Street," where he and his partner had operated a photography shop at 575 Castro Street. The shop was now a museum. So much of gay identity and activism, including the early response to the AIDS crisis, had begun around these streets.

My new friends helped me find accommodation in a wooden, three-story apartment complex on Mission Street, built in the 1930s. The large complex housed a fascinating mix of residents, rich in culture, language and the arts: all the good things that remained from San Francisco's counterculture renaissance. My new apartment was also located on the highest point of Mission Street. All I had to do was step outside and take one of the San Francisco trams. Imagine my surprise when I was riding on a retired W-class Melbourne tram; the tram I rode even retained the classic green colouring and markings. How homesick I felt riding it! I was transported back to Melbourne's renowned trams, making my way to St Kilda Beach and the cake shops of Acland Street.

The keys were available from the landlord, who lived on the premises. Gloria Jaworski was a consummate San Franciscan experience: an eccentric, joint-smoking, bona fide Polish princess. I was forewarned that she liked well-built boys, especially handsome Europeans with sexy and romantically expressive accents. Intrigued, I conjured up in my imagination a scene from Armistead Maupin's *Tales of the City*, which my seating companion and friend, Jason, had waxed on lyrically about during my flight to the U.S. He had described the characters that lived at 28 Barbary Lane, the fictional address of the marijuana-smoking landlord, Mrs. Madrigal, endeared to all because of her tolerance, wisdom and capacity in nurturing naive people into the cultured character of freedom-loving San Franciscans. Perhaps I too should meet a Mrs. Madrigal, I mused, to help me deal with all these new experiences.

Heading to Gloria's place feeling somewhat apprehensive, as I had never liked dealing with landlords. But that feeling was counterbalanced by the thought of sharing the third-floor apartment with two Shanti volunteers I had befriended at the Kinship Kampmeeting, and Anthony, the English dancer and free spirit from the earlier picnic on the U.C. Berkeley lawn.

I arrived at Gloria's apartment, number seven, which was somewhat hidden by the adjoining roof garden that boasted a profusion of gardenias, Madagascar jasmine, frangipanes in ceramic pots, and a few miniature Japanese maple trees. A note on the door directed visitors to pull the white rope next to the door, which I did. I could hear a deep, sombre gong softly humming inside, like sounds emanating from a Buddhist temple. An older woman opened the door. She looked like an aged version of Argentina's Eva Perón. One immediately sensed intelligence and a strong ability to love sincerely and unconditionally. I liked her instantly. Gloria complimented my tanned skin and blue eyes. "You obviously play some sport. Is it wrestling?" she asked in thick Polish-inflected accent. I was momentarily stunned but smiling. She continued drawing on her joint. I smelled the sweet aroma of marijuana mixing with the fragrance of the nearby gardenias and frangipanes.

Gloria asked why I had anglicised my name, Keith, from the Dutch. I explained that *Keith*, or in Dutch, *Kees*, came from the name Cornelis. Gloria offered to call me Cornelius, but I said that Cornelius was the English version of the name, Cornelis being the Dutch spelling. "Don't be a cheeky boy," she said in a friendly voice. I realised a few moments later that she was just playing with me. She must have noticed my reserved nature as she broke the momentary silence by mentioning that her brother, Erik, had been a Polish soldier fighting in the Second World War. He fought with the Allied forces liberating the Netherlands in September 1944, and was killed at Breskens during a German bombardment.1 I was taken aback by Gloria's story: my family was from that area of The Netherlands. I explained this to her, adding that my parents had often talked about the bravery and sacrifice of Polish soldiers. I remember Gloria smiling wryly, thanking me as she said, "But don't overdo it, dear. The Polish Communists weren't all that wonderful." Suddenly, Gloria hugged me, with tears in her eyes, and kissed me on both cheeks. "You look so much like my brother, please come in."

Once inside, she offered me vodka, gin, beer or a glass of red wine, with a *placki ziemniaczane*, a potato cake recipe handed down to Gloria by her mother, to which Gloria had taken the liberty of adding some hash oil. She must have assumed that because I was a Dutchman by birth, and therefore naturally tolerant of most things, I would accept the hash-infused potato cake. However, I had never tried any mind-altering drugs so I politely declined and asked for a coffee instead. Gloria was doubly surprised that not only did I not care for hash, I did not care for alcohol, either! To each their own was my philosophy. I could see that Gloria thought I was far too serious, and she gently insisted I should try a bit of hash so I could relax and assimilate in with San Franciscans. "You will need it going to work with all those GRID boys," she said with a smile worthy of the Mona Lisa.

Following my coffee, Gloria took me over to the shared apartment where I would be staying. Anthony, who did not join Shanti but began dancing full-time at a Folsom Street theatre and dance company, had already left his bags in the room. Gloria welcomed the other two housemates, one of whom I would be starting the Shanti induction course with at four o'clock that afternoon.

The first Shanti training session comprised an overview of the program and a quick introduction about caring for people with AIDS. We were also to meet some clients, all young men, who were living with the disease. Everything about this disease seemed mysterious to us, and no one knew much except for one thing: that AIDS was merciless and it absolutely killed.

My first stint on the job was to take some men to a recycled clothes shop to buy some shoes and a warm coat. Nearly every day, from May to August, the fog rolls in from San Francisco Bay; somehow it stops, not consuming the city entirely. The fog freshens the air, though its wetness and wind are chilling. Homeless people living with AIDS felt the cold even more intensely. The recycled clothes shops were heaven-sent, not only for clothes and blankets but for socialising. Many of them offered the homeless coffee or tea and a light meal of soup and bread, provided and served by volunteers.

Taking the homeless shopping required a degree of people skills. I had to learn to communicate without a judgmental or patronising tone, which emphasised that all humans deserve equality of treatment and access to goods and services. It was generally the mere recognition—expressions of love and attention—that seemed to buoy people's spirits. People with drug addictions are oftentimes ignored, causing hurt and isolation and driving them deeper into despair and self-destructive behaviour. A kind word, a funny joke, a gentle touch, a warm shower or bath and clean clothes: these acts, on the other hand, raised hopes and, more importantly, saved lives.

Anthony accompanied me on the second day of volunteering. The weather was warm and we had decided to entertain the volunteers and clients at the Shanti drop-in centre. Anthony danced salsa and sang some musical numbers. I joined in some of the singing but left the dancing to Anthony and another dancer. All in attendance were amused, a brief but welcome distraction from the grim reality materialising around us.

I look back fondly at those days spent in San Francisco. The circumstances were admittedly bleak, but the energy and commitment of those around me were inspiring and instructive. We had not yet seen the darkest days of the AIDS crisis. A crisis that would challenge volunteers' limits of energy and commitment, as well as the gay community's resolve to fight back against the stigma and suffering inflicted on its members by society. I was set to return to Melbourne armed with new skills and fresh perspectives, ready as I could be for the unknown future awaiting us all.

Picture; I drove my hire car back to Los Angeles. I did not
ride alone on the return trip, as this time I was joined by three
new friends whose presence was spiritually and psychologically
invigorating. They were educated Americans—articulate, energetic
and committed to doing something about this frightening
disease. They showed me around too, here is Stanly I loved
Art Deco and he took the time to the Queen Mary, so kind.

1. Zeelandic Flanders is a geographical region of the Netherlands bordering
Belgium and part of the province of Zeeland. Zealandic Flanders lies
alongside the river Scheldt, the gateway to Antwerp. The region was
liberated in September of 1944, largely by American and Polish troops,
and despite heavy resistance by the Germans. Breskens sits at the mouth
of the Western Scheldt.

Chapter 6

All cute Men are Queens

"The Australian sky and the sea with its shimmering surface were clear and blue. I was home away from the AIDS epidemic, or so I thought, until I picked up the local tabloid at the airport newsagent. The front page read: "Sydney Hit with Gay Plague." The reporting was sensational, as only a sleaze of a rag like an English tabloid could publish. But the fact remained: the crisis had come to Australia's shores."

I was feeling somewhat out of sorts, and certainly with a heavy heart, as I made my way to San Francisco International Airport. Not even the bright and balmy October day could lift my spirits departing San Francisco and the world I had only briefly but intimately come to know in California. Just as well that Gloria Jaworski sprung a surprise visit to the airport with her entourage of colourful "cheer-me-uppers," as she called them. She wasn't wrong, too. In a split second my spirits were lifted. There is something to be said for the Americans: when they do something, they do it well, and their enthusiasm is contagious. Truly, I was enamoured and bedazzled by their friendly generosity, then and during my time working alongside the Shanti volunteers.

Gloria's cheer-me-uppers not only brought their vivacious spirits to the terminal. They also bore small but meaningful gifts, including some cassette tapes to play in my Walkman during the flight over the Pacific. They knew I had become a fan of Willie Nelson and loved his rendition of "Somewhere Over the Rainbow." That song had an additional emphasis now. At first, I had associated it with Judy Garland, an ally to gay men in a world hostile to them, who first sang it in the *Wizard of Oz*. Now, the song was indelibly linked to the rainbow-bearing Pride Flag. Gloria pointed to the large Pride Flag flying alongside the tarmac, in full view of all who landed and departed. "The Star-Spangled Banner is our national flag with only three colours, but the Rainbow Flag has all of the colours of the spectrum," Gloria told me. "A symbol to all the girls and boys that they are not alone in the fight against AIDS. We're ready for the fight of our lives and you, lovie, are going to help us with this."

I briefly met Gilbert Baker, who designed the Pride Flag, at an AIDS volunteer workshop in San Francisco. He explained the colours to us: hot pink for sexuality (although this colour was later removed because of the unavailability of the fabric); red for life; orange, healing; yellow, sunlight; green, nature; turquoise, magic and art (later dropped as well); blue, serenity; and violet, spirit. This symbolic spectrum of rainbow colours strongly affected me intellectually and spiritually, as I had always acquainted the rainbow with the love of God. But this spectrum was no Biblical allegory for God's promise to Noah. Rather, this spectrum represented the diverse flourishing of gay life. The colours metaphorically reinforced my values and the positive direction of where my life was then heading.

Willie Nelson's version of "Somewhere Over the Rainbow" was sung in a high and quavering, manly voice. When I listened to it, the song flooded my mind with recent memories of the people I had met and cared for during my time in California. In fact, many melodies were flitting about my mind at the departure gate, each one associated with certain friends, acquaintances and occasions. The songs became intrinsically personal for me, just as the emotions of those I had encountered had become my emotions. This may have been what others called empathy, and if that were the case, I thought, there was a dearth of empathy worldwide in the early 1980s.

"Somewhere Over the Rainbow" took me back to Ricardo, the first person I met who was dying from AIDS-related complications. That conjured up another memory: I saw medical personnel dressed like spacemen approaching AIDS patients; food caterers refusing to deliver food trays to them, fearful of infection from merely breathing the same air. Horribly, they would instead leave the trays at the end of the hospital corridor for Shanti volunteers to take on to their friends. It wasn't hospital policy but ignorant caterers, filled with fear and revulsion, who simply refused to care. Having read some Dutch-produced brochures about safely caring for people with AIDS, I was careful to adopt strict hygiene and not to exchange any bodily fluids or touch any blood. I defiantly refused, however, to wear white protective clothing over my own clothes, as did other friends who were supportive. Uniforms under the guise of protection created fear, anxiety and distrust.

The most important thing that I had learned from my program and work in San Francisco was to cultivate our own emotional wherewithal while supporting patients and their concerned relatives and friends. After the passing of a young man—at that time, they were mostly young men: someone's partner, a son, a brother, a cousin or an uncle—his loved ones needed much help. It was difficult for many parents to say that their son had died of complications from AIDS. The diagnosis immediately implied that their son was gay and therefore a criminal, as by the early 1980s, many states in the U.S. and Australia had not yet decriminalised homosexuality, not like the Netherlands, where homosexuality had been decriminalised in 1811. Nevertheless, in the Netherlands, as in the U.S. and Australia, social stigma caused by the religious right isolated gay men and fractured their families. Thank God, then, that we could comfort them, usually by just being there for them, and not having to say much. A gentle touch was often all that was needed. Volunteers could also assist in rebuilding some harmony and trust between patients and families who received no support from their churches or communities. The volunteers were well aware of their own vulnerability. Not many, I observed, were immune from the risks of acquiring HIV themselves and each encounter led them face-to-face with their personal choices—and their own mortality.

To reach the plane at San Francisco's international airport, one had to walk across the tarmac. All the while my friends continuously waved to me from the viewing platform. Oh, how I disliked this bittersweet departure! One had to turn around to give a wave, then walk some more, then another wave, and another and some more, including blowing kisses. I bounded up the stairs like an athlete to the plane's entrance, turned around and gave my dear friends one last long wave.

The steward who welcomed me aboard commented that my waves were very royal. I waved like a real queen, he said with a wink. "All cute men are queens," he smiled. I pretended to ignore the flirtation, yet I was secretly pleased to have been noticed. I replied with a broad, friendly smile. I always smile when I don't know how to handle a situation, a sort of nervous response. Sitting near the window, I saw Gloria's large yellow and green hat that she had worn to put me into an Australian frame of mind. She had figured that yellow and green were our national colours, and it did the trick. I was transported to a different time, back to the Netherlands, aged ten, when my family and I waved goodbye to all my aunts, uncles, cousins and four grandparents as we set off on our ocean voyage to Australia. That was twenty years before San Francisco and yet the pain of saying so many goodbyes had never left me. This time, however, it was a different kind of goodbye. I knew I would see my new friends soon enough.

I had a holiday romance and he was also at the airport. The trouble with holiday romances was that while they were fun, it always hurt when saying farewell. One never knew, especially in those early days of the AIDS epidemic, if one would ever see someone again. That reality helped to explain why people clung to each other for support and affirmation. My holiday romance had given me a cassette with my then favourite group, The Manhattan Transfers, for the long journey ahead, and some English Leather cologne. I could have easily walked off that plane and stayed in San Francisco, except for the fact that I was down to my last dollar and did not have a visa to stay longer. Gloria had wrapped in rainbow gift paper four of her legendary potato cakes, with instructions that if I were to become sad during my flight, I was to eat them. They were hash potato cakes and if I were not to finish them before landing in Australia, Gloria instructed me to put them in the toilet and flush.

The steward who had welcomed me aboard approached me again to offer an upgrade to business class. I smiled and thanked him as he led me to business class, which was virtually empty. He placed me near the stewards' forward station. His name tag read Rod Dixson so I thanked him personally. I appreciated the extra leg room, which elicited a compliment from Rod, who offered me a drink on the house. We soon struck up a friendship.

Like me, Rod lived in South Yarra. In fact, it seemed like anyone who worked for an airline lived in Toorak or South Yarra. Rod also knew Umberto from Big Bunches. Out of the blue, he confided in me that he was worried about catching HIV, as he had a sailor in every port, so to speak. I stayed silent but nodded in agreement and asked him what he knew about safe sex. The concept was new to Rod. The aroma of Gloria's potato cakes wafted out of my cabin bag, which sparked Rod's curiosity. To my surprise, he asked whether the cakes were the handiwork of his Polish friend, Gloria Jaworski. I said that we should shake hands on his successfully guessing their origin. Rod laughed and said that, in that case, he wouldn't touch the cakes while on duty but that I should go ahead and try them. Which I did and soon I was in a pleasant dreamland.

Landing in Sydney relieved me of the melancholic mood that had briefly taken hold when first departing San Francisco. Hearing the reassuringly laid back Australian accents was like soothing music to my ears. I managed to make my way through Customs quickly, as I had travelled light with just one checked bag, which was not much larger than a cabin bag. I hated carting suitcases around and waiting at crowded baggage carousels. The Australian sky and the sea with its shimmering surface were clear and blue. I was home away from the AIDS epidemic, or so I thought, until I picked up the local tabloid at the airport newsagent. The front page read: "Sydney Hit with Gay Plague." The reporting was sensational, as only a sleaze of a rag like an English tabloid could publish. But the fact remained: the crisis had come to Australia's shores.

Terry had organised for a friend to pick me up at the airport. His name was Dirk van Sant, who worked at the Dutch Consulate in Sydney. I had met him once before, during one of the many entertaining dinners held at Terry's East Melbourne Art Deco house. Because there were always so many interesting people at those dinners, I had not had the chance to talk to Dirk at length, but I soon discovered that we had several important things in common. We shared the same birthday, March 24, and we were born in the city of Terneuzen, in the province of Zealandic Flanders. His mother even knew my mother! Despite our not knowing each other too well, Dirk gave me a big hug at the airport and offered to treat me to lunch on Oxford Street in Darlinghurst, which was just as well as I was nearly broke.

Walking and talking, we took a taxi to Oxford Street and ate alfresco at a posh restaurant, perfect for a superb Sydney day. I showed him the awful headline in the Sydney tabloid, *The Daily Telegraph*. Dirk acknowledged that these headlines on the "terror of gay plagues" were, in his words, "bloody awful." He produced a copy of a Dutch-language Belgian newspaper from his smart leather briefcase. Dirk was fashionable in every way and reminded me of Brian. He was sophisticated in a different sense than I was, although he had a certain, alluring air of pretention. I supposed it was because he worked for the Netherlands' diplomatic service. He also called me *Keesje*, despite my telling him not to call me that; he insisted that it was a term of endearment.

Dirk directed my attention to a story in the Belgian newspaper, which read that the majority of AIDS cases were heterosexual, and nearly all had links with the former Belgian Congo. Additionally, the symptoms of AIDS, for want of a better word, had been recorded in France and Belgium for the last ten years and the disease was transmitted primarily through heterosexual sex. There was no denying, however, that in Australia and in the U.S., the disease mainly affected young gay men. I took out my diary and noted that 1,100 victims had passed away so far in 1982; by August 1983, a further 2,304 would be lost, primarily in the American metropolises of New York City, Los Angeles and San Francisco. But could we fairly call it a plague? I didn't think so, especially in comparison to the bubonic plague of Marseille, France, in 1720, which killed over 100,000 people in under two years, or the Black Death, which wiped out as many as 50 million in 14th century AD Europe alone. What's more, the term itself, when applied exclusively to gay men, sounded pejorative, especially when coming from the homophobic tabloids. In fact, according to my diary notes, *The Australian* newspaper was the first newspaper in the world to use the term "gay plague" as the epidemic swept the U.S. Many times thereafter, I was confronted by the term "gay plague," as the Aussie tabloids sold copies by employing the term purely for sensationalism. By that point in time, anyhow, the disease had already been formally named Auto-Immunodeficiency Syndrome, or AIDS.

Dirk and I discussed why the European mainland newspapers were using less provocative terminology. Dirk said that the right-wing press knew that Australians are easily frightened; they saw fear in most things: fear of Asians, fear of Aboriginals, fear of Communists (later, in the present day, a fear of Muslims), which is why the Australian electorate voted to send their boys to Vietnam. The tabloids, in particular, would never let the facts or truth get in the way of a good story, Dirk added. Now it was the fear of gay men, and not simply of the HIV virus. The religious right locked onto the epidemic as well, suggesting that God was punishing the Sodomites again because of the modern gay "lifestyle." The Catholic newspapers suggested that gay men were a threat to innocent people. Only yesterday in Sydney, Dirk remarked, four haemophiliacs exhibited the same symptoms of AIDS as gay men had and the media went into top gear. I nodded in agreement feeling that the Australian media was addicted to crises it was their pipeline to increased sales.

The Dutch and Belgian medical authorities were saying that AIDS was not contagious outside of exchanging bodily fluids through sexual intercourse or open wounds (such as in the cases of blood transfusion and needle use). The authorities also issued guidelines, which Dirk had brought with him. There was simply no need for the panic that we found in the Australian and British press. AIDS would sell newspapers: the more shocking the news, the better. Gay men made easy targets, given we were socially marginalised in Australia, and male homosexuality was still a criminal act across the country, save for in South Australia, where my friend Terry had helped to decriminalise it in 1972.

Dirk asked me if I used "poppers." I didn't know what they were before I attended summer school in San Francisco. I had since learned that poppers were amyl nitrate, a substance discovered by Thomas Lauder Brinton, a Scottish physician and medical scientist, who recommended the drug as a form of treatment for angina. Sniffing amyl nitrate, or taking the drug in tablet form, relaxed one's veins, allowing more oxygen to flow through the body. This had an effect of sensitising the body all over, especially in the genital region, which, according to users, gave them heightened sexual pleasure. I mentioned to Dirk that poppers were actually vasodilators. Dirk said I must be a user given I knew so much, but I assured him I was not. However, there was not one scrap of evidence that use of the drug contributed at all to HIV transmission, which was the connection the tabloids were attempting to draw. It was not like Hepatitis B, which was transferred by contact with faecal traces. I asked Dirk that, for the moment, we move on with the conversation, as I was still enjoying my vegetarian meal of fried tofu, accompanied by a glass of my favourite Merlot.

Smilingly, changing the conversation to something more frivolous he asked what I thought of the 1983 Sydney Gay and Lesbian Mardi Gras festivities. He offered me a look at the *Antwerp Gazette* and the Dutch gay newspaper *De Gay Krant*, which both boasting lengthy articles about the Sydney parade. I admitted that I didn't know much about Mardi Gras. Except for having read a few lines in *The Age*, I found that practically no Australian media was covering it, despite its being the largest such festival in Australia, as well as the largest non-military parade, with thousands of visitors coming from overseas. I said that I thought that the Mardi Gras parade was somewhat over the top for my taste, with all the near-naked, gyrating men. I pointed out that heterosexuals didn't have a comparable public festival (at least in Australia, as Rio de Janeiro's Carnival might be well considered highly sensual). Dirk said that I was missing the point: Mardi Gras was a part of an international day of solidarity, a political show of support for gay rights worldwide. The first Sydney Mardi Gras, held in 1978, marked a show of solidarity with the riots at the Stonewall Inn in New York City in 1969, and the Sydney protests in June 1978 when police tried to intimidate gay protestors, who fought back. The protestors had not been breaking the law; it was instead pure prejudice and antagonism toward the gay community that motivated the authorities. The Mardi Gras parade was, and is, a celebration of liberation, the freedom of movement in society and personal self-expression. The police had miscalculated the determination of the gay community to fight for their rights, echoing something that my father, Piet, had instilled in me from a young age. You have to fight for your rights; no bastard will ever give them to you. Fighting for decency, justice and equality were some of the hallmarks of the Protestant Reformation, part of our complicated yet progressive Dutch heritage.

Dirk had a degree in Sociology and Ancient Greek History from the University of Leiden, the first Protestant university in the Netherlands, which was also renowned for its fight against tyranny and oppression. The university was founded in the City of Leiden by the Dutch stad holder, Prince William of Orange, as a reward for breaking the Spanish siege in 1575. With his expertise and knowledge, Dirk predicted that the gay community would be held under siege by conservative and ignorant forces in society. The scourge of AIDS, he continued, will be the biggest coming out of the gay community worldwide, resulting in many social and attitudinal changes. One thing was certain, he said: we would not go quietly into the night. It was refreshing to hear such an optimistic voice in those darkening days, as the AIDS crisis had only just arrived and its consequences, for gay men, for their families and loved ones, for society at large, were only barely known, let alone considered.

Indeed, AIDS would have a profound impact. In its wake, the Western world would undergo a social transformation in ways more powerful than the Counterculture of the 1960s, of which Gay Liberation was a major part. We were fortunate that the Australian Government under Prime Minister Bob Hawke and Health Minister Neal Blewett, himself a gay man (albeit closeted at the time), were taking the AIDS epidemic seriously. That was not the case in the U.S., where Republican President Ronald Reagan did not mention HIV/AIDS once in those early years, nor naming any of the thousands of victims anonymously claimed by the disease. Even worse, safe sex and needle exchange programs were opposed by the conservative U.S. Government. I told Dirk that we were relatively lucky in Australia. I had found many individual Americans inspiring during my time there; how ordinary gay men and women had mobilised support to comfort and assist the disease's victims and search for a cure. On the other hand, I had met some American evangelicals who were gay and had to face contempt and cold shoulders from their fundamentalist peers. The contrast of hate and love was astonishing, while the U.S. Government was doing little in comparison to what it could do to turn the tide against the spread of the disease and the hatred that the crisis was sowing in families and communities. So many gay men had been hounded out of their churches and families, and had fled hate and condemnation, only to be driven to all the wrong places in search of love and acceptance. The future was, for the time being, in our hands—the hands of ordinary gay men and women, with the support of their allies in the broader community.

Picture : On my return to Australia the tabloids
blurted...I thought what can better control the
unthinking masses than the thread of catastrophe.

Chapter 7

Everything Shabby and Grubby

"Some staff were fearful of catching HIV in their workplaces, which was revealed by common questions such as: Is it safe to sit on common toilet seats? What about the urine vapours when infected men urinate? Some had even asked for danger money to work alongside their gay colleagues."

Upon my return to work at Australia Post, Mary informed me that there was a new project for me. She had greeted me as "Mr Paulusse," which had put me on edge: no one, particularly no Aussies, referred to me formally unless they were strangers, desiring something from you, or angry! I was relieved to learn that it was such good news. Mary had complimented my team's work on the Equal Opportunity policy with Brian. The policy had been accepted by all stakeholders, including the unions. Now Mary was offering me to join the team that was going to address Australia Post's policies on sexual orientation and discrimination, especially considering the rising threat posed by the AIDS epidemic.

Mary had also read my report on the summer program in San Francisco and wanted me to debrief key stakeholders at that morning's meeting. She told me that the meeting would be no holds barred: I was to be candid about my experiences and recommendations, drawing from my time in the U.S. At the meeting, the stakeholders asked many good questions, especially about my volunteer work with Shanti and their caring for people living with AIDS, and my visits to the world's first hospital ward solely dedicated to handling HIV/AIDS at the San Francisco General Hospital.

My descriptions of the American horror story then unfolding were a vivid, albeit dark picture of the reality only then materialising in Australia. They proved to be insightful and thought-provoking for our purposes that morning, too. One attendee said my report read something like a prediction from Nostradamus, if what I wrote about came to pass. Mary likewise commented that the report's events were like something from another planet or time. Almost like a description of Daniel Defoe's novel, *A Journal of the Plague Year*, which I quoted in the report's introduction. Defoe's narrator, H.F., wrote about what he witnessed on the eerie streets of plague-stricken London following the death of over 200,000 of the city's denizens. The deserted homes of those who had died and those who fled the pestilence, the poor who barricaded themselves indoors, terrified of human contact and the vapours of the plague-stricken victims. Perhaps my report was an omen for what we were about to experience, Brian noted: an AIDS plague in Melbourne, and across Australia and the world more broadly. It was a terrifying prospect for a society that knew nothing yet of the magnitude of the problem. Perhaps we were headed the way of Defoe's great plague, although this time we had the benefit of medical science to aid in combatting the disease. Yet more than medical science was needed, someone at the meeting piped up: we needed to apply the science of social psychology to understand and overturn society's prejudices toward gay men. After all, homosexuality was only decriminalised in Victoria in March 1981, just over two years earlier. Prior to that bold move forward, such policies were out of the question, simply because being queer was in some sense illegal.

Browsing several recent sickness reports at Australia Post shocked me: 16 Post employees working in our mail centres exhibited symptoms of HIV/AIDS. Management had put them on sick leave with pay, a responsible decision as no one really knew at the time how infectious the disease was. By that time, the evidence seemed to suggest that HIV/AIDS was transmitted through bodily fluids including blood, a retrovirus as recently identified by Professor Luc Montagnier of the Pasteur Institute in France. Everyone was waiting on some direction from the state and Commonwealth health departments to manage and prevent HIV/AIDS from spreading in the workplace and in the community. Brian presented the meeting with another incident report, wherein a postman had almost been pricked by a dirty syringe while emptying a street posting box on Smith Street in Collingwood, a popular area for drug users. Luckily, he was not harmed. Oftentimes when chased by police, drug users would dispose of the evidence, depositing drugs and spent needles in street posting boxes, which were cleared twice a day.

The posting box incident highlighted the need for legalising injecting rooms and accessible disposal bins for needles. I had spoken to some Dutch AIDS experts about the successful needle exchange programs trialled in Amsterdam. Perhaps it was time for this program to reach Australian cities. The major hurdle here, however, was that the act of shooting up drugs such as heroin was illegal, as opposed to in the Netherlands, where the authorities treated shooting up drugs as a medical issue (trafficking drugs, on the other hand, remained a criminal act). All eyes focused on me as if to say, "It'll be your job to convince the authorities of a needle exchange program." I knew that changing the conservative, and often fear-laden, bureaucratic mindset was going to be an uphill struggle. Dirty syringes were a real problem for Australia Post and some staff had been talking of boycotting collections from street posting boxes around the drug-infested suburbs of St Kilda, Fitzroy and Footscray.

Some staff were likewise afraid of catching HIV/AIDS in the workplace, a sad fact revealed by common questions asked by nervous Post staff, such as: was it safe to sit on common toilet seats? What about the urine vapours when men used urinals? Some had even requested danger money to continue working alongside their gay colleagues. Our Human Resources Manager, Joyce Jones, said that four employees at Melbourne's General Post Office refused to work with gay men, who they feared carried HIV/AIDS.

Such ignorance and fear abounded. I placed the blame squarely on Melbourne's irresponsible yet popular sleazy tabloids, like the weekly *Truth*, which fed sensationalism and victim-voyeurism to their sex-obsessed readership. I showed Joyce and the others the headlines of the tabloids that I had been collecting: every day there would be an AIDS-related headline demonising gay men, aided and abetted by fundamentalist Christian leaders, spewing their hateful sermons that God was punishing homosexuals for their crimes of the flesh. All this sensationalism fed the growing fear, distrust and prejudice in the workplace, especially among those who could not wait to share their sundry prejudices with all. The more sensational and dramatic the headlines were, the more newspapers were sold and TV audiences would grow. AIDS was a money-spinner for the mainstream commercial media. Again, contrasting this with the Great Plague of 1665, the AIDS epidemic was smiting a much smaller fraction of the population, yet an overreaching hysteria was being fostered in Australia's workplaces. Imagine, I thought, what havoc it is going to wreak in the general community, in our homes and schools. It was clear so far from these distressing discussions and reports that the gay community was going to be a community under siege for the foreseeable future.

After this long yet energizing day, we capped it off with a welcome back to Oz dinner held just for me. It wasn't a planned affair; Terry was shouting dinner and had quickly organised an entourage, including a Federal Labor Party minister he wanted to introduce to me. "I told him all about your American adventures, which made him curious," Terry told me. "Now he wants to meet you in person." We met at Mietta O'Donnell's restaurant by the same name in Brunswick: Terry and Brian; Ken, the Vietnam War conscientious objector who I had met again at the University Club; and Keith Harbour, a lecturer from Melbourne Teachers' College. To think that I had only met these people a couple months ago at the University Club, and here I was again with this new family of friends. Rarely, apart from my own blood family, had I experienced such inclusion and love. Yes, it was about love. After all, everything about friendship involves love, acceptance, and recognition.

Yet tonight at O'Donnell's the atmosphere felt different. It was somewhat subdued and bordered on sombre. Our conversations were almost whispers. I had initially put it down to everyone winding down from a full day's work. Then the penny dropped: news filtered through that some friends we knew had developed AIDS, including Umberto from the Big Bunches Flower Shop. The one who had given me two nipple pink-coloured roses in the lift on the way up to the tenth floor of the University Club. It was an indescribably sad moment. Such a sweet man, I thought. Umberto had been asked to join us that evening. "He was impressed with you," Brian said. "And you might just be the one to cheer him up a bit. He'll be joining us for supper later."

Umberto had been experiencing bouts of pneumocystis pneumonia, which had caused Umberto to experience severe weight loss. "Be prepared when you see him," Terry forewarned us. It was a good thing to prepare oneself for the worst, so I started to practise expecting the worst that night. It usually transpired that the worst wouldn't eventuate, but it was a coping technique for all involved. The AIDS story was virtually never a happy story in those early days. In 1983, it was the sudden interruption in one's life when one had to make peace with losing a loved one far too early.

Umberto arrived as we were finishing our mains. We were met with a kiss and hug each, in addition to Umberto's cheery "hello, darlings!" addressed to all of us. Despite what we had prepared ourselves for, Umberto's genial appearance lifted our spirits. I did notice his drastic weight and muscle loss. He had been a "muscle Mary," as he had once referred to himself; now, there seemed to be little muscle left. He sported one addition to his look: a black moustache, which suited him and made him look like Freddy Mercury (although he had better teeth than Freddy). Nevertheless, I could sense the subtle changes in his tight-lipped smile and erstwhile twinkling eyes. They say the eyes are windows to the heart and our true emotional state. Umberto had depth in his dark blue eyes, indicating strength of character, sincerity, and sensitivity. Here, in Umberto's now plaintive eyes, I could see the pain and fear. Yet the most beautiful part of Umberto remained intact: his vivacious personality, his sharp and intellectual wit, his exuberant *joie de vivre*. Being Italian, he started off by asking us why Italian boys grew moustaches. In unison, as though in song, we answered, "Because they want to look like their mothers." The levity broke the remaining awkwardness and melted the ice of our own fears, aided in part by a few more rounds of port and coffee.

Umberto eventually told us the news, with all the candour and purpose he could muster. "It's official," he said. "I have AIDS and there is nothing anyone can do about it." Gasping for breath, he continued, "I just have one worry and that is I cannot pay for the funeral and I am paying off a business loan for my flower shop in the Jam Factory." He then turned his frightened, piercing eyes into mine, blurting out as he did, "It is all my own fault having AIDS! Now I am suffering because of my behaviour. It's a sign of God's disapproval!" His fingers and perfectly manicured nails fidgeted around his golden necklace, playing with the crucifix hung around his yet stately neck. Umberto asked me if his thinking was right. He sincerely believed that God was punishing him and therefore had inflicted AIDS upon him and his friends. That was what he had heard from his fellow Christians, including his priest who had told him to repent of his sins before taking Holy Communion again. For a devout Catholic, this was doubly humiliating: not only to be denied love from one's fellow humans, but also the promise of divine love.

I suddenly realised what a great evil this organised religion was, using spiritual blackmail on otherwise naïve believers who lacked critical thinking to question the tenets of their religious faith. Umberto had always been under the spell of the impressive, colourful rituals of his Catholic upbringing. I wondered if the irony had been lost on him as he participated in rich, emotionally provoking ceremonies in which priests donned white dresses, something of an ancient drag! I believed that I needed to provide a serious and informed rebuttal to these harmful diatribes, which amounted to public vilification of gay men who were suffering from HIV/AIDS. Most of this hate speech was coming from fundamentalist religious quarters, espoused by leaders of the Christian, Muslim and Jewish faiths. Their religious invectives were inducing guilt, shame, fear and panic among an already distressed community. Unfortunately, the AIDS crisis tapped into a mystifying need among many religious people's deep-rooted belief that one's suffering is tied to one's behaviour, and that God played a direct role in natural disasters such as the Ash Wednesday bushfires and this new "gay plague."

I put my arm around Umberto in a reassuring manner and said that he was an innocent victim of a modern plague, and that illness is never a sign of God's displeasure against one person or a group. Everyone is innocent: the gay men as much as the babies born of infected mothers or those who received blood transfusions infected by HIV. Church people had claimed that the Great Plague of 1665 was a token of God's judgment. If a cure for HIV/AIDS were ever found, as it eventually would be, I said, it would spell the end of this supposedly divine judgment. There was, however, always the law of cause and effect. Just as we know with a high degree of certainty that smoking cigarettes can increase one's risk of developing lung cancer, prolonged obesity to diabetes and heart problems, so it was that we knew unprotected sex with multiple anonymous partners heightened one's risk of catching any number of sexually transmitted infections. The advent of HIV/AIDS was a perfect negative storm and a wakeup call in the age of sexual liberation and urban migration. We drew physically close to Umberto as a token of solidarity with his suffering, and poured ourselves another round of port to toast his future. We promised that he, nor the others, would never face life alone, regardless of blood family and church, both of which had disowned him for the moment. In the most crucial moment of one's life, fighting for survival.

As it turned out, I shortly thereafter approached my parents about Umberto's situation. With a generous loan from them, I bought the Big Bunches Flower Shop at the Jam Factory in South Yarra for $7,000 in cash and took on a four-year lease. Umberto's funeral costs and business loans were satisfied. The financial relief had a positive effect on Umberto's immune system; worries reduce the white blood cell count, the soldier cells that are supposed to fight pathogens in our bodies. Consequently, Umberto remained with us. For the time being he continued to work part-time at Big Bunches, another fateful coincidence in life, one that was to shape the rest of my life and the lives of so many connected to this special flower shop.

Chapter 8

Imagination is doing something with nothing

"The Chapel Street precinct had its own demographics, best described as the new white multiculturalism. There were many second-generation Greeks, fashionable and well-educated, lived in nearby Prahran. They lived alongside hundreds of diverse ethnic families, including many second-generation Italians, who were always full of life. "Amore per la vita," as they said. Umberto, the former owner and newly appointed manager of Big Bunches Flower Shop, was one of these proud and vivacious Australians."

Driving up fashionable Chapel Street to the Jam Factory in South Yarra was always an adventure. You never knew who you might meet or what you would see: the latest in fashion designs, smart architecture, classical motor cars. Melbourne's finest was always on display down the busy thoroughfare. It was Melbourne's catwalk, our home-grown equivalent to London's Soho District or Kalvert Straat in old Amsterdam. And it was most certainly *not* typically Aussie in those days. One would rarely hear "G'day mate!" or "fair dinkum" or other Aussie country slang. That might have passed muster in the suburbs, but not fashion-conscious South Yarra.

The area had undergone considerable gentrification by the time I took over Big Bunches. Gone were the old brick-making factories, breweries, the Red Tulip Chocolate manufacturing plant, and, of course, a jam factory, all part of a radical urban transformation. The actual jam making factory had only recently closed. It had been converted into a shopping centre of the same name. The original machinery was on display, as were the pipelines running the length of the space overhead, through which hot strawberry, raspberry and plum jam used to flow. (One knew what flavour of jam flowed through the pipes by the colour the pipes were painted.)

The Chapel Street precinct had its own demographics, best described as the new white multiculturalism. There were many second-generation Greeks, fashionable and well-educated, lived in nearby Prahran. They lived alongside hundreds of diverse ethnic families, including many second-generation Italians, who were always full of life. *"Amore per la vita,"* as they said. Umberto, the former owner and newly appointed manager of Big Bunches Flower Shop, was one of these proud and vivacious Australians. There were not as yet many Asians or Africans living in Melbourne. It was only the early 1980s and the disgraceful White Australia Policy had been rescinded only seven years prior, when 2,500 Vietnamese made their way to Australia by boat over a period of years in the wake of the Vietnam War. Public sentiment began to swing towards allowing the migrants into Australia. Prime Minister Malcolm Fraser did the right thing by resettling them in Australia. How different from our country's current shameful policies toward asylum seekers and refugees at the time of this writing.

The other major demographic was the gay community, as evidenced by the many trendy businesses lining South Yarra's streets. One only had to look for the discreetly placed rainbow flag or rainbow stickers in their shopfront windows. I noticed that Big Bunches had some rainbow-clad markers too. Although I opined they did not need a sticker or a rainbow flag: the gorgeous, meticulously crafted displays of flowers said it all! The gay community found freedom and acceptance around Chapel Street and Commercial Road: things it did not find much elsewhere in Australia's otherwise conservative, straight society. The exceptions were Sydney's renowned suburbs of Darlinghurst and Paddington.

On Chapel Street, smart cafes opened up, Gary Whitelaw, his boyfriend Craig Longburn, and three other partners founded a Café-Restaurant called Soda Sisters and were easily the trend setters for the new burgeoning Café Society and Coffee culture situated down the street from Big Bunches at 382 Chapel Street. The Soda Sisters boys were pure eye candy at work, whooshing up to the customers on their roller skates taking menu orders serving tasty uncomplicated nutritious well presented food with flair and panache; without any doubt Melbourne had never seen anything like it. The Soda Sisters set the standard for other cafés in the neighbourhood, which tried to emulate its personalised service. I did notice that straights usually copied the art and esthetics started by Gay people and the copying of the Soda Sisters style was evidence of this. More remarkable, trend-setting establishments were soon to follow, like The Market Hotel on Commercial Road. The fashions forged on these streets were very popular with the peroxide bottle blondes and posh-accented women of Toorak, one notable exception being Big Bunches' famous customer, Sheila Scotter, then editor of *Vogue Living*, who kept her hair gracefully grey.

Big Bunches sat in the middle of the Jam Factory. Hot percolated coffees and fresh croissants were ready and waiting, our coffees often speedily delivered by the roller-skating Soda Sisters. It usually took at least an hour and an early start at 6:00 am to prepare the displays of fresh flowers, which were delivered daily from Melbourne's markets. We had what seemed like fields of Western Australian dried flowers, edged by a menagerie of sea shells and cages of chirping pink-green love birds. It took a certain amount of flair to set up the shop six days a week and this was Umberto's specialty. A new window dressing was required every day, which only Umberto and his fellow "style queens," as he called them, could create. Although I had purchased the shop, I would only work during the weekends. To be honest, I really knew nothing about flowers. Except that I liked the many colours and sweet fragrances and their innate power to allure, romance, and comfort. And as a Dutchman, I knew that tulips had made the Netherlands rich, very rich. Perhaps cultivating flowers was in our cultural genes.

Big Bunches was well-regarded as much for its personalities at the store as for its extravagant displays. It was a popular tourist attraction in South Yarra. Sales depended on the displays and the customers' desires and impulses. We were after their disposable dollar, after all, somewhat like the attractive people at my gym: the fit ones had the looks and got the attention, so too must the flowers attract in order to sell. There was some indirect competition from the Jam Factory's supermarket, but they sold cheap and bland flowers in comparison. Theirs were no match for the freshness and style of Big Bunches. Nor did they have the Umbertos of the world at their service. It would only be a short time, however, before the supermarket and the Red Tulip Chocolate Factory would close their doors.

There was still the prestigious Georges store, as well as many other unique shops. The famous Jam Factory boasted chic clothing boutiques, emporiums, delicatessens, bookshops, art shops and galleries, interspersed with restaurants. Many of these businesses were also customers of Big Bunches, thanks to Umberto's charm and that of his blond Aussie boyfriend at the time, Leigh, a window dresser at Georges. The large displays of fresh and dried flowers enhanced the catwalks of Melbourne's fashion shows and boosted the French Montmartre feel to the Jam Factory. All these valuable business clients were well looked after by Umberto. He had also surreptitiously hidden a couple of bistro tables amongst the flower displays, where his friends could have a quiet cuppa and a smoke (and not always tobacco). Umberto could somehow always manage socialising and doing business simultaneously, wrapping up big bunches as he went along.

On my first day of watching how the shop was set up in the early morning, I met Kees Tesselaar, a fellow Dutchman and my namesake, as well as Australia's premier tulip farmer. He had been visiting the Big Bunches boys for a while. He assisted them with valuable advice, especially in relation to tulips. Melburnians and thousands of visitors from out of town would flock to the Tesselaars' farm in Silvan, near the Dandenongs, for their annual Tulip Festival. The festival remains today one of the biggest tourist attractions in Victoria. The Tesselaars were also widely known as a generous, community-minded people, donating part of their festival ticket sales to the Red Cross and other charities. I had heard about this incredible family in 1961, while our family was living among thousands of recent European migrants in the Bonegilla Migrant Assimilation Camp in northeast Victoria. The Tesselaar story greatly inspired and encouraged many Dutch postwar migrants. Umberto had confided in Kees that he had sold Big Bunches to me because he had been diagnosed with AIDS. This disclosure led to a special friendship between Kees and me, as another of Kees's friends had been recently diagnosed with AIDS. Umberto had also befriended Kees' wife, Sheila, and the two enjoyed a close bond. Much later, the Tesselaars would become part of a large community caring for people living with HIV/AIDS.

Later that morning, back at the Australia Post office, Brian asked me half-jokingly if I had brought a copy of *The Herald*, Melbourne's evening newspaper. Indicating I was late for work. (In those days, there were two types of daily publications, with morning and evening newspapers aimed at the working crowds at rush hour.) I explained that I wanted to observe the boys setting up shop at Big Bunches and that I had at last met a famous Dutchman, Mr Tulip himself. Brian kidded that I should have taken the nickname "Tulip," but I hated nicknames.1

My mind was swirling with thoughts,especially those of coming to grips that I was now the owner of Big Bunches, my own beautiful flower shop. I was meeting these extraordinary, talented people while retaining my normal day job at Australia Post and later on at the Alfred Hospital. At the Post, I was still assisting the development of workplace policies to fight the tide of homophobic bullying and fear-mongering. In those early days of the AIDS crisis, it could seem like a desperate, uphill battle, but we persevered.

It was agreed between the Big Bunches staff and me that I would work at the shop on weekends. I employed Dorothy, a talented and traditional florist with good church connections, to assist. Dorothy had a very kind personality, the sort that attracts children and middle-aged, conservative women, a key demographic for the flower trade. I had only one initial fear: how would Dorothy accept gay customers, let alone work alongside gay men? I knew she attended a fundamentalist Christian church, the sort that preached any real joy in life was a sin. I need not have worried, however. Dorothy's quaint personality, combined with her colourful dress and hairstyles, were a surprise hit with many of our gay staff and clientele. Some of Melbourne's drag queens would even copy and exaggerate her sense of style. Her non-judgmental attitude and reserved religious disposition were her saving grace, so to speak. Although Umberto did not work with Dorothy, upon learning that Umberto had AIDS, she made a concerted effort to bring him homemade bread and vegetarian meals whenever he was at home not feeling well. In time, Dorothy's church friends became regular customers and Big Bunches supplied the Sunday flowers, arranged by Umberto, to her church and to the delight of the parishioners.

Meeting new customers was always exciting for me. I fondly recall one particular customer. He gave me a bold smile and said, in Dutch and all in one, long breath: "Are you Dutch? How much are your tulips? How much discount do I get for paying in cash?" I immediately told him not to be cheeky. If he could not afford my flowers, I said perhaps he could barter his diamond or rhinestone ring (I could not tell the difference from a distance!). That was how I met Bill Schreurs, who hailed from another well-respected Dutch family in Victoria. The Schreurs were major celery farmers. In fact, they practically supplied the whole of Australia with this healthy vegetable, of which I ate a lot as a vegetarian.

Bill introduced me to his handsome, reserved friend, Robbie. Both were living in a large house in St Kilda and were hosting a party that night. They came to Big Bunches looking for some large bouquets of springtime flowers: tulips, jonquils, daffodils and hyacinths. (Although Bill instructed me not to include too many jonquils. He said they might give an amyl-like rush to his guests, he was always light-hearted.) I always enjoyed meeting other Dutch men, a rarity in Melbourne, and meeting Bill was unexpected. After all, to be Dutch and gay was to be a minority of a minority. Unlike their straight counterparts in Australia, Dutchmen would give bunches of flowers to other men. Most Australian men were, on the other hand, fearful of the connotations, reflecting on their own insecurity and innate need for conformity.

Robbie could smell the strong coffee being served at the tables and remarked that he loved Dutch coffee, knowing we would not serve instant coffee but the real bean. He enquired where Umberto was that day. I responded that it was his day off. Not knowing how well Robbie and Bill knew Umberto, I felt it inappropriate to reveal that Umberto had been experiencing difficulty breathing. He feared that it might be the beginning of the dreaded PCP, or pneumocystis pneumonia. Robbie confided in me, however, that he was aware of Umberto's HIV-positive status and confessed, with all the usual fear and sadness in his eyes, that he was also afflicted. "Don't tell anybody," he impressed upon me. I wouldn't. Yet it was painful to watch so many beautiful young men being forced to live in the closet twice. First, in a hostile world, secondly as victims of this awful disease.

I would see Bill and Robbie regularly at Big Bunches. On one occasion that Bill called in, he mentioned that he had been talking to a friend of mine named Dolf who was a sergeant with the Victoria Police and a second-generation Dutch-Australian. As was usually the case when the Dutch meet, they asked each other which boats took their families to Australia. Dolf's parents arrived here in 1949 from the island of Texel. They sailed on the famed MS Volendam, a Holland America Line ship that was torpedoed in the Second World War with hundreds of war orphans on board. No one perished, thankfully, as there were enough life boats, and, beyond anyone's expectations, the ship did not sink under the steadfast command of the Dutch captain and crew. In fact, the vessel and its hardy crew survived two torpedos attacks. After extensive repairs, the *MS Volendam* was later used as a migrant ship sailing to Australia. Dolf had confided in Bill that he had been diagnosed with HIV/AIDS. He added that Victoria Police was having difficulty coping with HIV/AIDS diagnoses among police officers. After all, the police still frequently raided gay nightclubs and bookshops, and went undercover at gay cafes and hotels. Like the MS Volendam, Dolf refused to sink despite the odds. There were enough life boats in the gay community to ride out the coming waves of AIDS, to fight this dreaded and deadly disease in every way possible. I determined privately in my own mind to do my part and to offer lifelines of hope, cheerfulness, inclusiveness, and practical personal help. Twenty-six years ago, Dolf developed High Grade Non-Hodgkins (Burkis) Lymphoma, an AIDS-related illness. And yet, he has been one of the fortunate ones. Dolf is still alive at the time of writing. He lives a healthy life in country Victoria, with an undetectable viral load and zero risk of transmission.

I experienced that many gay men wanted—in fact needed—to tell someone about their status. They confided in those who they perceived to be sympathetic. Sympathetic ears were, of course, hard to come by in those days. The tabloid newspapers had done a thorough job of demonising people living with AIDS. Their sensationalism had stoked fear and ignorance among the gay community and the public at large. A chief worry was that of trust: who could these vulnerable gay men trust? The cruelest thing that could happen was abandonment. When a person living with HIV/AIDS confided in a partner or someone they trusted, their partner or friend could immediately end the relationship. Partners, at times fled their loved ones, afraid that they, too, might have been infected. Friends, fearing their own mortality and the repercussions of knowing someone with AIDS in a judgmental society, did as well.

Before any support organisations existed, people diagnosed with AIDS frequently led isolated lives. Yet they would put up a brave front. One of the Big Bunches customers, Brendan, a sweet, sensitive man of twenty-two years, was afflicted with Kaposi Sarcoma. I noticed his condition when looking at his heavily powdered face. It was a desperate attempt to mask the small purple lesions dotting his otherwise handsome face. Discreetly, I took him for coffee to converse with him freely he said that he had recently lost his job and was now couch surfing with friends or sleeping with strangers in lieu of accommodation, and because he was physically showing signs of AIDS, many of his so called friends had deserted him. We helped to turn his situation around immediately. Dorothy, together with the Sisters of the Good Shepherd, organised care and a roof over his head. His own church, the fundamentalist Exclusive Brethren, had disowned him. Christmas was nearing and Big Bunches needed Gum Nut wreaths to be made. We employed Brendan to take on this job, first gathering a variety of Gum Nuts dropped from Eucalyptus trees around Melbourne's Botanical Gardens and around the Shrine of Remembrance. Afterwards showing him how to glue the gum nuts in tasteful patterns on foam rings ready for others to prepare and decorate them further, completed for our local customers and export market. Brendan would stay on with us for six months, until.

A few days later Robbie visited again and told me that he had spent some time at *Fairfield Infectious Disease Hospital* and did not want to return there. He enjoyed managing his own business again, hiring out rooms in a large boarding house in St Kilda. For him visiting the Fairfield Infectious Diseases Hospital was a frightening experience, seeing once beautiful young men, often his friends, in the prime of their lives disfigured by

Kaposi Sarcoma or mentally by the onset of early dementia, or severely malnourished due to the disease's scourge on their body's ability to function and not keeping food down anymore. Many were walking skeletons it's so awful as he determinately reiterated not going there anymore only to brutally face his own mortality, he viewed it as a scene out of the worst footage of the Holocaust. I had silently agreed, too often I had to prepare myself mentally to continue with the regular visits as the sights were distressing. But the visits were also joyful my friends appreciated them so much, though little was often said. Love can be silent and a gentle touch more meaningful than words.

Many times, too many times, I reflected on me meeting these men suffering from AIDS. I wondered to myself whether I could withstand grieving for so many who, in 1983/84, were more than likely destined to die. Yet my heart was stronger than my fears. Although I never became accustomed to the deep dismay experienced by these young men, their dreams suddenly dashed by a diagnosis, yet our lives were enriched by the precious moments we shared. The memories that I have carried to this day, now memorialised in writing here.

Our tight knit family at Big Bunches began to ramp up its efforts in the gay community because at the time, there was not much in the way yet of formal organisations dedicated to meeting the daily challenges of the AIDS crisis. The monumental, oftentimes harrowing, tasks of physical, mental, economic and emotional support was largely left up to individuals like us. It was a task we bore with no pleasure, except for the pleasure of bonding and altruistically supporting our brothers and sisters in very dark times. Those were the days when we, gay men and women, forged a new front against society's longstanding stigma and prejudice. We had to look out for each other.

Vaughan Lenny, a doctor in South Yarra, dropped in one time when he saw some of the boys chatting in the shop. Dorothy offered everyone a cup of percolated coffee (I've noted that in my daily diary I began keeping fastidiously at the onset of the crisis). Vaughan wanted to order some flowers for a funeral. He explained that they had to be special flowers for the coffin of a special friend. It was enough said. He asked whether we could arrange a selection of tulips coloured like the rainbow.

I reassured him that it was a simple order we would happily fill. Vaughan also mentioned that, some months back, he had attempted to discuss the AIDS crisis with the Victorian Health Minister Tom Roper. Roper's office had unfortunately told him that the Victorian Government would not have anything to do with homosexuals and the unfolding crisis. Vaughan and I talked at length about how we might manage to set up a meeting with Roper and relate my experiences in San Francisco to the minister.

Big Bunches started hosting informational nights for health and wellbeing, as well. The programs were set up by Umberto and his new boyfriend, Angelo there seemed so many new boyfriends I lost track of them all. I assisted with the logistics. We hosted several immune-building nutrition sessions, which demonstrated to people living with HIV/AIDS how to make healthy foods and drinks. The boys designed beautiful posters to advertise the sessions. One poster read: "An evening at Big Bunches amongst the kiwi fruits, apples, berries, ginger, citrus, and leafy greens and the aroma healing power of flowers' essence." I was somewhat cynical of alternative therapies but kept my mouth shut because I was ignorant of what benefit the therapies might provide. Besides, healthy food meant healthy bodies and I was a big proponent of healthy eating. The presenter was my friend Cynthia, a flower therapist who believed that the essence of flowers stimulated physical healing and made one ware of mental and spiritual imbalances.

The poster had a great effect. The alternative therapies movement helped lead the healing charge at a time when wider, more formally organised AIDS responses were only beginning to get programs underway in the community. And all of this happened in absence of any guidance or support from the government health departments and the medical establishment. Things would change, but for the time being, people were desperate for community and healing. In light of all we know now about HIV/AIDS, the immune-boosting nutrition of 35 years ago may sound like a false hope. Yet, at the time, it was a struggle for optimism. We hoped, perhaps against hope, that the awful disease could soon be managed, and in time, if we could help it, defeated.

Despite this, or perhaps because of it, some of my newer friends had started calling me Zsa Zsa behind my back, after Zsa Zsa Gabor, the iconic Hungarian actress. Apparently, according to my friends, when I was tired late in the evening my accent mirrored hers. I didn't appreciate at the time that it was a term of endearment, but it was somewhat difficult to appreciate when, for instance, a person called out to me on the tram once, "Hey, Zsa Zsa, come and sit here with us!" Alas, all I could do was ignore the innocent attention. Better, I suppose, to be noticed than ignored!

Big Bunches sat in the middle of the Jam Factory, it was always a hive of activity including fashion shows. It usually took at least an hour and an early start at 6:00 am to prepare the displays of fresh flowers.,

Chapter 9

He often spoke in Wildean wit.

"I had worked Umberto out by now. He was not unlike Oscar Wilde, who he loved to read. He often spoke in Wildean wit, putting his own twist on memorable adages, like "There was only two bad things in this world: having AIDS and not being talked about."

Big Bunches specialised in Australian native flowers. The rich aroma of frangipani filled the shop and mixed with the heavy scent of Western Australian boronias. The frangipani flourished in the heat of the Jam Factory. Umberto would quietly hum a tune while arranging bouquets. One time, I recall he was humming a Bach melody as he made a bouquet for a special person. Umberto simply said the person was someone who had "given up on life." According to Indian custom, Umberto noted, frangipanis were said to extend life. At the very least, the sweet flowers were destined to lift his special friend's spirits. Umberto had also stuck a frangipani flower behind his right ear, which, he said, indicated that he was seeking a relationship (not that many people would know that, unless perhaps you were a Polynesian woman).

I had worked Umberto out by now. He was not unlike Oscar Wilde, who he loved to read. He often spoke in Wildean wit, putting his own twist on memorable adages, like: "There was only two bad things in this world: having AIDS and not being talked about." Umberto exuded self-confidence, even in the face of death. His resilient energy drew many customers to Big Bunches. He still had his good looks, too, despite the ravages of the virus. A strong, rugged face with the body of Adonis. I learnt early in the piece to compliment people's best features and character traits. It was an antidote to any negative self-image they developed about themselves because of AIDS. But Umberto was in no need of false flattery. I genuinely complimented him on his smooth skin, coal black hair, and the natural beauty of how he struck a pose. He was as artistic a creation as the bouquets he fashioned himself. I knew he sensed his own vanity, but he was a charming man nonetheless.

Our gay customers frequently introduced us to their parents, albeit usually in a hushed manner. The parents would join them on a trip to Big Bunches. Umberto would make a warm, genuine fuss of their old folks and offered tea or coffee. I would take them out for a cup of coffee; well aware that they did not just come down to look at flowers or the colourful peached faced parrots our in house love birds. No, they wanted connections with their sons' friends and sought out empathy and support. These parents had too often experienced the double shock of simultaneously learning about their sons' medical condition and sexuality. Their concerns were not only for their sons but for themselves: How would other family members react? What would they tell their friends? For some parents, especially those from conservative religious or cultural backgrounds, it was also a question of legacy. They feared they would not become grandparents. Worse still, the family name might be extinguished. All these fears and anxieties were heaped, consciously or not, on their children, a burden far too large for their children to bear and wrongly, too.

Religious parents had the most difficulty coping with their sons' condition, as they had no support from their so-called "Church Family." They felt completely isolated, not to mention disappointed with the absence of *agape*, the unconditional love that Christians are supposed to provide their brothers and sisters. Instead, it became the opposite of unconditional love: everything became conditional. People only loved others if they conformed to their religious ideals and ideological values. Some parents told their friends that their sons had cancer instead of AIDS. For them, that was the safest thing to say despite it being false. Nevertheless, the white lie meant that the parents obtained some sort of temporary psychological peace of mind. Yet they would continue to bear their guilty consciences as the truth remained hidden. I would counsel these distressed parents that there were times when one cannot really be uncritically open. Privacy was as important for them as it was for their children struggling with AIDS. To be open about their personal issues, considering their religious communities' wholesale and unapologetic rejection of them and their sons, would often do more harm than good.

The boys usually took only their mothers to Big Bunches. Many of the mothers had not met any outwardly open gay boys before. Not that the Big Bunches staff had name tags alerting, "Hi, I am Umberto and I am a gay man!" but there was a certain *je ne sais quoi* around the flower shop. However, meeting openly gay men was a revolutionary act. The mothers were fascinated to meet living human beings who challenged the unwarranted and distorted portrayals of gay men in the media and popular entertainment. Here, at Big Bunches, the boys could live comfortably within their own skins. In joining their sons and overcoming their initial fears, the mothers (and some fathers) who came down to Big Bunches found they, too, could live a bit easier in an affirming and non-judgmental environment. Together, we could face down this awful disease and the broader community's stigma against gay people and their families. Oftentimes the mums would say something along the lines of, "Oh, if only my husband could meet you." Alas, the politics of the closet.

Visitors frequently dropped in to Big Bunches out of the blue. One such personality was Dirk van Sant, the Dutch diplomat whom Terry had introduced to me en route back to Australia. Dirk had sprung a surprise visit to Big Bunches one day, sneakily burying his face in a cluster of frangipanis so that we wouldn't easily recognise him. He laughed in wonderment at Umberto's beautifully coloured and fragrant bouquet, and flirtingly said hello to Umberto. We all, of course, recognised him. His was a warm and memorable personality. Dirk was in Melbourne to interview potential Australian diplomatic interns. He heard that the Victorian AIDS

Council (orVAC) had been recently formed, and that Commonwealth Health Minister Neal Blewett and his department were taking steps to halt the advance of HIV and cooperating in the urgent search for a medical response. Dirk also wanted to introduce me to several AIDS-focused doctors and medical researchers, who had travelled to Australia from the Netherlands. One of them was a young doctor named Joep Lange.[1]

Dirk, Joep, and I joined several Australian AIDS medical professionals for a few coffees at the Jam Factory. Joep asked what I thought of Australians: were they easy to get along with? I recalled telling him that Australians were uncomplicated to get along with. But, I mentioned that most professionals in Australia were firstly concerned about covering their arses and then worried about doing their real jobs. That's just called office politics, Joep laughed.

I also met Arjen Broekhuizen, a Dutch journalist who specifically covered the latest medical research on HIV/AIDS. Arjen was constantly traveling the world and attending conferences. He was a journalist for the *Gay Krant, a* gay newspaper in the Netherlands. He also recorded a weekly broadcast on Australia's public SBS Dutch Radio, relaying current events in the Netherlands to the station's many Dutch listeners living in Australia.

Arjen brought his partner, Martin Golding, to Big Bunches. It turned out, in fact, that I had forgotten I had met Martin in 1976 when he was a student waiter at Café Paradiso in Carlton. One of the Soda Sisters had introduced him as a fellow Dutch speaker. Martin told me he was studying the language at the University of Melbourne. I came to learn that he was an Australian cultural attaché who lived part of the year in The Hague. Martin was a handsome, highly intelligent man, full of witty repartees, and a quick thinker, too.

It was through meeting Arjen and Martin that my understanding of the AIDS crisis deepened. Martin was one of the first diagnosed cases in the Netherlands. The couple had moved from The Hague to Son en Bruegel, a pleasant country town near Eindhoven, where Philips Electronics had their headquarters. Their hope was that a quieter life and healthy country living would improve Martin's quality of life, and his chances for a longer life despite the grim odds. In 1989, however, Martin returned for good to Australia, so his mother could care for him. I also met

Joan and her husband, Ron Golding. The Goldings were a middle-class Australian family, with an Anglican background, living in Warrandyte, then a sleepy Australian country town to Melbourne's northeast. Ron was a scientist at the CSIRO and Joan a homemaker who made exquisite quilts. They were a churchgoing couple. On first meeting them I wondered how they would grapple with their son's AIDS and homosexuality. However, much to their credit, they did well, with the assistance of the VAC's care groups, and Martin's gay friends who would visit the family to offer their encouragement and support. Martin passed away later in 1989, without Arjen by his side. Arjen was alone back in the Netherlands. Martin's death hit him hard and he took a long time to reconcile with his distant loss.

After Martin's passing, Joan became involved as a volunteer worker with the VAC and the Churches AIDS Pastoral Care Program, which assisted and counseled the families and friends of those living with HIV/AIDS. She also eventually co-authored a book, *Coming Out, Coming Home*, intended for the parents of gay children. I admired her courage in getting involved from the very beginning in the VAC. In her book, Joan said as follows:

> When I first volunteered to work for the Victorian AIDS Council, I was greeted with great suspicion by the mainly gay male people who ran the organization at that time. One of them even asked me, what is a well-meaning middle-class grandmother like you doing in this scene? Their method of trying to discourage me was to shock me with everything in their armoury, from explicit illustrated literature to videos on gay sexual practice. They let me in only when I was able to convince them that I didn't intend to invade their territory and that I would be able to care for people they had neither the time nor expertise to deal with – families affected by HIV/AIDS.

The VAC provided Joan with a little car in which she crossed Victoria for over six years, visiting families and friends affected by the AIDS crisis. She was truly heaven-sent. On Australia Day 1994, Joan was awarded the Order of Australia Medal for her work. Joan is still alive and well at the time of writing in April 2018, and recently became Facebook friends with me. She lives in a coastal fishing village along Port Phillip Bay, now aged 93.

Joan is still alive and well at the time of writing in April 2018, and recently became Facebook friends with me. She lives in a coastal fishing village along Port Phillip Bay, now aged 93.

Arjen wrote to me in 1988 to say that he had applied for a housing mortgage, only to have to undergo a health assessment. It was because he was HIV positive. He was suffering personally as well. He came from a strict Dutch Reformed Calvinist family. His parents could not accept that their masculine son was a gay man. Arjen's mother was an ardent watcher of *De Evangelical Omroep* (Evangelical television broadcasts), and she had learnt to believe that one could "pray the gay away." Yet she also loved Arjen and Martin very much, and after her husband unexpectedly died at age 73, her views softened towards them. She often stayed with the boys at the Australian Diplomatic Residence in The Hague. She had the time of her life.

In the end, Arjen's physical suffering became unbearable. He was not eating anything, yet continued to vomit. He was permanently cold despite wearing three jumpers and two woollen trousers. His legs were swollen so much that he could hardly walk, a painful condition known as bilateral lymphedema. His other, ever-present difficulty was taking around 27 different medications every day. A medical cocktail that practically became a full-time job.

The saddest part was that Arjen felt lonely. Even though he was surrounded by loving carers. He deeply missed Martin and felt horrible about not having said proper goodbyes. I talked briefly with Arjen about the subject. Did he believe that he would run into Martin in the afterlife? He did not answer me directly, but tossed the ball in my court. He said he believed there will be a resurrection of the dead. He asked whether I thought the two of them would be reunited. I replied that I did not know the answer, and that it was something unknown to anyone. He could believe by faith alone. Faith is, according to Hebrews 11:1 in the New Testament, is "the substance of things hoped for, the evidence of things not seen." I encouraged him just to have the will to believe and he would see Martin again. It was his one emotional bulwark against the ravages of this disease.

This loneliness caused by AIDS unfortunately occurs when all of one's friends fade way. Many cannot cope with the visible degradation of the body, and often, the mind. Personalities change under the duress of coping with the disease. That was the hardest part. So many young friends came face to face with what could soon be their own plight and mortality. They would stay away from seeing and experiencing what made them afraid, a reaction that always distressed me. It was a cruel, self-inflicted punishment, but AIDS cast a dark shadow on one's mind. Here was Arjen, a popular and attractive gay man. A well-respected professional. Yet at the end of his days, he felt alone and heartbroken.

Picture;The boys usually took only their mothers to Big Bunches. Many of the mothers had not met any outwardly open gay boys before. Not that the Big Bunches staff had name tags alerting, "Hi, I am Umberto and I am a gay man!" but there was a certain *je ne sais quoi* around the flower shop.

1 Joep, together with five other Dutch AIDS researchers, sadly perished in the Malaysian Airlines MH17 crash, when it was shot down over the Ukraine on 17 July 2014, on its way to the International AIDS Conference held in Melbourne, Australia. I had not seen Joep since 1998, when he was by then a world-renowned AIDS expert and working very closely with Australian HIV-AIDS researchers.

Chapter 10

Fear is Petrol

"I contemplated how to approach this painful family situation. I had learnt from my parents and my own experience to keep all my senses together. Most people feared the unknown. They thought the worst and the improbable, and wasted so much time caught up in anxiety and distress."

The phone rang at six o'clock at my apartment on St Kilda Road. It was a particularly cold winter's morning. The phone sounding at that dark and chilly hour felt ominous. It was surely too early for any dramas, I thought, as I groggily made my way to the phone. It was Dorothy and she sounded agitated, which quickly roused me from my sleepy state. I listened as she mumbled something. Her pastor's son, Dale, had been diagnosed with HIV/AIDS the day prior. According to his doctor, it was one of the first confirmed cases in Victoria. After I had some success calming her down, she explained that Dale's parents and siblings were devastated. They felt as though the judgment of God Almighty had rained down on their son and brother. What's more, they hadn't known that Dale was gay, a fact his doctor impulsively divulged without a smidgen of discretion. Incidentally, I knew this doctor: a real moralist and homophobe. I had attended a Bible class with him once. There, he made disparaging, inaccurate and offensive remarks about gay men. I challenged him then and he lost his cool and, consequently in my eyes, his dignity. He also belonged to Dorothy's conservative church. Dorothy told me that the vulnerable gay men in her church needed my help and support. I agreed: They needed *any and all* help.

First, however, there had to be a change of doctor. One needed a medical practitioner, not a wolf in sheep's clothing. Dorothy was pleased when I said I would call my friend Dr Peter Meese, who specialised in gay men's health. I had met Peter at one of Terry's dinners, and he would often drop by the flower shop for a chat, usually about health issues, purchase flowers, or the quality of the coffee. Most importantly, we would discuss his insight on the latest AIDS research. Umberto would join us occasionally as Peter was his doctor, too.

Dorothy pleaded for me to talk to Dale's father. He apparently wanted to meet me, as well. He had read my Kinship Report. The report documented my time with Ricardo, my friend from San Diego suffering from Karposi sarcoma, and the others struggling with AIDS at the Kinship Kampmeeting. I was no friend, however, of fundamentalist pastors of any stripe. My experience was that many of them were self-righteous control freaks and moralists, obsessed by the subject of sin instead of preaching love and goodness. Most of them, likewise, loathed their bête noire: the gay community. How little there was of what the disciple John had exhorted of Christians, that there was no fear in love and that perfect love drives out fear. They could have learned a thing or two about unconditional love from the gay community. However, I agreed to meet Dale's father and told Dorothy that I would call him to arrange a meeting.

After I finished speaking with Dorothy, I made coffee and picked up my copy of *The Age*. Gordon Archer, the director of the Sydney Blood Bank, had publicly announced that men who had sex with other men should refrain from donating blood. He intimated that the gay male blood supply was already contaminated, for which he presented no evidence. (In those days, bear in mind, homosexuality was still criminalised in New South Wales.) While I believed Archer was trying to act responsibly to protect the integrity of the blood supply, the way his message was broadcast publicly was entirely irresponsible. It fed a public backlash against gay men.

Many Australians historically feared a bogeyman: the Asian Yellow Peril, the Communists, later the Muslims. Now, in the 1980s, it was the gays' turn in the harsh public limelight. Incidentally, in 2016, men who have had sex with other men in the preceding 12 months are still not allowed to give blood, out of fear of contaminating the blood bank. It is, sadly, not an uncommon position worldwide.

I received another phone call that morning before I could finish my coffee and the news. This time it was Umberto. He was talking rapidly as well. Several of his friends had recently lost their jobs because their employer suspected them of being gay and deemed them health risks at the workplace. His friends wanted to do a morning cuppa with me at Big Bunches and discuss their plight and new job opportunities.

During my coffee with the boys, Kees Tesselaar stopped by Big Bunches to deliver flowers. Some of the boys asked him if there were jobs going at the tulip farms, in the packing sheds or even picking tulips. I chimed in that the boys would look good tiptoeing through the tulip fields. I can't recall whether Kees was able to assist these particular boys, but it had dawned on me then that Big Bunches was not only a flower shop. It was fast becoming a place of moral support, as well as a resourceful refuge for gay men.

I had written Dale's name on the top of my to-do list that day. That meant ringing Dale's father as I had promised Dorothy. I planned to offer meeting with them that evening. I would have to forgo my usual run around the lake in Albert Park with Terry (there are, after all, only 24 hours in a day). Since acquiring Big Bunches, my workload had increased and my free time and socialising had taken a hit, although I was mindful of maintaining my exercise regimen.

When I spoke with Dale's father, his tone was civil. I could sense, however, fear and worry coming through the telephone line. Irrationality had taken hold of him. I tried to be uplifting. I said that the AIDS situation was shaping up to be very different than any normal health emergency. All of us, I stressed, should prepare ourselves to move beyond our previous spheres of experience, and to suspend all judgments. In the world of AIDS, all the previous rules and experiences no longer applied. There was equally no use quoting the Bible here and there. I cannot recall what he said in reply, but I clearly recall him swallowing heavily and what sounded like the crunching sound of his Adam's apple.

We agreed to meet for coffee near their home in Canterbury. I knew an excellent European-style café on Maling Road called Gezelligheid, with private booths and dimmed lights. I had met the charming owner, Bram, at the University Club. He was Dutch, too (of course!). The café's name was a well-known Dutch phrase, meaning a happy serendipity where ambience, food and drink, and human warmth converged in one happy space and moment. A powerful word! Gezelligheid would be the perfect, calming atmosphere and ideal for a confidential conversation. The right atmosphere was absolutely critical. It could not be anything like a clinical space or sterile medical consulting room. I knew how to create a positive attitude and a trusting environment with people in distress. My mum Bets had taught me well.

On my way to meet them, I contemplated how to approach this painful family situation. I had learnt from my parents and my own experience to keep all my senses together. Most people feared the unknown. They thought the worst and the improbable, and wasted so much time caught up in anxiety and distress. My first line of approach was to listen empathically, although often people came to a counsellor or a friend expecting a word of comfort and support. Above all, I would offer my unconditional empathy . Many friends with AIDS could not verbalise their anxiety and were often paralysed by it. They felt terribly inadequate in dealing with the many obstacles and difficulties the disease presented. As it was, hardly anyone back then knew how to respond to a crisis of seemingly epidemic proportions. To protect my own mental health, I quickly learnt how to dismiss doubt and replace any negativity with positivity. I would not allow myself to be paralysed by others' fears.

I had met Dale once before, at a Christian Youth Camp years ago. He was a former footballer, just shy of six foot, with an athletic build, dark brown hair and piercing blue eyes. He played tennis when the football season finished. He was a handsome bloke who did not fit the effeminate stereotype of a gay man. His father looked like an older version of his son. I shook hands with him and was about to do the same with Dale, when

Dale made a gentle move to hug me instead. We embraced. I could smell his fragrance, English Leather, my favourite. Dale smiled shyly and sat down, but did not look directly at me. He seemed more focused on his father, who was very ill at ease.

Bram brought over some hot coffees and a hot chocolate for Dale. Bram was a friendly and attentive host and the venue was indeed welcoming—*Gezelligheid* at work. The ambience helped our focus to stay in the present, and not to jump to the future or the past. Dale clutched his hot chocolate. He said he was still coming to terms with his diagnosis. His father listened quietly in the meantime and looked intensely at me. Suddenly, he burst out in anger and fear, with what I suspected was also a tinge of guilt.

"Do you have sex with men?" Dale's father asked me brusquely. "That causes it, you know. That's what gave it to Dale." I did not respond. Responding would have been futile; his emotions were obviously agitated. Calm was needed. Dale continued to enjoy his chocolate as he said that his main worry was other people's reactions, especially his father's and the parishioners'. These were the same folks who professed to practise inclusiveness and unconditional love, the hallmarks of Christian faith. The reality, however, Dale said, was that they practised their prejudices against gay people and AIDS sufferers. They ostracised gay members of the church, which upset him greatly. I nodded in agreement. Dale was much more relaxed by now, and his father had gone quiet. Speaking to Dale's father, he agreed that he lacked compassion for his own son, and lamented that he could not genuinely accept his son's diagnosis without judgment. I encouraged him to find the courage in himself to help his son and others like him.

Dale had arranged an appointment with Dr Meese the next morning. Before leaving the café, I invited Dale to attend the Metropolitan Community Church the following Sunday, and invited him further to come with us to to Pokey',s *at The Prince Of Wales Hotel in St Kilda after the service so that his spiritual and social needs were equally catered for, I added. My intention was to introduce him to others like him living with HIV/AIDS, although there already seemed to be a deep sense of solidarity within him identifying with other AIDS sufferers.

I also handed Dale a brown paper bag containing the first edition of *Outrage*, a new gay periodical that had just hit the shelves. * It was a stellar publication that would provide a steady resource for the latest developments in the AIDS crisis. We hugged again. Dale and I would meet many times subsequently, including with his father, who by now had told me to call him Bob.

In 1983/84 "time" for me was an issue of concern, time, for some was diminishing fast, I was glad for some early stirrings to organise broader efforts in the gay community. My mum Bets brought a community notice to my attention. The Alternative Lifestyle Organisation (ALSO) called a public meeting to galvanise the community behind the fight against HIV/AIDS. It was organised for June 16 at the Dental Hospital Theatre in Melbourne. The plan was to formalise our individual efforts into some coherent framework. Bets thought it would be good for me to attend, so we could work collectively and beyond our efforts to date at Big Bunches. She had witnessed the great amount of time and care we were investing in people who were showing symptoms of HIV/AIDS, but who were not yet sick enough to be admitted to hospital. Other community-wide efforts would soon be underway. In the meantime, I would continue with my personal outreach as I did with Dale and the boys at Big Bunches. However, I was never alone in the effort.

Umberto had introduced us to a lovely couple, Pearl and Suzan, who had been together 20 years by then. He had met them at Pokey's. Both women were in their mid-50s and longtime regulars at Big Bunches, where they depended on Umberto's expert services. The couple owned a pub as well. Pearl was the chef and they served fantastic counter meals, although not vegetarian ones. They had little time for that rarest of tastes in those days! Nevertheless, they were down-to-earth and practical people. Both women joined us at the nutritional information nights the boys had organised at Big Bunches. It was there they came to know some of the boys who were no longer working and needed help at home. Pearl suggested that they deliver frozen meals to them several times during the week. They also began picking up some of the boys for social visits held at their pub. In time, Pearl and Suzan became surrogate mothers to many young gay men living in distress.

It was not always easy to look after people in the early days of AIDS. Deterioration of the mental and physical states happened so quickly. Here today, gone tomorrow. It was, for all intents and purposes, a wartime scenario with daily casualties.

Pearl, Suzan and I met Billy another airline steward. Billy was diagnosed with toxoplasmosis, which caused advanced dementia. In his case, the disease had changed his whole personality. At times, he would greet his friends and helpers with volatile cursing. He would call Pearl "a big butch dyke" and Suzan worse, and then in quick succession, he would become as sweet as pie. These were difficult days and one thing we knew was not to take anything personally. We would support each other emotionally through talking and laughing often. What else could one do besides educating ourselves about the disease? Frivolity became an important ally against despondency.

There were times when I had to excuse myself when visiting sick friends. My excuses were rarely genuine. Kaposi Sarcoma would disfigure once-handsome young faces and Pneumocystis Pneumonia would ravage the body, converting the most robust of frames into walking skeletons. The boys were mentally crushed when they realised that they had lost their former beauty. There was no use tut-tutting or offering patronising clichés such as "You'll be right soon." Again and again, I learnt not to be paralysed by fear. I appreciated that we were in uncharted waters. Many who became de facto AIDS carers held no formal qualifications for dealing with the disease. I was a counsellor, but I was unprepared for the devastating speed and unsettling ramifications of the AIDS crisis. All of us, including doctors, were on a steep learning curve. We would get our hands on the latest reports and clinical studies. But the most important tools remained what we could provide immediately: our compassion and empathy.

IT'S MELBOURNE'S BIGGEST EVER REGULAR GAY VENUE.........

WITH THE SHOW THAT SETS THE PACE IN MELBOURNE.

Campaign Gay Guide MAY '78

FEATURING BEST OF POKEYS

Sunday 6 till 10

POKEYS

Prince of Wales Hotel
Fitzroy Street,
St. Kilda

DISCO FLOORSHOW PIANO BAR

Pokeys Newspaper advertisment 1978

Pokeys was the ritzy drag cabaret club at The Prince of Wales Hotel
in St Kilda. Doug Lucas, one of the performers and the compere,
was a friend of mine, as was Jan Hillier, the business doyen behind
the Pokeys phenomenon through all of its 14 fabulous years.
Pokeys was a safe haven for the gay community and, in particular,
those affected by the AIDS crisis. There, they could enjoy the
opulent productions and extravagant costumes, make new friend,
and, above all, momentarily forget their pain and suffering. Pokeys
raised the funds to purchase all the TV sets at Fairfield, Jan Hillier
thought it awful that patients should have to pay TV rental.

Chapter 11

Controlling the unthinking masses
through fear of catastrophe

*"There was a sad urgency to the occasion, too, as Ian feared he had
not much longer to live. I wasn't surprised, as I knew other gay men
living with AIDS who wished to marry their partners. I attended six
such services in one year alone."*

B ig Bunches's atelier was a quiet place situated in one of the Jam
Factory's small laneways. Visitors could stop by the cosy workspace
to have a chat, or to idle in one of the chairs adorned with colourful
cushions. They were constant conversation pieces because of their
embroidered floral designs. Oftentimes, people would come in to quietly
watch us craft floral arrangements. Lately, however, the atelier had become
a place to listen to gay men with suspected symptoms of HIV/AIDS
discuss their feelings of exclusion and fear. Many of them were agitated
by the hatred spewed out by the religious organisations. The AIDS crisis
had opened my eyes to the cruelty of many churches, which had proved
themselves to be impervious to facts and reason and, above all, empathy.
As a practising Christian, I was sadly disappointed.

Dorothy was preparing bridal bouquets for a wedding one morning,
while I made the rose lapel pins for the men, when I caught the light blue

eyes of one Ian Harris. Ian and I had met some weeks prior at the gay-friendly *Metropolitan Community Church* on Toorak Road in South Yarra. A mutual friend of ours, Mary Bodnik, had introduced us. Mary was a well-known artist and had painted the Big Bunches flower shop in the style of Van Gogh's Montmartre series. Van Gogh had painted the famous Parisian district's coffee shops and popular haunts, which were not unlike the scenes around the Jam Factory. Mary also made portraits and sketches of handsome men and others of interest who visited her at the church. (I suspected that she thought Ian and I would make a good match.)

Ian approached us in a shy manner and upon greeting us with a subdued but cheery hello, he got straight to the point of his visit. He told me of some recent homophobic press releases from several Australian churches, which had been published wholesale and without apology by the country's sensationalist tabloids. Ian was outraged. With a twinkle in his eye, he said he had prepared a talk to rebuff the fundamentalists for once and for all. The subject of the talk: Jesus's wet dreams! I couldn't help but chortle at the idea and agreed to read his draft notes. We made plans for later that day, when the shop wouldn't be as busy.

Ian was a thoughtful, philosophically inclined young man. He was the youngest of three children and the only son. He was always genial and never set in his ways. Ian's slight build, brown hair, and blue eyes were becoming of someone of English decent. He also sported a robust and cheeky sense of humor and saw the good in people. One thing he could not tolerate, however, was injustice, toward any human being or animal.

I knew Ian was HIV-positive from our first conversation at the MCC. He was not overly worried by the question of the hereafter, and chose instead to focus his energies on the cruel homophobia practised and preached by so-called leaders in the Christian community. During our conversation at Big Bunches, he gave me a copy of an article written by the infamous New South Wales preacher-politician, the Reverend Fred Nile. Nile's article was published in the *Sunday Telegraph*, where he also appeared as a regular columnist, spouting his diatribe of anti-gay ideology. He would repeat his assaults on the gay community on his other platform, the talk-radio station 2GB. Nile would inveigh against gay people and demanded that they be ostracised because of the AIDS crisis and more generally because of who they were. He reminded listeners that homosexuality was still illegal in New South Wales. Ian was particularly concerned about the effect of these inaccurate, hateful articles attacked on defenseless young gay men suffering from HIV/AIDS, who could not defend themselves while they were physically and psychologically weakened. Then Ian reminded me that it was the tenth anniversary of the firebombing of an MCC church which held their services in a Gay Bar named the *Upstairs Lounge* in New Orleans. It happened on the 24 June 1973,thirty two parishioners died the assistant Pastor Mitch Mitchell was a friend of Ian's. I knew that Mitch and his boyfriend Louis Broussard both died in the fire, their charcoal remains showing them clinging to each other. I quickly concurred that we needed to promote and conduct a memorial service for these early Gay Christian Martyrs to remind the community that such attacks were encouraged by fundamentalist sick religionist who spewed hate and discord against the Gay Community; sadly this homophobic attack against the MCC church received virtually no media coverage, the police investigations were sloppy and were barely interested and the Christian Churches completely ignored it. There was a twist to all this hate as well. The assault on gay men by Nile and other Christian leaders coincided with the ongoing exposure, from 1983 onwards, of sexual abuse and pedophilia in the Christian churches, across all denominations. Ian intended his talk, which was to be delivered at the MCC, to counteract the damaging disinformation campaign waged by the fundamentalist preachers by exploring Christ's own humanity and struggle with sexuality. Ian also wanted to expose the child abuses in these religious organizations.

As an aside here, in November 2017 the Royal Commission into Institutional Child abuse establish by Labor Prime Minister Julia Gillard in 2012, presented its final massive 17 volume report to the Governor General in November 2017 detailing the culmination of five years of hearings into of abuse by mainly Christian Churches of all colours listing thousands upon thousands of child abuse victims perpetuated by the enemies of the Gay community over a sixty year period. Karma has caught up with these self-righteous ones., Ian would no doubt be smiling that justice will be done and that such evil was exposed.

There were of course sympathetic Christians. For instance, the Sisters of the Good Shepherd, who made their facilities available to offer palliative care to people living with AIDS. Countless Christian individuals fought in the trenches alongside their gay brothers and sisters. Then there was the example of the Commonwealth Government's intervention in Premier Joh Bjelke-Petersen's Queensland, when the archconservative aspiring autocrat refused to distribute federal funds for AIDS education. The federal Labor government funnelled the critically needed moneys through the Catholic Sisters of Mercy, whose work was also praised by the then federal Health Minister, Neal Blewitt.

Ian's other reason to see me struck a joyful chord: he was marrying his partner, Layne. He invited me to their private (and, at the time, legally unrecognised) commitment ceremony, to be held at their place on Park Crescent in the leafy Melbourne suburb of Alphington. It would be, for all intents and purposes, a traditional Western wedding, with the till-death-do-us-part vows, readings, an exchange of rings, and, of course, a wedding cake. There was a sad urgency to the occasion, too, as Ian feared he had not much longer to live. I wasn't surprised, as I knew other gay men living with AIDS who wished to marry their partners. I attended six such services in one year alone. Ian had also arranged the pastor of the MCC to officiate the ceremony. I hugged Ian and said I would be delighted to join them for the big day.

I had already met Ian's partner, Layne, at a recent VAC support group meeting. Layne was an enthusiastic collector of antique clocks and the proud owner of a lovely large cat named Amadeus. I agreed to watch Amadeus during Ian and Layne's honeymoon. I won't soon forget having to call the Fire Brigade to rescue this hefty feline from high up one of the trees in the couple's yard. No amount of prodding or food could entice Amadeus down! Layne had also arrived in Australia from the United States aboard the Dutch liner *MV Johan van Oldenbarnevelt*, the same ship that had ferried my family and hundreds of other Dutch families to the southern continent. In fact, so many of the gay men I had met over the past three years had also sailed on the Johan that I swore it must have been because of the famous ship's elegant style!

Ian and Layne were fortunate to enjoy two more blissful albeit challenging years together. Ian succumbed to complications arising from AIDS on 10 December 1988. Layne paid tribute to his beloved at the funeral service:

He was not just an ordinary man but a wonderful man. A wonderful man with beautiful eyes and brown hair. His name is Ian. A man not yet in his 30s. A man with great courage and faith. A man who lived his life in 27 years. A man with faith in his God and maker. A man who thanked you for all he received. A man who loved life. A man who could love everyone. A man who God will love. A man whose memory will never fade or die. A man for whom I will ever thank God. A man I will love forever. Thank you, Ian, for sharing your life and love with me. For your love has made me more loving and a caring person.

Layne took Ian's surname shortly thereafter, becoming Layne Ramon Shoebridge-Harris. As of the time of writing, Layne now lives near Hobart in Tasmania.

There was a sad urgency to the occasion, too, as Ian feared he had not much longer to live. I wasn't surprised, as I knew other gay men living with AIDS who wished to marry their partners. I attended six such services in one year alone.

Chapter 12

More then death they feared decline

"Robert would later come to stay with me for three weeks for emotional support. Every day I would give him a fresh bunch of flowers. Flowers were potent weapons against the ugliness pervading our lives."

It was nearing five o'clock on a Saturday morning at Big Bunches and what a sight to behold! The flower shop was overrun with five hundred hot pink tulips, exquisitely arranged for delivery to Olympic Park ahead of Gay Day, Melbourne's first-ever gay festival, organized by the ALSO Foundation. The festival was then entering its second year in 1983. If its inaugural year was any indication of future popularity, this Gay Day promised to be bigger and better.(The festival would give way to the current annual Midsumma Festival,) which was first held in 1989. After all, it was Big Bunches' first time participating in the festival! Many gay businesses were showcasing their services at Gay Day and had stands around Olympic Park serving refreshments, including by the ever-popular Soda Sisters and their uniformed roller-skating boys.

We had the pink tulips specially flown over from the Netherlands for the occasion. I was nervous as our reputation was at stake. When it came to important events like Gay Day, one needed a keen eye for beauty and perfection – the same qualities that Big Bunches' gay clientele demanded from us. Our customers were fastidious in their requests for floral arrangements. Gay men only wanted the best flowers, and, above all, they had to be stylishly presented to make the right impression. I was confident that our hot pink and graceful tulips would not only do the trick at Gay Day: they would be the talk of the town.

We were busy setting up the fresh flower displays at Big Bunches that morning, before the regular customers began to arrive in the early hours. It was well-known that I only worked at the shop on weekends, when most of my friends, like Terry, Brian or Ken, would buy their flowers or some seashells or other plants to decorate their homes. Each friend usually brought some coffees for us to share whilst we caught up on the latest news. My friends also enjoyed listening to Umberto's amusing repartee with his cool clique of customers. Just as well the coffees kept coming: I had (and have) a high tolerance for caffeine, something many Netherlanders would understand. Besides, at those early hours, coffee was a natural mood enhancer!

A very dear friend, Robert, was the first to rush in that morning, carrying a breakfast of freshly baked almond croissants and two short black coffees from a nearby bakery at Prahran Market. The pastries were still warm from the oven and filled with the most delicious almond paste, which reminded me of marzipan, my favourite Dutch sweet.

Seeing Robert and smelling the croissants put a wide smile on my face. But Robert was not in a good mood and hadn't slept the night before. He had come to Big Bunches straight from Mandate, one of Melbourne's alternative dance clubs popular with the young gay set. Amidst the shop's roses, tulips and long-stemmed gerberas, Robert flashed his lower legs to me, exposing several serious-looking dark blue blotches. His dark brown eyes dimmed and showed a deep sadness. He lacked his usual cheeky sparkle. Robert then sat down while I continued to serve customers in between having coffee and listening to him. He asked whether I thought the blue lesions might be the start of Kaposi Sarcoma, a common affliction for AIDS sufferers. I was not a medical doctor and not about to offer a medical opinion glibly. But when I compared Robert's lesions to what I had seen in the AIDS wards in San Francisco, they were a worrying sign. Of course, I wasn't about to tell Robert that myself. I calmed him down, offering a somewhat laughable excuse for the lesions. I suggested he might have bumped into something in the dark corridors at Mandate. I asked when he first noticed the lesions. When leaving Mandate in the early hours that morning, he said. I encouraged him to see a doctor urgently just to be sure.

Suddenly, Robert asked whether I still found him physically desirable. The question didn't take me aback: I heard scores of young gay men fretting over the cruel diminishment of their once beautiful looks. It was a common fate for many living with AIDS in the days before effective treatment. Robert's conscience was doubly punished by the homophobic tabloids and the guilt that the sensationalist stories induced in him. He felt alone and dirty. I looked surprised and put on a Sisyphean smile, the type to save one from falling into despair. I said that his question was the best news I had heard all day: his wanting to be desirable indicated to me that he had not lost his erotic passions. That his psyche had not devolved into self-loathing, as would happen to so many young gay men. The Dutch have a much better word for this kind of passion: *hartstocht*, which means something akin to "the heart's journey." Robert's simple question revealed, I said, that he was still on a journey of the heart.

I asked in turn whether he enjoyed feeling attractive. Robert said yes. An answer that had been reinforced, no doubt, by compliments he received from several men the night before at Mandate. A few asked him out for coffee, and he had a dinner invitation, too. But Robert feared that he would become less attractive, and therefore less desirable, as his condition worsened. He felt that his HIV/AIDS status would be hindrance itself and asked whether he should inform his potential partners about his status, to which I gave a resounding yes. One thing that had sustained the gay community was a common sense of altruism, born of our personal struggles and the difficulties facing our community. I recommended that he move away from casual sexual encounters and look for a more lasting relationship. Though I knew my view on casual sex was not popular at the time, I saw few other ways to put an immediate stop to the spread of HIV/AIDS.

Umberto joined us for his coffee break. He enriched our dialogue by relating his story of dealing with his AIDS diagnosis, and how he coped with low energy and feelings of self-loathing and depression. He pointed to his strong friendships and good conversations, things that sustained his self-worth and confidence despite handling a terminal illness. He also enjoyed going to Steam Works, an all-male sauna, to feel desired by other men who frequented the sauna for casual sex. The compliments boosted his mental state: Umberto compared going to Steam Works or Pokey's on a Sunday night to therapy or having a holiday. While they were safe havens for gay men who had lost family and friends due to their sexuality and for those diagnosed with HIV/AIDS, the downside, I hastened to add, was the absence of safe sex at those venues, despite the ample condoms available there.

As we finished our coffees, I encouraged Robert to check his self-criticism and reach out to his friends for conversations and platonic but affirming physical contact, sort of like a "bromance". It wasn't the perfect medicine, but in those times and even more generally, it was an effective strategy of nurturing a healthy, positive frame of mind. Umberto also complimented Robert on his sense of humour. It was incredibly valuable having Umberto's presence at Big Bunches. He was a jack of all trades in business and a sweetheart and confidant for those who needed both.

Robert would later come to stay with me for three weeks for emotional support as he gradually accepted living with his condition. I would give him a fresh bunch of flowers every day, I believed that flowers were potent weapons against the ugliness pervading our lives. As Robert's condition deteriorated, his body's physical degradation caused him to have panic attacks. At times, he thought he should give up on life. He likewise feared a lifetime of discrimination and rejection. It was at these low moments that he could be restored by a hug or back rub, or merely being held. I had learnt from studying Evolutionary Psychology about a hormone called oxytocin, without which there was no romantic desire or appetite to bond with another (or, for the men, have erections). The neurotransmitters in our endocrine system are the bodies' chief communication system and cause the release of hormones like oxytocin. The release only happens through an act of intimacy, such as physical touch, or through other psychological mechanisms, like a romantic chat with a loved one. Persons with low levels of oxytocin can suffer serious mental illnesses, such as deep depression and anxiety, and may have less empathy for others. During these supportive experiences with Robert, his brain's neurotransmitters were triggering the release of oxytocin, reducing his fears and anxiety.

We shared many positive memories and indulged in bouts of nostalgia, for instance dancing to Grace Jones. Robert, like hundreds of other frightened young gay men, needed to realise that the circle of affection was not broken. A positive diagnosis was most alarming. After all, at the time, in most of cases, AIDS equalled death. That was not the only factor: many came from religious backgrounds, from churches that made them feel dirty, undesirable, and guilty. In this way the churches ensured that gay men were the modern equivalent of lepers. Most of all, Robert and the other boys wanted to talk. When the boys came to have coffee at Big Bunches, it was always an active brainstorming session. They shared and discussed their personal strategies to survive the battlefield that was the AIDS crisis. It gave us a sense of empowerment at a time of intense homophobia and sex negativity. Ideas were flushed out in the open about the new sexual counterrevolution that this disease was initiating. Francis Bacon once said that knowledge is power. We needed to build an armoury of knowledgeable rebuttals to combat ignorance as well as homophobia. It was becoming a matter of urgent self-preservation.

We explored ways to make safe sex erotic, at a time when safe sex practices were not commonly practised in the gay community, the perception being that a condom reduced the physical enjoyment of sex. Erotic safe sex education, however, was for everybody, not only for gay men. Heterosexuals were at risk of contracting serious sexually transmitted infections. A perfect illustration was the case of cervical cancer, which was caused by the Human Papillomavirus, or HPV. Like HIV, HPV was transmitted via bodily fluid encountering infected sperm. In the 1980s, hundreds of Australian women died each year from cervical cancer, at a much higher rate than gay men were dying of complications from HIV/AIDS. Yet there was no sensationalism in the daily tabloids. No mass HPV panic. Instead, journalists concentrated with voyeuristic zeal on the sexual lives of gay men while women died in large numbers from HPV. Sadly, in the days before an HPV vaccine, 965 new cases were reported in 1982 alone. Over 400 women died of HPV that year.

The situation may have been totally different to the stigma facing the gay community but the blowhards' rhetoric surrounding HPV was eerily familiar. In 2004, when an HPV vaccine finally became available in the form of Gardasil, the Australian Government was the first in the world to vaccinate schoolgirls. Fortunately, fatalities from cervical cancer began to decline. Nevertheless, Christian fundamentalists and their political allies on the Right protested. They did not want young women to be vaccinated, absurdly believing that taking this precaution licensed sexual promiscuity. In 1985, these same moralists and so-called religious leaders complained about a safe sex erotic video entitled *Chance of a Lifetime*, released that same year by the Gay Men's Health Center in New York City. The NSW Attorney General prevented the film from being shown in the state, on the grounds that the video contained publicly offensive material. At the time of writing, history was being repeated: the NSW Minister of Education Adrian Picolli bowed to pressure from conservative moralists in 2016 and banned the showing of *Gayby Baby*, an Australian film about children raised by gay and lesbian parents, in the state's public schools. Under a right-wing government, the Australian Government also withdrew funding for the Safe Schools program, which promoted inclusive sex education and anti-bullying. Little has changed since the 1980s in this respect: in Australia, right-wing governments have habitually catered to the sexual fears and anxieties of the Christian Right. The battle for equality and dignity was and remains a constant battle.

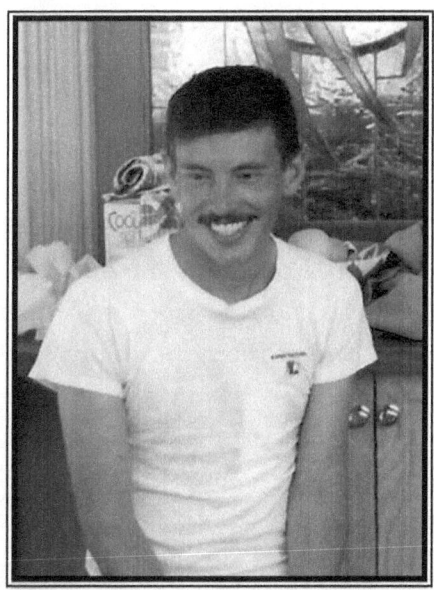

My very dear friend, Robert, was the first to rush in that morning, carrying a breakfast of freshly baked almond croissants and two short black coffees from a nearby bakery at Prahran Market.

Chapter 13

Under siege, coming together in a time of grave crisis

It reminded me of my grandparents' retelling of Dutch families working together during the Second World War to hide their sons from the Nazis and deportation to the camps. This, too, was an effort to save lives: gay lives and all those affected by AIDS.

On 16 June 1983, the Alternative Lifestyle Organisation held its major community-wide public meeting on the unfolding AIDS crisis. Umberto and Jason joined me at the meeting held in the Melbourne Dental Hospital lecture theatre. My mum Bets was especially pleased that I was attending, as she hoped to pass on any useful information to her church community. In particular, her church's pastor, the Reverend Williams, was in dire need of enlightenment, and not only because his son had AIDS: a fact Bets alone knew and for which she was sworn to secrecy. Much later, the Williams family would set up the David Williams Fund, one of Australia's largest charities assisting people living with HIV/AIDS.

Well, there was not one empty seat that night: as they say in Australia, it was chockers! It came as some relief recognising so many faces in attendance as well. Some fellow union members of mine smiled and nodded my way, while several Big Bunches customers blew us kisses.

Our good friend and clinical psychologist, the now late Bruce McNichol, sat with us and introduced his partner, Mark. It was practically a family affair, albeit a family under siege, coming together in a time of grave crisis. It reminded me of my grandparents' retelling of Dutch families working together during the Second World War to hide their sons from the Nazis and deportation to the camps. This, too, was an effort to save lives: gay lives and all those affected by AIDS.

The meeting brought together many professionals: lawyers, nurses, health educators, including Drs Vaughan Lenny and Peter Meese. Lenny and Meese were frequent visitors to Big Bunches. They enjoyed talking over coffees while purchasing flowers. We would often discuss AIDS and their hopes for a way out of the crisis. Lenny and I had a mutual American friend whose situation we discussed that night as well. Our friend was an advisor to the Australian Air Force on the F15 fighter jet. He had been diagnosed with AIDS and the RAF was at panic stations. We agreed to see him after the public meeting and discuss how we could support our friend.

I recognised several people who produced *Gay Community News* and *Outrage*, both monthly gay newspapers that published the latest AIDS information coming out of the United States. My eyes also fell on a person whom I absolutely admired: Jamie Gardner from the Homosexual Law Reform Coalition. I thanked Jamie personally afterwards for all his and the group's hard work. It was good to be amidst such respectable people. We were not a lonely, insignificant community, but a robust, talented and dependable one. How different from the conservatives and religious fundamentalists who hurled hate and abuse at us!

My friends and I felt empowered simply by attending the meeting. I am sure that was the case for all in attendance that night. We met many future leaders and visionaries, people who were coordinating our community's holistic approach to the growing crisis. I admired the political acumen of young activists, some with links to the socialist and trade union movements, who took the stage that night to speak. Activist luminaries such as Phil Carswell, Adam Carr, Lee Visser, Chris Gill, and Alison Thorne. Thorne proved the catalyst for action when she spoke, declaring: "What we need is an organisation." We all nodded a quiet amen of agreement. We needed an organisation to publicly advocate on behalf of all the communities most affected by AIDS: the gay community, haemophiliacs, and intravenous drug users. We also needed these activists' political knowhow to grab the politicians' attention. If we didn't strategically pursue our agenda, our adversaries—and this horrible disease—would walk all over us. The Victorian AIDS Council (or VAC) would emerge from these early collective efforts. A few weeks after the meeting, in the dining room of the popular gay Laird Hotel in Collingwood, Adam Carr proposed a motion, which carried, that the VAC act as the official representative voice on behalf of the Victorian gay community.

Yet I was, by nature, skeptical of formal organisations. As much as they could do good work, they could also stifle autonomous initiatives and frustrate otherwise organic community-level responses. Australians had a reputation for hiding behind rules and regulations before taking any action. Then again, I didn't have much political nous at the time. Nor did I understand much of the political process, although I had a strong sense of what social justice should mean in terms of appropriate government policies. After all, we were fighting for the recognition and fulfillment of human rights and the decriminalisation of male homosexuality.

One key item on the agenda was indeed legal reform. Male homosexuality had only been decriminalised in Victoria in March 1981, years after, in 1975, South Australia, thanks in part to my friend and politician, Terry, and the Australian Capital Territory. The Northern Territory would follow suit that year, in 1983, then New South Wales in 1984. In Western Australia and Queensland reform came much later: the states decriminalised male homosexuality in 1989 and 1990, respectively. Tasmania lagged even further behind. The Tasmanian Government refused to budge until a team of Tasmanian activists—including the likes of future gay rights champion Rodney Croome and his then partner Nick Toonen—took the state to court. The future Greens Party leader Bob Brown helped, as well, as the activists fought the conservatives all the way to the High Court of Australia. It was only Nick Toonen who went to the United Nations Human Rights Committee, where he won, that the Tasmanian Government capitulated to pressure from the federal government and decriminalised male homosexuality in 1997.

When organisations first start there can be a scramble for positions.

Egos are stroked and destroyed. This is all too common to any organisation, religious or secular. Remarkably, however, I don't recall there being many birthing problems in the early days of building the AIDS coalition. Phil Carswell was elected as the first President of the VAC. Phil was an astute leader and drew from his experience organising as a teacher with the Victorian Technical Teachers' Union. He was down-to-earth and proved capable of turning a diverse, and often divergent, group of activists into a formidable organisation for advocacy, education, and practical support. He also knew how to stroke and temper egos and make everyone feel like a valuable contributor. No small feat for any leader!

The VAC soon opened its first office on Rupert Street in Collingwood. The office was named the Peter Knight Centre after Peter Knight, an early fighter for the AIDS-affected community. It was Peter's idea that gay people should look after their own and provide home support services. He went on to become the first convener of the VAC Support Group. Peter, who could no longer work full-time due to complications from AIDS, joined us for many discussions at Big Bunches, too. He was always entertained by Umberto's catty, clever repartee of witticisms telling nosey friends that sexual satisfaction had washed every part of him clean. Many customers were charmed by Umberto's sexual magnetism, and his contagious humour was a great medicine to lift flagging spirits (Not to mention all the eye candy that would saunter past the shop, as the boys pretended to smell flowers and talk to the peach-faced lovebirds.)

The boys and I became regular attendees at VAC functions. I recall one Sunday afternoon, at Club 80 on Peel Street, where Peter held a screening of videos he had obtained from the U.S. as part of the VAC volunteer induction training for support group members. The videos contained images of gay men ravaged by AIDS. They were so very raw and uncensored, like viewing a Dantean hell scape up close. The men depicted in these videos reminded me of the emaciated frames of men and women as they walked out of the Belsen Concentration Camp. Belsen was a horrific slaughterhouse but not a guaranteed death sentence; for AIDS sufferers in 1983, a positive diagnosis was practically terminal. As we watched the videos, I noticed a rapid change in the attendees' mood: one of utter sadness underscored by an eerie silence. After all, many volunteers were facing their own mortality because of the disease and had not yet learnt how to discuss it openly. They bottled up their feelings instead, although they were betrayed by their distressed body language, which exposed their underlying fears and negative emotions. The aftermath of viewing these tapes was such that we held debriefing sessions afterwards. Several young men were crying, Robert among them. Peter himself could barely talk because, as for so many, he saw his own diminishment in these painful videos. It was difficult for all to behold. I felt a lump in my throat thinking of the people immediately around me.

Shortly after the VAC launched, a call went out for volunteers. It set up a skill and experience register for people who had already volunteered, along with an AIDS telephone information and counselling service hotline. There were specialised groups for lawyers, nurses, and educators. The VAC Support Group was the largest of these groups, headed by Peter Knight. Every volunteer contributed their skills, experience, and personal networks to the massive effort to provide care to people living with AIDS. Prospective volunteers were required to attend Peter's memorable VAC induction course, while I introduced them to the organisation's rules, procedures, and values. The VAC drilled into volunteers the importance of maintaining confidentiality, and taught them how to properly clean up infected blood and bodily fluid, and how to get along with difficult people (dementia was no small problem for some with AIDS). There was also an influx of straight women volunteers, which challenged some of the gay men. At times, especially in the beginning, they viewed the women as "fag hags," a term for straight women who enjoyed socialising with gay men. While this initially caused the group a degree of stress, we knew this was a time of transition. We were forging new alliances and learning how to cope in the process. In the end, the issue faded.

Nurses and health educators from Fairfield Infectious Diseases Hospital taught us how to manage patients and about medical terminology. The lectures were transcribed and included in our training manuals. We were also joined by several Fairfield medical doctors: Anne Mijch, Ron Lukas, Alex Wodak, David Bradford, Ian Goller, David Plummer and others whose names escape me. All this valuable information was added to the formidable database of AIDS-related information that the VAC

Support Group was steadily amassing. Updating the database was a great responsibility as our knowledge of AIDS (and eventually HIV once the vector became known) was evolving rapidly. Old was soon replaced by new, which made for plenty of work in the days long before Google.

Bruce McNicol headed up the training for another initiative, AIDS Mates, and I was his assistant. Hundreds of volunteers undertook months of learning how to personally care for people living with AIDS. How to cook for them, clean them, physically move them, make coffee for them: the volunteers had to do practically every daily chore that the person could no longer do themselves. Above all, we were there as their friends, a lifeline in dark times. The first AIDS Mate training course took place at Big Bunches, as we had the space and, more critically, it would save money that would otherwise be spent on renting a hall, money that we did not have then.

The Big Bunches family also became increasingly involved in providing care and support outside of the VAC. I hosted vegetarian dinners at my place twice a week. Dorothy was especially good at preparing meals that were beneficial for the immune system. The boys regularly asked for her recipes. Our foods were packed with flavour and spices: basil, coriander, rosemary, thyme, sage: the list went on and on. All these spices improved the aroma and flavour of the food and, more importantly, awakened our friends' struggling appetites. It was also a welcome departure from the food that many of my Anglo-Australian friends were accustomed to: the three veg and a chop cooked by their mothers and grandmothers. I was fortunate to know my friend Raja Dasa, who was a Hare Krishna, a vegetarian chef, and a closeted gay man. Dasa taught me most of my cooking repertoire, including kebabs made with cottage cheese, oats, yogurt, and raisins: by far, my most popular dish. Stuffed baby eggplants with pine nuts and secret spices, with a sauce made from tamarind pulp and lemon juice: a true aphrodisiac, the recipe was guaranteed to raise slack libidos. Our regular Friday night spread made regulars out of many young gay men who joined us.

My friend Peter Knight the founder of the VAC Support Group, for one, saw the delicious, wholesome vegetarian dishes that Dorothy and I prepared for Umberto, Ian, and the other boys and asked if we could prepare some for him, too. When his mother flew in from the United Kingdom to be with him during his last days alive, I had Peter, his mother and their friend Bill join us for the dinners at my home. Bill did not dislike vegetarian (or "fake") sausages, but with a sly wink you knew he preferred the real thing. He especially loved Dutch-style mashed kale, *stamppot*, with a big *Rookworst*, the Dutch national sausage, which he enjoyed eating like I ate: with one large fork, mashing the food together like real men do, he said. It reminded Bill of living in Amsterdam with his Dutch boyfriend. Perhaps that is why we got on together so well. It was through food, caring, and solidarity then that our community grew united and survived.

We worked hard and quickly to lay the groundwork for handling the AIDS crisis, as we anticipated that hundreds more would soon be diagnosed with AIDS. That would not be the case yet in the early 1980s, but it was the calm before the storm. While we couldn't know it with any certainty at the time, the storm would come.

According to government figures for Victoria, 500 people were diagnosed with HIV/AIDS between 1983 and 1985. To those of us volunteering, the official figures seemed low. It was a time of immense paranoia in the gay community (and, in other ways, more broadly). In 1983 alone, many frightened and likely infected boys had visited Big Bunches displaying telltale symptoms. Hundreds more gay men remained untested. I was not a medical doctor (nor an expert in anything much!) but I had a gut feeling that the reality on the ground was already much worse than we knew. I knew from working in San Francisco that the disease had a long incubation period before definite symptoms emerged. My friend and AIDS research journalist Arjen Broekhuizen also suspected, from what he knew—and he knew far more than most—that more people were living with HIV/AIDS than had yet died of AIDS. Due to the general paranoia and the strict confidentiality imposed on people's statuses, the scope of the problem was kept largely hushed. It wasn't until April 1984 when the first AIDS patient was admitted to the Fairfield Infectious Diseases Hospital. Within a few years, into the late 1980s, when 10,000 cases had been diagnosed overall, there was no doubt that without the early leadership of the VAC and other AIDS organisations across the states and territories, alongside a proactive Commonwealth Government, the fight against the spread of HIV/AIDS would not have been as effectively contained.

Many governments worldwide, however, deliberately ignored this deadly disease, which by the late 1980s would devastate whole communities in Africa, Asia, the South Pacific and Papua New Guinea. Right-wing Christian missionaries and a conservative Polish Pope exacerbated the problem by forbidding the use of contraceptives and speaking negatively of sex and sexuality. AIDS organisations everywhere had to fight disinformation campaigns and widespread ignorance and bigotry, while publishing the latest research on available antiviral drugs and educating as to what worked and what didn't. In Australia, we were very fortunate to have a Labor Government with a gay man as Minister of Health (though Neil Blewett was closeted at the time). The Australian Government sponsored many AIDS-related programs. Some programs were beneficial, others a step back, like the controversial TV advertising campaign for AIDS awareness, *The Grim Reaper*. Many of my colleagues identified the Reaper in the advertisement as standing for a gay man living with AIDS, an unfortunate but unintentional symbolism. Fear was one tool employed to change people's attitudes toward unprotected sex. Perhaps the advertising campaign was detrimental, yet these were desperate times. The urgency of stopping the advance of AIDS was as vital as our cultivating nonjudgmental compassion towards those affected by the disease. I don't know how effective the campaign was in preventing overall HIV transmissions, but it certainly stigmatised people living with AIDS.

As it was, Australia would become an example to the rest of the world with one of the lowest HIV infection rates in the West, bar the Netherlands, which had a similar population size and the lowest rate. Nevertheless, given the resistance the Australian gay community faced by the Christian Right, it was a spectacular feat of the community and its allies' collective efforts.

Picture; My friend Peter Knight (standing lhs near window,) the founder of the VAC Support Group, for one, saw the delicious, wholesome vegetarian dishes that Dorothy and I prepared for Umberto, Ian, and the other boys and asked if we could prepare some for him, too. When his mother and brother seated at the table, flew in from the United Kingdom to be with him during his last days alive, I had Peter, his mother and their friend Bill join us for the dinners at my home.

Chapter 14

Diversity our strenght

"It makes me sad and happy all at once, remembering all of those sweet young men who sang for Aunt Dolly, knowing that each one had since passed on soon after. None made it over thirty years of age, Robert and Umberto among them. We had one life to live and we lived that life together fully"

The first meeting of the VAC support group at Big Bunches was more of a social event so organisers and volunteers could mingle. Dorothy, Umberto, and several others acted as hosts. It happened to be Umberto's birthday, too, but he told me to keep that a secret. Many of our friends came, including Pearl and Suzan, who rode into town on their spotless chrome Harleys. Dorothy flourished in her role welcoming and introducing the attendees that night. She took a genuine interest in everyone, although sometimes her country nature was misunderstood by some as being nosey. She was dealing with some particularly colourful characters at one point in the evening when she noticed Russell, a young man in black leather chaps and a leather vest sporting a Jackeroo Club insignia. She asked him whether he was into motorcycles. "Excuse me, Keith," Dorothy called out amid the crowd, "Russell wants to know if we have a hazing or initiation test. You'll have to help him, love. I don't know what that is!"

We had a diverse crowd at the launch. People were chatting. I overheard some admiring each other's tattoos and piercings, others discussing health and fitness. I was raving about vegetarian diets and vegan cakes. The bonding process was well underway. Umberto told me that it was the kind of extended family he had always wanted. He then became morose thinking about his condition and fell silent. There were to be plenty more such moments in the years ahead when we did not know what to say; a gentle smile or a slight caressing silent touch or hug usually soothed the dissolutionment of the moment.

Dorothy and I continued to mingle with the new volunteers, filling up glasses along the way. A short while later, I went to the music system and put on Umberto's favourite gay anthem, "You Make Me Feel (Mighty Real)" and switched off the lights. Suddenly the darkness gave way to Robert, who looked resplendent in his Ansett Airlines uniform with his endearing smile, carrying a birthday cake adorned with 24 candles and sparklers. I hadn't kept Umberto's birthday much of a secret after all! The gathering broke into a spontaneous "Happy Birthday," followed by "For He's a Jolly Good Fellow" and an outpouring of hugs and kisses and hands ruffling Umberto's hair. Everyone enjoyed the rich, creamy black forest cake, which was baked and donated by Mordecai, a baker who ran a cake shop on Saint Kilda's famous Acland Street. I had been drinking coffee and eating the best Vienna cakes in his shop for years, although I would only learn later that Mordecai was gay, too.

There was no doubt that the VAC provided psychological security and a feeling of belonging for its members and our vulnerable community. Prior to the VAC's formation, our young community of activists and caregivers was in danger of splintering, or worse, annihilation. We were no longer fighting as individuals in a solitary battle against AIDS: the VAC became our collective effort and an easy point of reference for the gay community and society at large. We were fighting for our lives and dignity amidst daily worsening strife. The news from San Francisco was increasingly ominous: gay men began to die in droves, the HIV virus (which was only identified in 1984) frequently having a long incubation period before any noticeable symptoms manifested. This urged me on to get our support group trained and skilled up and working in the community right from the start. While we had fun in the moment, we never lost sight of the serious urgency of the times.

In these early support groups, there was a common hope for dreams, for laughter, for an expansion of love. For some, the support groups replaced blood or church ties for gay men and women whose families had disowned and abandoned them. I wondered (and still do) whether these men and women were hated because of their sexuality or for the simple fact that they were non-conformist in a highly conformist society. As a whole, many of the gays and lesbians and the sprinkling of straight people aiding the VAC operation were creative, outside-of-the-box types with artistic and innovative mindsets. They did not suffer from apathy toward social ills as conformists do, nor did they accept the status quo, in keeping with many queer souls over the course of history: the trendsetters, leaders, artists, scientists that have revolutionised our world. It deeply saddened me to think that all this talent was dying in the thousands around us.

Our newly unified tribe was no pack of cowards, either: we were fearless fighters up against a mainstream society that had devolved in the early 1980s into a mass of infantile finger-waving and hysterical scapegoating, plagued by ignorance and paranoia. That sadly was the Australian community then, and in ways that are not the subject of this book, today, too: with respect to our society's treatment of Indigenous Australians and migrants locked up in our offshore concentration camps.

Tabloid newspapers and commercial news media reminded us daily that we were dirty. In 1984, three babies died in Queensland from receiving HIV-infected blood. Of course, the gays were collectively responsible. The famous, otherwise untouchable Hollywood star Rock Hudson died in late 1985: "he deserved what he got" was the gist of the tabloid media's message. That same year, the NSW government supported the discrimination and effective ostracising of a four-year-old toddler, Eve van Grafhorst, who had been infected by an HIV-contaminated blood transfusion. She was banned from her preschool because fearful, narrow-minded people made life hell for the Van Grafhorst family, who eventually fled to New Zealand, where they were welcomed by the government and people. The VAC volunteers and the leadership of the Australian AIDS Council were committed to changing the paradigms in our society along with the laws and regulations.

They did not know it, but as they were dying, gay Australians were creating a legacy that would forever change Australia, as their brothers and sisters were doing in their own countries worldwide.

As we participated in the VAC training courses, we learnt new rules and regulations and received sensitivity training to assimilate new values associated with the fight against AIDS and the stigma against the gay community. We learned of legal responsibilities such as the duty of care. The law required the keeping of accurate medical records, privacy, and the maintenance of confidentiality. These were now serious aspects of our daily work: there was no room for loose cannons or "tabloid cheap speak," as I called it. Umberto, for one, took the new norms and values to heart. He repeated the truism that "a standing cock has no conscience," and with that newfound awareness, he asked the Jam Factory management to install a "No Loitering" sign in the public toilets. I was surprised but delighted that he initiated such a request. He went even further, asking carpenters to reclad the toilet cubicles to close off the glory holes. "We have to do it for the sake of saving lives," he told me. I hugged him and said I was happy that the safe sex campaigning and the VAC education group were having their intended impact on changing risky sexual behaviour. I later got into a heated argument with the manager of the Jam Factory, who sent me the bill for the "No Loitering" sign and the recladding of the male toilet cubicles. Management said my shop was attracting the undesirable elements to the Jam Factory, although the manager hastened to add that he wasn't homophobic; his only problem was with "girly poofters." I took exception to his comments and refused to pay the bill. That was the end of that.

The influx of new friends was good for Big Bunches, too. Business increased and many more cups of coffees were poured while we spoke about the near- and long-term future of the gay community in the wake of the AIDS crisis. Dorothy was overworked. She would often get grouchy, as would Umberto, whose health began to diminish. His remaining time would be short. We needed more staff as well, and what better choice than to employ some of Melbourne's smart transgender men and women? It would support our business and their lives, affording work and community for those facing incredible social stigma. Dorothy had no clue that we had employed two transgender women. One was a gorgeous dancer from

Pokey's. She called them both "her beautiful girls" and I agreed: they moved about with unparalleled grace and style, exhibiting authenticity and respect for their own bodies. Surely, I thought, they embody the aspirations of many Australian women. They modelled the way of beauty.

Nor should the diversity of VAC volunteers be overlooked. I particularly remember a lovely Orthodox Jewish woman from Balaclava, where many of Melbourne's Orthodox Jewish community resides. Hannah was a friend of Mordecai, our Jewish baker on Acland Street. She wore a wig to cover her real hair in keeping with the customs of her religion. Hannah volunteered at VAC for one reason alone: her unconditional love for humanity compelled her to do what she could for a community under siege. Our Jewish friends in general showed a lot of sympathy to the gay community. As a Dutchman, I also felt an affinity for the Jewish people, primarily because of their centuries of suffering and persecution across Europe, not unlike the gay community then worldwide. The Netherlands was the only country in Western Europe that had welcomed the Jews with an open heart for over 500 years whilst they faced persecution elsewhere. The Netherlands thrived as a result of accepting Jewish people into their communities, intellectual life, and businesses. Could Australians learn this lesson by opening their hearts to their gay brothers and sisters?

Personally, the coming together of many diverse subcultures within the gay community presented a steep learning curve for me as well: Bears, Chubs, Drag Queens, Leather, S&M, Androgynous, Pansexual, Bisexuals, Queer, all in the same boat and on the same page to defeat AIDS. If the readers will excuse a moment of levity, all of this integrating into and involvement with the wider gay community came as a cultural shock to my middle-class but liberal Dutch upbringing. The names, o Lord, the names! Hannah was also a friend of Betty Butt Plug—yes, many of the volunteers had outrageous, personally liberating names, which were only disclosed after we knew each other better. I had learned by then to hold my peace, even when the nicknames got to me. The nicknames were descriptive of the individual personalities: here was Betty Butt Plug with his partner, FiFi. Loose Fart and Limp Wrist. Then there was Ice Cream: he was so sweet you'd like to lick him. Our group called Keith Harbour, one of the VAC heads, Mother Superior because he was an older and wiser gay man who had been around the block a few times. Ursula was a female volunteer in our group who liked hanging out with bears, a subculture within the gay community, but I called her Goldilocks. Some of the couples who volunteered also had nicknames for each other: Buttercup, Sugar Lips, or simply Dear. I was, of course, Zsa Zsa.

Our support group meetings were not a piece of cake. There were always difficult people to contend with and one had to be mindful interacting with them. Some could be suffering from a mental health condition, not uncommon among so many vulnerable men and women. Empathy and silence were important watchwords, as was good humor. It was essential to be able to laugh even in the bleakest circumstances. But while not everything was easy, there were blissful moments and a sense of optimism was ever present. There was the happy process of adopting new brothers and sisters, parents and grandparents, such as Martin's mother, Joan Golding, or Dorothy, whose freshly baked country pumpkin scones filled our rooms with their rich aroma. The presence of cakes and bread rolls, and the love that went into providing these treats for sustenance contributed to a general feeling of homeliness and belonging.

Our meetings normally started with a greeting, followed by a discussion about our respective weeks. For most, it was a story of a daily war, an existential as well as physical struggle. We grappled with each other's problems: for instance, what do you do when you are called a poofter at work? There were no anti-discrimination laws to help us in those days. However, gay people had two strengths: our ability to ignore hatred and persevere, which is often the best in the most dire circumstances; the other was our "verbal advantage." A well-read, witty gay person could demolish a straight person with a few choice words, as I discovered when my compatriots would deliver a swift repartee of retaliation by calling straight aggressors a slew of names: breeders, rednecks, tampon busters, closet cases: the list went on! The language was often harsh and impactful, but after all, was not the physical and verbal violence directed at us worse and more pervasive? We saw no harm in shocking our straight counterparts, if it meant shocking them out of their complacency and privilege.

While our volunteers came from all walks of life and subcultures, above all what we had in common was a conscience and the will to help each other survive the daily pressures and onslaught of hate and depressing news. Umberto once teasingly asked me to do two things because, in his words, he "loved my bitchy analysis." He asked me to do an off-the-cuff personality analysis of the people in his support group, and an overall group analysis. I obliged with a group analysis, as that was an easier task and I could generalise (one had to generalise because there is always and ever the exception). The people in our group—Tony, Alby, Paul, Hannah, Robert, Bruce, Pieter, Bob—all proved to be passionate lovers of life, free spirits who all possessed a questioning mindset, which occasionally led to butting of heads with the professionals in the VAC office. While some volunteers suffered because of their personal circumstances—circumstances, because of AIDS, often outside of their control—many possessed an insatiable curiosity, extraordinary resilience and courage, and an indomitable spirit.

...

La Cage Aux Folles

Like any healthy family, our VAC support group liked to do activities together. We had all manners of fun: we held picnics and barbecues, hosted movie nights, had drinks out on the town, attended events at sporting clubs—yes, gay sporting clubs! In the 1980s, many Aussies had difficulties accepting gays openly playing in sports; same with the Australian armed forces. There simply could not be poofters in the armed services or, for that matter, in the local football clubs!

The main event of 1986, however, was the Melbourne premiere of the world-renowned, highly entertaining gay musical, *La Cage Aux Folles*. The evening's proceeds were being donated to Melbourne's AIDS-affected community efforts. In the early years of the AIDS pandemic, when there was little or no government funding, we had to raise every dollar, and much deserved praise goes to the VAC fundraising operations. These were professional boys with strong networks in the entertainment industry.

It was a big deal for all of us in the Big Bunches family to attend the opening night of *La Cage Aux Folles*, which told the tale of a gay couple who owned a Saint Tropez nightclub on the French Riviera by the same name.

"La Cage Aux Folles" translates into English as "a cage of crazies"; *folles* is also French slang for queens. *La Cage* began on Broadway in 1983 and went on to become a major success at home in the U.S. and internationally, winning six Tony Awards, including for Best Musical, Best Score, and Best Book. I had won a raffle for a luxury night out for 15 persons, including a free bar and barman and limousine to take my party to opening night. The whole Big Bunches bunch could come along: Umberto, Angelo, Robert (who went in his airline uniform), Dorothy wearing her yellow polka dot outfit (I often joked that she would get buried in it as she loved wearing it so much) and her hat designed by Paris, a young gay hat designer. We were joined by a friend of mine named Rita, my work colleagues at The Alfred Hospital and Australia Post, and my Aunt Dolly and Uncle Kees, who were visiting from the Netherlands.

On opening night, the limousine was waiting out front of my St Kilda Road house and all the Big Bunches crew and invited guests were ready. Aunt Dolly looked the exact image of Princess Grace Kelly of Monaco and her reputation for kindness and openness preceded her. Whenever she visited town, Aunt Dolly would help sell flowers at Big Bunches, and often prepared *RijstTafel*, a Dutch-Indonesian type of yum cha, for the VAC support group. The boys absolutely loved her and she lifted up their spirits. Some people just have grace as a gift; Aunt Dolly was one of them. Several queens would sing "Hello, Dolly!" whenever she entered the room.

All of us could fortunately fit in the stretch limousine, including a paramour of mine at the time whose name I have shamefully forgotten. The champagne served in the limo did its work: in no time at all, we were singing the musical's theme song, "I Am What I Am," on our way to St Kilda's renowned Palace Theatre. We already knew the songs by heart, having learnt and sung them at our personal growth weekend retreats. The theme song had become a popular gay anthem for the troublesome 1980s, as we were fighting for our lives. Jerry Herman, an openly gay man, composed "I Am What I Am" in 1983, a couple years before he was diagnosed with HIV-AIDS. He also wrote the scores for *Hello, Dolly!* and *Mame. I Am What I Am* was about honesty, being true to oneself, living an authentic life with integrity: a difficult thing to do for many Australians, who were mired in groupthink and conformity. The song's lyrics were very powerful, a personally liberating experience for thousands across the world, people who found meaning in accepting themselves without fear:

I am what I am

I am my own special creation

So come take a look

Give me the hook or the ovation

It's my world that I want to have a little pride in

My world and it's not a place I have to hide in

Life's not worth a damn

Till you can say, "Hey world, I am what I am"

I am what I am

I don't want praise, I don't want pity

I bang my own drum

Some think it's noise, I think it's pretty

And so what, if I love each feather and each spangle

Why not try and see things from a different angle?

Your life is a sham till you can shout out loud

I am what I am

I am what I am

And what I am needs no excuses

I deal my own deck

Sometimes the ace

Sometimes the deuces

There's one life

And there is no return and no deposit

One life, so it's time you open up your closet

Life's not worth a damn till you shout out

"Hey, world, I am what I am"

As soon as the limousine pulled up in front of the Palace Theatre and its doors opened, Umberto was first to alight. He bowed and did a quick tap dance as our the rest of us filed out of the car. As Aunt Dolly emerged from the limousine, the group started singing: *"Hello, Dolly, it's so nice to see you again…"*. I will never forget this scene as long I live, and I often recall this memory fondly. It makes me sad and happy all at once, remembering all of those sweet young men who sang for Aunt Dolly, knowing that each one had since passed on soon after. None made it over thirty years of age, Robert and Umberto among them. We had one life to live and we lived that life together fully.

As soon as VAC formed I met all the different sub cultures within the Gay community, and it was a steep learning curve to learn all the nicknames were descriptive of the individual personalities: here was Betty Butt Plug with his partner, FiFi. Loose Fart and Limp Wrist. Then there was Ice Cream: he was so sweet you'd like to lick him. Our group called Keith Harbour, one of the VAC heads, Mother Superior because he was an older and wiser gay man who had been around the block a few times.

Chapter 15

Mind-Body Medicine

"Firewalking, Jack explained, revealed that our state of mind reflected a preconceived set of thoughts and beliefs. Those thoughts and beliefs in turn manipulated our perception of reality. Much of our perceived pain, he concluded, was all in the mind. With that, our boys began to walk across the hot coals, and in doing so conquer fear itself."

There wasn't much in the way of positive news for medical treatments in the early 1980s. Thanks to Adam Carr, the assistant editor and a writer for *Outrage*, the premier gay and lesbian magazine in Australia, the gay community received the latest information about ongoing medical research in the race to cure the disease, or at least prevent its transmission. The global news, however, made for disconcerting reading in the early days of the AIDS pandemic. This was before AZT, the first drug for the treatment of AIDS, which the U.S. Federal Drug Administration approved in March 1987. In 1985, nothing of the sort was available at all. There was eventually the ELISA test kit to screen for the telltale antibodies. All lived in anxious hope and clutched at straws, especially when that awful sinking feeling occurred, a fear that, in the absence of major intervention by governments worldwide, things were only going to get worse. And they were.

As more gay men fell ill, the Big Bunches bunch joined with other

VAC friends seeking alternative therapies. Tablets, powders, potions and lotions, with little in the way of assurances given by medical doctors, sold widely. AIDS was strange to all of us, including the doctors. All sorts of people came out of the woodwork offering hope where there was despair. The controversial American motivational author Louise Hay was one of the most popular, with her 1984 book, *You Can Heal Your Life*, promising people that the solution to many of their ailments lay within themselves. Many Eastern-influenced medicines and practices sprang up as well, in my opinion often raising false hope and unrealistic expectations to people diagnosed with AIDS. However, I respected people's choices to try these alternative therapies, as I could see the glimmer of hope in their eyes. Our friends with AIDS would ask me what I thought of such-and-such therapy; my usual answer was to say there was no harm in trying.

Robert was already on a daily regimen of Chinese herbal medicine. Following his doctor's advice, he concocted a mixture of dried goods: mushrooms, ginseng, grasshoppers, seaweed, and some other pungent herbs. I assisted him by squeezing his nose shut as he swallowed the mixture. It smelled awful, but his doctor was confident that the medicine would boost his immune system. While we had our doubts, Robert's health did improve and he privately told me that that the medicinal concoction had also restored his libido. He felt desired again. "That counts for something," he would say to me, which always made me laugh. Robert's enjoyment of physical touch returned, which he had avoided since his condition first deteriorated. So many other boys were looking for anything remotely promising. Some even drank their own urine first thing in the morning: a practice known as urotherapy, apparently borrowed from the ancient Egyptians and Native Americans, whose thousand years of medical wisdom and traditions should not be forgotten. Yet these ancient remedies' applicability to halting AIDS was highly doubtful.

One VAC support group member, John O' Hare, suggested that the group run an alternative remedies weekend, inviting various practitioners to demonstrate their restorative therapies and wares. We canvassed the idea with our membership and people living with AIDS, and given a positive response, we went about organising the retreat. Not many leaders among the professional VAC staff were interested in assisting us. Nor would you have read much about these alternative healing events in any newspaper or from any AIDS organisation. The leadership was no doubt (and rightfully) looking after their jobs and dared not rock the boat too much. One can imagine the medical profession's response if they had discovered we were promoting potentially questionable alternative therapies. I remember the case of Dr Ian Brighthope, who gave vitamin injections to his AIDS patients in 1984. Dr Brighthope's controversial treatment caused a big stir internationally, with much debate over the expensive course of vitamin injections, which was alleged to do little to stop the progression of AIDS. Yet, at the same time, I knew firsthand from friends who received the injections that they felt better upon receiving the treatment. Their quality of life, however momentarily, improved. For some that fleeting reprieve from the fear and devastation of AIDS was worth it all the same. Nevertheless, in the end, they died as quickly as anybody else who didn't receive the injections.

We organised a three-day weekend retreat with Umberto leading the charge, as he knew a large network of alternative healing practitioners who could attend. I volunteered to help with the vegetarian cooking and work with nutritionists in assembling the retreat's menu. We chose as our venue the Uniting Church's Burnside Camp at Angelsea. We did not have to pay camp fees, courtesy of the Uniting Church and the Reverend William, whose son David, as you know, had developed AIDS. At the opening session and in advertising before the retreat, we stressed time and again that these alternative therapies would not cure AIDS. They might improve one's quality of life and sense of wellbeing, but there was, we made plain, no panacea, no "magic pill." Some attendees were skeptical about the alternative therapies, others more open. All, however, were curious enough to explore any options for relief from the physical and mental anguish caused by the disease.

Over the course of the three days our guest practitioners introduced us to a range of therapies. I was suspicious of many of them personally, as they had little to no scientific confirmation through peer reviews and adequate testing. Nonetheless, I gave weight to the anecdotal evidence provided by my friends and others at the retreat as to their positive, if merely psychosomatic effects. In one demonstration, I witnessed crystals being placed on a person's stomach while the practitioner chanted. The crystals were apparently placed over different *chakras*—the energy centres or nodes in the body, according to Ayurvedic practice—and radiated a healing energy. While it was impressive to watch the practitioner at work, I could not understand how crystals relieved any ailment or affected the virus itself. I accepted that the rationale was by faith alone, a powerful but, insofar as AIDS was concerned, impotent palliative for the suffering.

Other practitioners demonstrated a variety of body therapies such as Chinese acupuncture, Reiki, and Yoga, along with meditative therapies designed to reduce anxiety and pain. The ancient practice of acupuncture was said to release certain pain-relieving chemicals in the body. The Reiki method—a Japanese technique—was very popular over the weekend, although that may have been in part due to the two very handsome Reiki Masters, Liam and his partner Joshua, both HIV-positive. Elkie, one of our Big Bunches regulars and HIV-positive, swore by her daily one hour of Reiki. The technique used the practitioner's palms through which its advocates claim *qi* (pronounced "chee"), a universal life force, is transferred to the patient. Patients report experiencing a healing and calming effect. For our part, Liam's and Joshua's palms radiated a warm, emotional healing energy over many that weekend, including myself. I found the practice, the touch of skin upon skin, comforting.

Some people believed that there was power in a vitamin pill. While I was no expert, I was not too sure, having studied the effect of food on the mind and body in my nutritional science studies. Taking virtually any vitamin tablets is a waste of money, as the human digestive system can't absorb most of the vitamins. Fresh fruit and vegetables are vastly more effective in providing vitamins and minerals for absorption. Nevertheless, some believed in the therapeutic benefit of taking supplements. Several medical practitioners presented their research on supplements such as garlic and St John's Wort, which some took for depression. Many supplements, like echinacea, ginseng, and bitter lemons, appeared to be safe; other exotic herbs, we learned, could interfere with conventional medications. The doctors also provided evidence that dangerous nitrates contained in cured meats could interfere with the efficacy of certain medications. Supplements were not wholly controversial: doctors often recommended calcium (and sunshine) to improve bone health; fish or flaxseed oil to reduce cholesterol; selenium to slow the progression of HIV and some whey, soy, or nut protein to support weight gain.

Then there was medical marijuana. One of our Dutch doctors, an AIDS specialist, had brought a secret supply with him—unbeknown to the police, of course. Marijuana was then, as now in most of Australia, illegal to possess or consume. Several HIV-positive boys at the camp suffered severely from nausea and vomiting and were unable to keep food down. My friends, including Umberto, Dale, Shane, Robert, and Jason, used high quality Dutch cannabis oil to alleviate their symptoms. The cannabis oil's results were nothing but phenomenal, virtually providing instant benefits to our retreat attendees. They felt much better and, more importantly, their appetites returned. We ensured food was a central feature of the retreat experience. All of our cooking was vegetarian and we had chefs specialising in vegetarian cuisine preparing our meals. Everything was fresh: nothing processed or out of a packet. Medical doctors regularly monitored our medical marijuana users, which continued for a period of four weeks following the retreat. Our Dutch doctors present during the long weekend could not understand why Australia did not tolerate medical marijuana. I thought that Australia should adopt international best practice, as demonstrated by the Netherlands, and quickly decriminalize the medical use of marijuana. We also needed a general shift in the Australian attitude toward regulating drugs that were already approved in other Western countries with equal or higher standards. Of course, as far as culprits for Australia's backward drug policies, we could point to the pharmaceutical companies, which feared the loss of profits to a natural competitor. There was also the moralism behind condemning drug use. Besides, not all nations were as enlightened and practical as our West European counterpart.

At night, before dinner, the attendees participated in firewalking, an exercise designed to conquer fear through the power of the mind. I must say that the leaders of the firewalking exuded immense confidence; they clearly were not dabblers and knew exactly what they were doing. Jack van Leer led the group and was himself HIV-positive, having been diagnosed early in July 1982. It was now December 1986 and he remained the healthiest specimen around: fit and the most beautifully sculpted person I had ever seen.

Firewalking, Jack explained, revealed that our state of mind reflected a preconceived set of thoughts and beliefs. Those thoughts and beliefs in turn manipulated our perception of reality. Much of our perceived pain, he concluded, was all in the mind. With that, our boys began to walk across the hot coals, and in doing so conquer fear itself. "It's no different than parachute jumping," said Robert, who was the first to volunteer, casually moving over the hot coals—and receiving not a single burn. That night, all the boys walked across the fire without any burns or injuries. They had conquered fear after a lifetime of being preconditioned to experience, and expect, pain. They had proved the opposite. It was in a sense a rite of passage, from fear to courage, and our boys were now ready to move forward.

We continued to sit around the fire, which by midnight had become the scene of a makeshift camp, with the sounds of the Bass Strait pounding against the steep cliffs off Anglesea. A flickering, crackling fire does something to people: we sat low on the ground, our body language open and encouraging, some singing, others storytelling. No one felt left out or vulnerable. It was a time for sharing intimate feelings, as much a bonding exercise as a time for healing: something that our modern culture was quickly forgetting. Some meditated.

I recall one evening in particular. It was a full moon on a clear night. I retreated to the edge of the cliffs. I knew the area well, but the sounds of the sea and the full moon awakened my consciousness even more than I had ever appreciated before. The thought dawned on me that life was like a game of chess: one had to make the right moves. Upon arriving back at Melbourne, I had tested myself for HIV. I was negative. I thought to myself: did I make the right moves or was it luck of the draw?

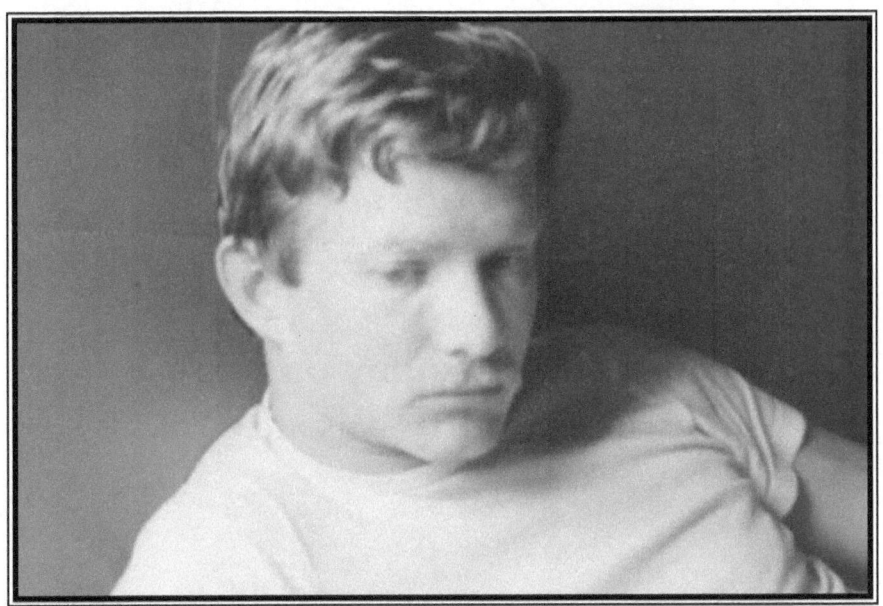

This is my friend "Pixi" he walked on the hot coal cinders for two meters without any burns on his feet, his confidence was restored and he believed a HIV-diagnoses could be overcome with positive thinking strengthening his immune system, may be he did have a point..I would not discount his positive thinking.

Chapter 16

Beauty and harmony only arose when rigidity was shed

"When I was young / I never needed anyone / And makin' love was just for fun / Those days are gone / Livin' alone / I think of all the friends I've known / But when I dial the telephone / Nobody's home"

Of course, I will never forget meeting Jason on my Pan Am flight to the United States. In 1983, he became a medical researcher at Monash University's Clayton campus in Melbourne's eastern suburbs. When we first met, Jason had just been ditched by his Dutch lover, and as it was, here he was, finding himself sitting next to another Dutchman. He was enamoured with me, and I with him, likely because, as he admitted to me then, I reminded him of his first Dutch love. We spent our flight together talking about the strange new plague, then in its early stages, known to us in those days as GRID. Jason predicted the death toll would be high. I wish Jason had not been a Nostradamus in that instance. But here we were now, in mid-1986, and gay men (and plenty more innocent lives) were dying in droves all around the world. The news was continually bad. Big Bunches was providing flowers for far too many funerals of young men, many of whom I knew. My attendance at these funerals had also painfully increased.

For a while, my involvement in the AIDS-affected community was the only thing in my life. It was a relentless battle against the disease and all the cruel hysteria pushed by the tabloid press, which continued to spout their nonsense untruths that gay men and drug users had brought this dreadful disease upon themselves. Many Australians now legitimised their prejudice against homosexuality with spurious beliefs about how the disease operated. Some believed (as some no doubt still do) that one could catch the disease by proximity alone. I recall a woman being scared because she discovered that the plumber who fixed her leaking tap also happened to be a gay man. Some Roman Catholic churches stopped offering the chalice of wine to gay men at Communion. Several Telstra technicians refused to fix telephones at a gay men's health clinic, fearing in their ignorance that somehow they might catch HIV/AIDS from simply handling the wiring. In this way, AIDS presented a toxic confluence of events and aspects of human life: our fear of death, mixed with self-preservation, fuelled by the churches and tabloids, each chasing their own agenda, the first their control over believers' lives, the latter their pursuit of profits gained by all the sensationalism. It was an ugly portrait of human beings' darker side, only challenged by the generosity of millions of others who fought for love and understanding.

Although business at Big Bunches remained as brisk as ever, we still faced the regular onslaught of hate and derision. Some referred to us as "the poofter AIDS flower shop"; Umberto and some of our more feminine boys were targets as well. We ignored all of these comments out of hand. Perfect love casts out fear was our guiding principle, and besides, we had our own community for support. And yet, now more than before, I found myself in a melancholic mood: so many friends had already passed away, and many continued to fade. My mood, however, was buoyed by the VAC support groups, as it felt like there was at least now a caring and functional community, especially for its most vulnerable members.

But one had to be perpetually prepared for the worst news. One day the phone rang at Big Bunches. I answered the phone as I usually do, with an effusive burst. "Hallo!" I'd near shout, being an enthusiastic person by nature. "Keith speaking, welcome to Big Bunches!"

"How's my little tulip going?" answered the person on the other line. I immediately recognised Jason's voice.

I told Jason that this little tulip was wilting a little that day, as Umberto had become quite sick. It seemed that the disease had finally taken its toll: he was fast losing weight and experienced difficulty breathing. Both he and his partner, Angelo, had also been hospitalized with what X-rays revealed to be pneumocystis pneumonia, an opportunistic infection that ravaged the lungs of people with AIDS. I had medical powers of attorney for both and knew that neither wanted to be revived or kept alive by artificial means. More bruising for Umberto and Angelo was their being placed in separate hospital rooms, unable to see each other. It caused them both great anxiety and stress. I asked Jason whether he could ask, as a respected medical lecturer and practitioner at Fairfield Infectious Diseases Hospital, that they be put in the same room, or at least able see each other. I had asked Dr Anne Mijch, a doctor at the hospital, myself some weeks prior, but had yet to receive any response. I understood, of course, that everybody at the hospital was being run off their feet, and that many doctors and nurses were doing their best in the circumstances. Jason promised to make enquiries, and then invited me to dine that night.

Jason was hosting Vito Russo, a gay American filmmaker and writer, who had come to town for the Melbourne Gay Film Festival. Russo wanted to meet me after Jason told him about me and what we were doing at Big Bunches. Jason had given our flower shop high praise for our dynamic community spirit, inclusive of all sexualities and openminded personalities. He joked whether Dorothy was a drag queen, with her bright red hair and oversized earrings. I chastened him as I was very protective of dear Dorothy. After all, she came all the way from Natimuk, in country Victoria, and had tried her best to fit in with our community, and by doing so, she was a welcome addition to our community. Vito had apparently wanted to discuss the possibility of making a film about Big Bunches, in a similar fashion to the previous year's hit, *My Beautiful Launderette.* He accepted my invitation to stop by the hospital to visit Umberto and Angelo that night, too. I knew that he had once fancied Umberto several years prior, although I cautioned him that Umberto's condition had caused his looks to rapidly deteriorate.

No sooner than I had finished speaking to Jason on the phone, police officers arrived at the Jam Factory, along with an anxious, barking police dog, and headed straight to the male toilets. Someone had apparently tipped them off to men loitering at the toilets and funny noises coming from the stalls. And their body language! They marched about like a pack of marauding invaders, shouting orders to those around them. Law enforcement had become ever more reactionary since the AIDS crisis began, confirming for many of us that prejudice was alive and well in Australia. It was a futile overreaction on the part of the police, as if they could somehow stamp out the disease by rounding up gay men caught in the act. In fact, their conduct would only drive risky public sex further underground, which would in turn worsen the crisis. That much was readily apparent even for, of all people, the editorial staff at the otherwise conservative *Herald Sun*. Nonetheless, there had been an increase in police raids on gay establishments and homes across Melbourne and Australia more generally. Terry's house in East Melbourne was no exception, with four policemen visiting one night on the pretence that there had been reports, all of which were false, of naked men seen in his garden.

I received a visit from another friend, Andrew, later that day. Andrew was preparing for a ice-skating championship and asked me to prepare bouquets for the winners. He asked after Umberto, saying that he had a ticket for him to Vito's movie. I explained Umberto's unfortunate predicament. Jason arrived shortly thereafter, accompanied by Vito, who turned out to be a delightful man. I had Vito sign my copy of his book, *The Celluloid Closet*. I invited Andrew to dine with us, and to come see a new film, *Buddies*, the following evening with Jason and Vito, our friend Rita, and me. I thought Andrew was a closeted gay man, living as he was with his conservative, strict Serbian parents. I knew them as they were practically my neighbours: they always seemed to frown disapprovingly when my support group met at my place. One time I had asked whether there was any issue with my friends parking their cars out front of my place. They replied that while they didn't object to the cars, they objected to the sort of company I kept. I pitied Andrew for having parents like that.

After a wonderful evening out with Jason, Vito, and Andrew, Jason and I paid a visit to Umberto at the hospital. Dr Mijch explained that his condition had improved: his breathing was normal and colour had even returned to cheeks. Umberto asked to join us for the following night's film viewing. The happy change of events delighted all of us. We made arrangements to have Umberto dropped off at the theatre.

Jason and Vito came to my place the following evening, from where we would catch a tram into the city. Andrew joined us, and despite my opinion about his general state of being, he was charming and polite. He did ask Jason, however, whether AIDS was contagious by merely being close to someone. The question seemed to bother Jason, who brushed away the question with his sharp tongue. "Only if you fuck him without a condom," he told a startled Andrew, who replied that he was not into anal sex. I added that at the time it was best to limit any exchange of bodily fluids until more was known. Judging from Andrew's body language throughout the evening, it was clear that he was experiencing an internal psychological struggle with his sexuality.

Once at the theatre, we enjoyed some coffee and snacks before attending a pre-viewing talk. It was helpful to have Vito's company, as he gave us insight into the film without giving anything away about its plot. Vito also revealed to us that he was living with AIDS. He noted that the film was a somewhat depressing, but necessary portrait of contemporary life for many gay men. *Buddies* followed the intimate relationship between two men grappling with the AIDS crisis. The film's writer, Arthur Bressan, wrote *Buddies* in five days and filmed and directed it in nine days. He knew that his own struggle with the disease left him little time. It only took minutes into watching the film for it to grab our full attention. Within ten minutes, it seemed like the whole audience was dabbing tears from their cheeks. I shared a box of tissues with my friends. Jesus wept.

The film finished with the audience in silence. Suddenly, Umberto began to sing softly, a tune called "All by Myself," written and sung originally by John Carmen in 1975, and set to the *Adagio sostenuto* second movement of classical composer Sergei Rachmaninoff's *Piano Concerto No. 2 in C Minor*. I knew the song well. To our surprise, Jason walked over to the piano in the theatre and played along perfectly, having known the music by heart. It was a powerful performance to cap off a poignant night. Ian Harris, a friend from Melbourne Community Church, asked afterwards why Umberto had chosen to sing that song. Because of past regrets, Umberto confessed. I looked on sympathetically and squeezed Umberto's hand in my own.

When I was young
I never needed anyone
And makin' love was just for fun
Those days are gone
Livin' alone
I think of all the friends I've known
But when I dial the telephone
Nobody's home

I was then asked about my reaction to the film. I said the character Dave resonated with me: he was a buddy volunteer who visited a man, Robert, who was himself dying of AIDS and had virtually no support from his family or parents. Robert's sad predicament reminded me of the situation facing many of my own friends. Dave, on the other hand, had strong support from his parents, as I did from mine. We were alike in many ways, with the exception that Dave, unlike me, was in a loving monogamous relationship with his boyfriend. Yet, like Dave, I developed strong feelings and an even deeper sympathy for my dying friends. I internalised almost everything they experienced, as one so often does when we share our emotions with others. I was particularly touched by one scene in *Buddies*, where Dave, who is a typesetter by profession, reads Robert some fundamentalist Christian literature denouncing gay people in a horrific way. Robert becomes distraught while listening to Dave read the homophobic vitriol, as it reminds him of his own judgmental fundamentalist parents. It was a far too common situation for many gay Christians.

Andrew also received his fair share of attention from the film crowd. He was a well-known and handsome figure skater, a real heartthrob for the girls and, I should add, the boys. He dressed stylishly as well, wearing a tight, well-tailored white shirt, fitted blue jeans, and black Italian boots. Although we were friendly and sociable toward him, Andrew viewed me with some suspicion, finding me, I imagine, far too opinionated. He had once remarked that all the Dutch boys he had met were supercilious, and that our only saving grace was that most of them were blue-eyed, tall, and blond. I understood his feelings, as he had been burying his true sexuality for so long. I, as an openly gay male, intimidated him.

Andrew was sitting very close to Umberto, virtually almost on his lap, with his hand gently tapping Umberto's knee and a naughty glimmer in his eye, as if to say, "Aren't you going to ask me how I found this film?" Vito must have picked up on Andrew's curiosity, as he did ask for Andrew's reaction. Andrew explained that Robert's situation affected him greatly. He was buoyed by Dave's assistance in providing Robert with empathy and friendship. Andrew spoke of how while Robert's looks and energy diminished, his character and personality had sustained him. It meant there was more to life than one's looks and sex, Andrew said. He seemed taken aback by his own candour. *Buddies* had inspired him to be honest with himself, and revealed that living a life of pretence is ultimately destructive. Several of us had been earlier discussing a new concept then floating about: *pronoia*, which was the opposite of paranoia and fear. It was the belief that everything in the Universe was conspiring to support us, an idea that appealed to everyone in those desperate times. The haters were becoming the minority, with only the extremely religious remaining paranoid, while the educated and enlightened mainstream was turning away from homophobia. All of this had come home to Andrew, including the reassurance that he could now depend on his new friends. We would genuinely affirm his worth, even if his biological family rejected him. Andrew looked clearly relieved by the end of the evening. He turned to me at one point and told me that now he was truly free.

A Book Launch

An order came in one day to provide native flower arrangements for a book launch at the VAC main office, gay activist and academic Dennis Altman's new work, *AIDS and the New Puritanism*. We made a spectacular arrangement of bright red banksias, which were dyed a deeper red to deliver an even more pronounced impact. We were also invited to the book launch, which excited me, as I was so thankful that Denis had written this book that would enrich our understanding of current events. As a twenty-year old in 1971, I had purchased Dennis's first book, *Homosexual Oppression and Liberation*. I never forgot how, when I was purchasing the book the shop assistant asked if he should put it in a brown paper bag. When I asked why, he replied that it was a pornographic book! (Although he admitted that he had not read it, demonstrating that not all ignorance is blissful!) That book taught me plenty about the problems facing so many in our community that I had not personally faced myself.

According to my diary, the book launch took place on Thursday, 3 April 1986. The who's who of the gay community was in attendance, in addition to some other interesting sorts, such as our early champions among the straight community—a man named Allen, then a Liberal member of the Victorian parliament for seventeen years, with his wife who was the secretary for our VAC support group.

Picture; Big Bunches was a joyfull attractive place in the Jam Factory, people came and played their music or simply exchanging conversations ideas. Several of us had been earlier discussing a new concept then floating about: *pronoia*, which was the opposite of paranoia and fear. It was the belief that everything in the Universe was conspiring to support us, an idea that appealed to everyone in those desperate times.

Chapter 17

Valentine's Day was a high energy day

Both Jason and Robert had such amazing personalities. They always made everyone feel special, which is what also made them so attractive. I often thought how death could soon take these boys away, which churned my stomach each time. Just the idea of living without them was beyond the pale.

985 was not an insignificant year for gay men. AIDS was at its most destructive since the beginning of the crisis, as evidenced by the increase in AIDS diagnoses worldwide. Before and during Valentine's Day that year, Big Bunches employed more staff who would prepare the large volume of orders and flit about town delivering them. Our flower delivery boys rode on pink bicycles for local deliveries in the neighbourhoods of South Yarra, Prahran, and Richmond. Everybody noticed eye candy on a bicycle and people talked about it. After all, everything at Big Bunches was designed to make an impact. For deliveries outside of the bicycle routes, we had two delivery cars driven by girls dressed in pink skirts that came down to just two inches above the knee. It was the French "baby doll" look personified by Brigitte Bardot knee, and admittedly it made our shop popular with our more conservative customers. We were a money-making business, after all, albeit one that strove to live up to our principles and commitment to creativity.

It took three hours to create a spectacular Valentine's Day display, and with around $10,000 worth of fresh flowers! I was praying for a profitable day after spending so much money, which was also a bank overdraft. I also hoped that this Valentine's Day would not be a sizzling hot February day, which would wilt the fresh flower stock in mere hours. Fast movement of stock was therefore essential when we opened the shop at six o'clock that morning. Customers were already waiting and we served them croissants, orange juice, and coffee as they browsed our beautiful offerings for the special day. The fragrance of fresh flowers permeated the whole of the Jam Factory, attracting clientele like bees to a flower's scent. Fragrance was an important aspect why humans buy flowers, as it usually triggers the release of oxytocin, the hormone associated with love and an essential for Valentine's Day.

The Big Bunches staff had to be as equally attractive as the fresh flowers, looking neat and clean and exuding warm personalities. That was real attractiveness, which was not being merely defined by one's having good looks. Big Bunches employed all types and shapes; we had employees who were older or larger as well as muscled and toned, all being desirable in their own way.

Jason helped for a few days around Valentine's Day. He figured that working in the flower shop would give him a welcome break from his medical research in laboratory. It was always fun to have him around, too. Jason was one of those rare sorts who always livened things up, and besides, he stroked my ego by giving me attention, as I gave him in return. Robert joined us as well, despite being on medical leave from Ansett. He was eager to interact with customers on Valentine's Day; he said it would take his mind off his condition. I gave him a sedentary job as he would tire quickly and begin panting for air. Things were deteriorating fast for him. Both Jason and Robert had such amazing personalities. They always made everyone feel special, which is what also made them so attractive. I often thought how death could soon take these boys away, which churned my stomach each time. Just the idea of living without them was beyond the pale. Both boys also gossiped quite a bit at times. I remembered catching the two in the act, asking them, "Are you two queens gossiping again?" It was never malicious gossip, of course, but for this reason, and some of their more colourful humour, I never let them compose Valentine's Day messages. They delighted in suggesting naughtier messages, far more than "Roses are red, / Violets are blue,/ Poems are hard and so is my penis." Nevertheless, they knew so many people in Melbourne's gay community, whereas Dorothy and I only knew a few in comparison.

Umberto could not work that Valentine's Day. He was sick again at the Fairfield Infectious Diseases Hospital, which was a bad and a good thing. Despite his illness, Umberto was spoilt by many secret lovers and received no less then eleven bunches of flowers and a kilogram of handmade Belgian chocolates, specially imported and airlifted by KLM from Antwerp. Hopefully the chocolates would get his weight up. He enjoyed the indulgence and all the attention. Each time he received a flower bunch or a box, he telephoned us on one of the four landlines at Big Bunches, asking who his secret admirers were. I was, of course, sworn to secrecy.

Valentine's Day was a high energy day, filled with emotions and pregnant with romantic hopes. It was a day of capturing hearts and for sending subtle messages to secret crushes, or for some, imaginary loves. I fondly recall Nathan, one of my favourite regulars, a funny man who had come out of the closet twelve months earlier and had more recently been diagnosed with AIDS. He told me that he might have caught the disease while on the beat at Melbourne's Fitzroy Gardens, then a notorious cruising ground for anonymous sex. Nathan felt pressured by society to live a double life, and often wished that Big Bunches had been around then. At least, said, he would have had someone to talk to. Nathan's excitement for the object of his affection was evident when we helped him compose a poem. He imagined what joy his paramour would experience receiving it. He added that his heart's desire was also a man whose health was fast deteriorating. He sought me to reassure him about what he had written on the card for Monty, the name of his beloved. It read:

> *your seclusion, come My dear friend, my fair and beautiful lover, come to me! Come, you shy and modest hunk, leave into the open.*
>
> *Let me see your face, let me hear your voice.*

For your voice is soothing and your face is ravishing.

Signed - a secret lover

An hour after Nathan had placed his order and left, another young man, with the most sparkling, friendly blue eyes I had ever seen, introduced himself as Monty Van Doren. Monty was accompanied by his mother, who in a typical Dutch manner shook my hand and just said her name, "Irene Van Doren, pleased to meet you." I had not met Monty and his mum before but there was an immediate bond and a lot of warmth between us. They carried with them a deep cultural sophistication, yet deep down, I sensed that there was some sadness. I suspected from the start that this was the Monty who had caught Nathan's fancy. Monty chose a large Nautilus seashell, the type you can put to your ear and hear the crashing sea or even the imaginary voices of people or lovers. Monty said that he hoped that his secret lover could hear his longing voice when cupping the shell to his ear. Irene was speaking to Dorothy at the time and did not hear the conversation between us. She returned with a bunch of rainbow tulips to go with the Nautilus shell. Monty asked if I could help him with a verse. I replied that I could, with a smile in my heart as I knew the likely intended recipient. Monty wrote as follows:

Dearest Nathan,

I am secretly thinking this about you, my fair-haired man...

His face is rugged, he smells like fresh sage, his voice, his words, warm and reassuring.

Fine muscles ripple beneath his skin quiet and beautiful.

His torso is the work of a sculptor, hard and smooth as ivory.

His words are kisses, his kisses words.

Everything about you delights me, thrills me through and through!

I veered toward using the love songs of Solomon as I had done for Nathan, but Monty was altogether unaware. One of the most erotic and romantic books of the ancient world, Solomon's book of songs in the Old Testament were a testament to the expression of erotic love for one's heart's desire. Needless to say, our shop's copy was worn down from the hundreds of eager fingers flipping through its pages.

Placing a Valentine's Day order was practically a sacred ritual for many and we took our time to personalise the transaction with the assistance of each customer. We sat down with them to formulate a unique message for their intended lover, as I had done for Nathan and Monty. We would prod them along by suggesting amorous words to trigger emotions and verbalise what the heart was feeling. Some of the boys brought little tokens of affection to include with their flowers or chocolate delivery. This never failed to touch my heart and cause a tear or two. In the early days of AIDS, we had to be much more aware about tomorrow's stakes and alert to how many tomorrows were so suddenly snuffed out. The messages had to be meaningful and uplifting, and create hope urgently where so many other messages would sound trite.

Irene was a tall, slim Dutch woman and asked if I spoke Dutch. We spoke at length in our native language about her concerns for Monty, who had not been able to keep down his food, no matter what the doctors tried. She thought his days were numbered and desperately wanted to travel back to the Netherlands to be with their family, in particular to see Monty's Opa and Oma. The Fairfield Hospital doctors, however, had advised her against any travel for Monty. She feared that the doctors' advice was of limited value because, unlike in their normal practice, they were facing an epidemic with a virtually terminal diagnosis. While I could not assist with Monty's migration issues, I gave Irene a vial of Umberto's cannabis oil, with instructions for how to administer it. It was a matter of providing comfort, whatever its legality, for our suffering brothers and sisters, which outweighed any risk of a criminal record or jail time.

Monty and Irene visited again four days later. He looked healthier and reported that he had been able to keep his food down and was eating seven small meals each day. Yet we had to stay hushed about his miracle treatment and only whispered the good news among friends. Even his medical doctors were not told. Irene and Monty eventually travelled back to the Netherlands, but it would not be the last I would hear from them.

Another of our regulars was Jeremiah, a handsome 29-year-old and a Mormon. Jeremiah came from a particularly conservative background and had, or so he told us, three wives: Lilly, Lucy, and Livy. I shall never forget their names, as I had to write them down on three separate cards, all the while keeping a straight and serious face while Jeremiah told me all about them. He asked whether I had a wife as well: I replied that I had a husband, which his heterosexual-blindered mind failed to register. I continued with his order, writing out three separate addresses—how could I ever forget! He told me to keep it a secret as he paid for three Valentine bunches of our tulips, roses, and carnations. With his Valentine cards, he included a verse or two from *The Pearl of Great Price*, one of the Mormon texts. We did not blink an eye at each other's idiosyncrasies. As Gertrude Stein said, a dollar is a dollar is a dollar.

Beverly, or Bev, as we knew her, was Dorothy's sister and another of the extra set of hands on deck for Valentine's Day at Big Bunches. Bev was not religious like her sister and instead put her efforts into social justice work. She was also a member of the Australian Labor Party, twice divorced and three-times married, and now lived with her partner, Les. She told me that she had known many men, "more than youse'll ever have," she said in her broad nasal accent. "Oh, you're so lucky, Bev!" Robert exclaimed and we all laughed in unison. Many Australian straight men, Bev added, didn't know how to romance women without alcohol. The only romantic notion that most Australian straight men knew, she added, was a standing cock. Dorothy would grimace and look down at her shoes whilst Bev regaled us with her romantic life. Meanwhile, the boys and I were trying to compose ourselves, finding her conversation extremely entertaining. We agreed that Australian men in the 1980s were hung up on being touchy-feely. They rarely hugged or kissed other men, yet ironically, they delighted in Dame Edna Average, performed by the male and heterosexual comedian Barry Humphries, a cross-dressing Australian icon. (I remember, too, how Humphries used to mockingly throw gladioluses, "gladdies," as he called them, to the audience sitting in the cheapest seats at his shows. As a result, few people bought gladioluses at Big Bunches!)

Receiving a Valentine signalled that one was loved and desired, which made it ever more intriguing if the Valentine came from a secret admirer. The secrecy surrounding some of the Valentines excited Dorothy, who wondered if at her age if she would ever receive one. There was a lot of truth to her fear, sadly, as a Valentine was rarely sent to an older person (as I have learned in my older age!). Alas, they were a tool of courtship reserved for the young.

Valentine's Day wasn't just for romantic love, as we celebrated many kinds of love at Big Bunches. And whereas most florist and chocolate shops in 1980s Australia only catered to heterosexual romantic love, we embraced all forms of mutual love. We were also painfully aware that many people were overlooked on Valentine's Day, particularly those suffering alone with AIDS. They were so often deserted by family and friends. At Big Bunches, we devised a plan of action. For those we knew who struggled with AIDS and were not likely to survive the coming year, we ensured they each received a bouquet of their favourite flowers or a chocolate box from a secret admirer. They would know they were loved and cared for. That was, after all, what Valentine's Day was all about.

These are Dutch friends typical of the 1970/80 Gay moustache
trend. The Dutch community were strong supporters of the
work Big Bunches was doing and some of their sons such
as Monty and his mum Irene were frequent visitors.

Chapter 18

The pleasure of entering into other people's lives and adventures

Almost everyone was invited to the Big Bunches gatherings on Friday nights, where we talked in a social setting about issues that concerned the LGBTI community .It was a time when the cerebral met the emotional.

The Jam Factory space had a warm and inviting ambience. It was the polar opposite of a common shopping centre: there was nothing plastic or pretentious about it, nor were there any large chain stores. All of the specialist shop owners were sole proprietors, and even the big Georges supermarket was unique. The commercial centre resembled more a small village covered by a glass roof, with beautiful wood and old brickwork throughout, populated by an interesting assortment of shops and their patrons, and many a curious visitor. Mainstream tastes were certainly *not* the norm in the Jam Factory of the 1980s, either. The Jam Factory's clientele exuded a strong sense of style and they valued difference; many were *avant garde* types when it came to fashion.

Due to its charming atmosphere, the Jam Factory attracted many younger gay people who didn't know much about the broader gay community (or where to even begin looking for one). They often wandered into Big Bunches, looking shyly at the staff, and when eye contact was made, darting their gaze elsewhere at the fascinating displays of flowers or our exotic seashells, sourced from all over the world. We would try to engage with them as they window-shopped. Perhaps we'd ask what shells they liked, or, if they were adoring our pair of friendly peach-faced lovebirds, I'd usually comment that as they were made for love, we had two lovebirds, not one (which, I'd add, would have been cruel). The lovebirds were a good conversation starter. Humans similarly operate better when they have someone to love, just like our pair of lovebirds. Some people are alone by choice and do well, but it is sad when people are searching for a lover and fail to find one. We made sure to have on offer some good-looking bunches of flowers for a couple of dollars, so our customers wouldn't feel bad taking up our time without having made any purchases. Few people left Big Bunches empty handed emotionally or when it came to leaving with some fresh flowers to brighten their day.

Many of our younger gay visitors were obviously looking for friendship and a place to belong, a place where they could talk openly. Almost everyone was invited to the Big Bunches gatherings that we held on Friday nights after nine o'clock, where we talked in a social setting about issues that concerned the LGBT community. It was a time when the cerebral met the emotional. Our young attendees also wanted to know more about gay history and to meet positive gay role models. Terry had suggested that I start the group along the lines of the dinner parties that we held at his house in East Melbourne. It was, after all, during those memorable nights, where I had been virtually apprenticed to Terry, that I learned how to throw a proper dinner party (as well as be head chef and dishwasher). His dinner parties, however, were not cheap affairs; my socials would need to be somewhat less expensive, yet maintain a level of sophistication to honour our guests. I chose to serve finger foods and some quality wines and fruit juices. Anyone who was non-judgmental and supportive was welcome to join us at Big Bunches afterhours. I made a point to invite straight divorcees, too, as they were shunned by their co-religionists in a way not dissimilar to how gay people had been ostracized by their religious communities. I felt a lot of empathy for the divorced and their experience as second-class citizens in traditional Australia.

Above all, we wanted to cultivate a unique, inclusive space for the gay community. Gay nightclubs often functioned like meat markets, which was daunting for some younger people and those who were only coming to terms with their sexuality. I was also mindful that some of the potential influences at the clubs were not in gay men's best interests; the overuse of recreational drugs and alcohol, and the frequency of anonymous sex with multiple partners. The club scene was not always the best introduction to gay culture, especially for vulnerable members of the community. Of course, with time and better socialisation, going out at night was ideal for bonding with new friends and enjoying a freer life. I loved attending the gay entertainment clubs Pokeys and Mandate, as well as dining at gay-owned restaurants like the Soda Sisters and the Market Hotel, where we would often take our newfound friends.

Our Friday nights after nine at Big Bunches became very good fun. Especially popular was my grandmother's secret potent Dutch punch, a recipe dating from 1676, and said to have been first concocted by the legendary Willem Van Der Decken, otherwise known as the Flying Dutchman (who, incidentally, came from my hometown of Terneuzen). New friends always asked for Keith's Flying Dutchman punch; some even reckoned the punch was better than taking ecstasy! Before the age of Google and social media strangled modern discourse, we enjoyed long discussions on a range of topics. These were fascinating times, which were reflected in our discussions. Many gay people from all walks of life and religions joined in, and oftentimes, famous gay people visited the Big Bunches bunch to tell their stories, and to model their lives to motivate and encourage others.

Our first Big Bunches discussion focused on the question of what caused same-sex attraction. We answered it by posing a counter-question to the group: what caused opposite-sex attraction? If we understood heterosexuality, we reasoned, we would understand homosexuality, too. Sexualities don't have a cause, they are what they are, said Dale, a Seventh Day Adventist teacher who had recently been diagnosed with HIV and immediately kicked out of his church and family. They spend too many millions on pseudo-research just to prove homosexuality is sinful, Dale added. Another visitor chimed in that Dale's church obviously did not believe that "perfect love casts our fear"; a thoughtful response.

Former South Australian Labor premier Don Dunstan joined our group several times, as he was living near me at the time. He was also the then Victorian Tourism Commissioner. When asked what was the catalyst for decriminalising homosexuality in South Australia, Don replied that it was the murder of a young law lecturer at Adelaide University Law School, George Duncan. Don described George as a cultured, kind, and highly intelligent young man. George, who could not swim, was thrown into the Torrens River in May 1972 and drowned. Yet under the then state law, George was potentially a criminal for having sex with other men; in effect, being gay was a criminal act, a law that was then on the books across Australia. Australians were appalled by George's death and the serious allegations swirling about that several policemen were involved in his murder.1 This was the necessary stimulus for action, and in 1975, South Australia became the first Australian state to decriminalise homosexuality. Don added that George did not die in vain as his murder helped to transform Australian law.

The South Australian Government later commissioned a report by Scotland Yard detectives that included circumstantial evidence suggesting that George Duncan may have been thrown into the river by undercover police.

Another famous guest joining our discussions was the centenarian Monte Punshon, who was 103 years-old when we started holding the weekly gatherings. Monty was a retired school teacher in art and drama and had taught Mandarin and Japanese as well. She became an honorary Japanese citizen for her work with Japanese prisoners of war captured by Australia during the Second World War. Whenever Monte came, we had a full house of young gay men and women who adored her. She was an articulate and refined woman who never missed a beat. Yet she did not label herself as a lesbian: Monte did not believe in labels, commenting once to us that labels "were for jars, not people." Margaret Taylor, a friend of mine from the Metropolitan Community Church, was her partner and carer at the time, and always accompanied Monte.

Monte was asked whether she had ever fallen in love. The question came from Alice, a young lesbian of 19 years of age, who was finding herself among the Big Bunches bunch. Monte said she fell in love several times. Her first big love was her girlfriend, Debbie, in 1910. They were together for twelve years, until Debbie left Monte for another woman. Monte complained of the intense heartache, which took years for her to recover from. She eventually met other women, adding that she "liked men, too, but not like I do women." I remember her warm laugh as she said that she liked "big strong men who carry me in their strong arms." Monte also told us that, back in the day, if one were suspected of loving a person of their own sex, they were said to have a "streak of lavender." She said she herself had been kindly referred to in the past as having a streak of lavender. Monte was also one of the first women to vote in the State of Victoria, in 1908, and she was the first woman to obtain her motorcycle licence.

Margaret spoke to the group as well. She shared her observation that people in the 1980s were far more concerned about who slept with whom than she recalled from the days of the First World War, when soldiers used to sleep and dance together (as women would do, too). Her comments reminded me of the story of the American president, Abraham Lincoln, who, in his younger years, shared a bed with a male acquaintance, Joshua Speed, for four years. Joshua would eventually marry (and later divorce), causing Abe a near nervous breakdown, according to their exchange of letters. Did this mean that Abraham Lincoln was gay? Who knows, but that wasn't important. What was notable, however, was the intimacy between men that, by the 1980s, would frighten many straight men. Modern Australia had become obsessed with sexuality, at a time when homophobia and bigotry were rife, especially in private and religious schools and institutions. Even with decades of public education and a growth of critical thinking and empathy, many Australians harboured ignorance and prejudice against their gay brothers and sisters.

Monte was 105 years old when the Queensland Government, then under the control of conservative strongman and National premier Joh Bjelke-Petersen, appointed her a star ambassador to the 1988 World Expo in Brisbane. She felt honoured because she had been to the Melbourne International Exhibition in Melbourne at the age of five in 1888. When Bjelke-Petersen learned that the centenarian honorary ambassador was a lesbian, his government wanted to sack her immediately. However, the international exhibitors were horrified and criticised his response as backward and narrow-minded: not a good look for Australia. The Aussies couldn't backtrack quick enough! Bjelke-Petersen may have also forgotten that lesbian sex was never a criminal offence. (According to apocrypha, Queen Victoria had said that female same-sex did not exist). Yet men having sex with men *was* a criminal offence in 1988. It took another two years until, in 1990, the Labor Government led by Premier Wayne Goss decriminalised homosexuality in Queensland.

Oftentimes, people just wanted to tell their story at the Big Bunches gatherings. They experienced a great deal of relief in doing so, and others could reach out to offer their love and sympathy.

Shane was a friend of Big Bunches who attended our gatherings. He was the son of Hillsong Pentecostals, who said they believed in unconditional love and received a daily anointment of the Holy Spirit. But in Shane's experience, their love was extremely conditional, superficial even, and there was a decidedly unholy spirit in their household. Shane's parents had imposed a condition, he explained, that they would love Shane only if he underwent "conversion therapy," another term for psychological abuse, which purported to turn a gay man straight, or at least rid the person of same-sex attraction. When he had come out to his mother, she put on a performance familiar to many young gay children, lamenting that *she* was hard done by his coming out, having to explain his sexuality to her church. I counselled and encouraged Shane not to undergo the so-called therapy, but to live the way he needed to openly.

I recall when Shane first told his story to the Big Bunches group. He explained how his family had abandoned him, how he lost his job at a Christian bookstore, how everyone he had formerly known had ostracised him for being gay and HIV-positive. Shane told us that he would rather die than live a fake life. It was at that teary point that Jason got up and sat next to Shane, putting his arm over his shoulder, a sweet gesture and a touching scene. We were all comforted by the sight of open love and acceptance.

Shane would later work for us at Big Bunches. We put him in charge of the export section at Christmas time, preparing 250 gumnut wreathes destined for sale in Singapore. He was always so thankful for "his new family." That was the truest, and healthiest, form of love he or anyone of us could know.

Shane would later work for us at Big Bunches. We put him
in charge of the export section at Christmas time, preparing
250 gumnut wreaths destined for sale in Singapore.

Dirk, our Dutch friend and diplomat, joined us whenever he was down
in Melbourne. He was also an Ancient Greek scholar and would teach us
about the gay influences throughout history, much of it whitewashed from
popular history because of its taboo content. We learned, for instance,
that Zeus, the mightiest of the Greek gods, fell in love with a young man,
Ganymede, and brought him to Mount Olympus as the gods' wine-bearer.
Zeus later sent Ganymede to the stars as the constellation we call Aquarius
today. We gay people are likewise special, Dirk said. The famous German
poet Johann Wolfgang von Goethe even wrote a poem about the love
Ganymede had for Zeus, which the young composer Franz Schubert put
to music in Opus No. 3 D. 544. Schubert died at 31, Dirk added, the
suspected cause being mercury poisoning, as mercury was then used to
treat syphilis—a lesson for all of us, he said, to practise safe sex!

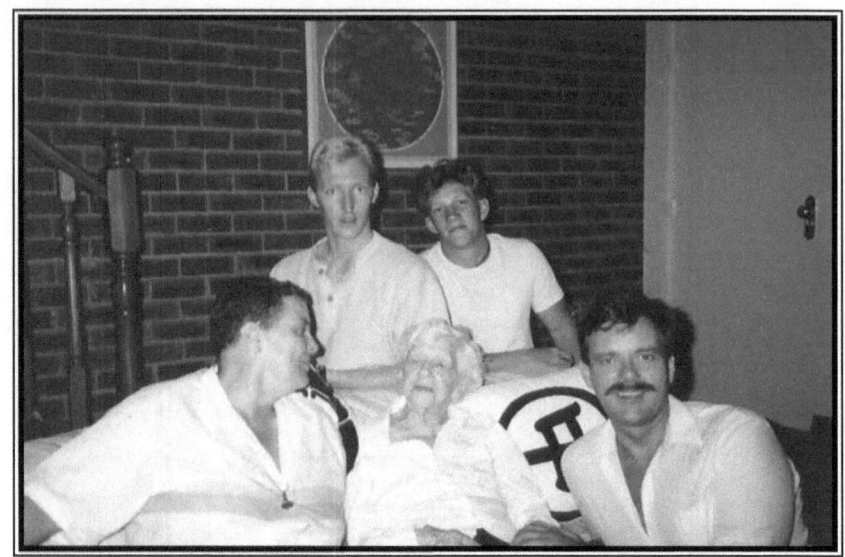

Another famous guest joining our discussions was the
centenarian Monte Punshon, who was 103 years-old
when we started holding the weekly gatherings.

Chapter 19

Whatever gets your attention gets you

Those personal growth weekends at Porto Bello were indeed magical: they smashed negative attitudes and destructive self-images that attendees had inherited from their earlier lives. Here many learnt for the first time about their secret fetishes, good and bad, and their obsessive compulsions. Here we talked about everything important in life.

M y late friend and psychologist Bruce McNicol had asked me to assist him with arranging personal growth weekends at Porto Bello, a stylish retreat in Melbourne's Dandenong Ranges. Porto Bello's grounds comprised large gardens with many old rhododendron trees, which were themselves a tourist attraction "befitting a passel of queens," as Umberto put it. Its architectural style was smart, with wooden buildings designed in the style of the iconic American architect Frank Lloyd Wright, stained glass windows depicting local flora and fauna, the varied and vivid colours providing a spectacular display, interspersed with eucalyptus trees hundreds of years old. The bellbirds sang, evoking calm and mystery, amid the warbling of magpies and what sounded like talking cockatoos. The ambience at Porto Bello was one of peace, healing, and hope.

Attendees at the weekend retreats were challenged about their views on sex and intimacy, family, spirituality, assertiveness. They would learn how to accept genuine feedback and understand the difference between affirmation and a mere compliment. The difference was subtle: affirmation offered a person more than a fleeting expression of praise. For example, I recall the case of one attendee named Adele. Adele was one of the few women who contracted HIV through a blood transfusion, yet she bore no ill will toward anyone. Her body was ravaged by AIDS and life's stresses. Her grey hair hung formless over her cheeks and neck, looking like a mess of spider webs, which she continually swiped away from her face with her hand. Her teeth were in poor condition, with large gaps between them. Her dark eyes had an angry look about them. Adele confided in me and asked if there were anything desirable about her. I affirmed that she had a rare kindness and empathy for people and gave her several examples of her generosity. I knew she had provided a home, free of charge, to a person with HIV- AIDS who had no money. She always went out of her way to be kind, her dark sad eyes conveyed compassion toward others.

We would throw out ideas for discussion to the attendees and then model our discussions on what attendees said. One time, Bruce asked me who I found attractive in the group. I replied that I found Garry attractive, prompting Bruce to ask further why I found him attractive. I referred to Garry's personality, and cited our first meeting the previous day, when he reached out and shook my hand, gave a warm smile, and said, "Nice to meet you, my name is Garry" and offered to help me with my heavy backpack. That sort of genuine, friendly kindness warmed my heart. He was a passing pleasure for both body and mind. Bruce continued by asking whether I found Garry physically attractive, but I apologised and insisted we moved on to the next question. I wanted to demonstrate to the group how to be assertive in a polite manner.

All sorts of people attended the Porto Bello weekends. To be honest, some were difficult to get along with, as in the case of few well-intentioned Catholic nuns who attended some of the weekends. They wanted to look after people living with AIDS in their palliative care nunnery. Some of them, however, were bossy and patronising, exuding a degree of certitude when it came to moral matters, which I found hard to deal with. They told me I had defensive body language and suggested that I relax, but these sisters were not going to get me to say a thousand Hail Marys! I accepted that I might have been acting defensively and said that I desired to be open and approachable at the retreat. After all, one never sees oneself as others do. But Sister Immaculate Mary, who was also a trained psychotherapist, did not let up, and remarked that the way I ate a raw carrot indicated a personality problem. I suspected she saw the carrot as a desirable penis, and throughout the weekend, she kept on about my carrot eating. Overall, I thought I deserved a gold medal for showing patience and kindness towards the nuns by keeping the peace. There were other, younger straight women who attended, all of them having gay friends who they wished to help. However, some women were just as high maintenance as the nuns, seeking attention for themselves. We understood what was happening much better when some of the women revealed in small working groups that they were sexually abused as young girls by straight family members. Our weekend retreats brought up many issues arising from dysfunctional or abusive families.

My purpose there was not to smile at people, but to give them genuine emotional support. Many of the boys did not have long to live. They often had a hard time dealing with unresolved emotional turmoil and depression. Unfortunately, Australian male culture was akin to the English stiff upper lip, where one suppressed their emotions and was not encouraged to be authentic. Many had lived fake lives, unknowingly imposed on them by repressive families who prized conformity to norms rather than having good mental health. I am sure we have all heard of the "tyranny of family" syndrome, well put by the iconic gay singer Peter Allen in his lyrics: *Don't cry out loud / Just keep it inside and learn how to hide your feelings / Fly high and proud / Then if you should fall, remember you almost had it all.*

I attributed this unresolved emotional turmoil and depression to the education of men in Australian schools. Personal emotional development was not usually encouraged; rather, the education system emphasized group conformity and team loyalty. Sport became a substitute for knowing yourself, at the expense of a deeper understanding of the self. There was little thought given to developing individual consciences or aesthetic taste, nor were mindful solitude and critical self-reflection part of the normal Australian male upbringing. Decades before, when I was a postman in Portarlington, I made friends with original ANZACs. The veterans would regularly break down at the letterbox and tell me, a young boy of 16, their painful stories of loss. They were suffering from what we call today post-traumatic stress disorder. My mum Bets and her friends would visit them regularly. She noticed the same disorder in young men diagnosed with HIV/AIDS, which encouraged her to show empathy and openness to them. Everybody needs to be loved, physically and psychologically close to another, and Australian homes and schools weren't providing love to everyone. As a result, far too many gay men committed suicide. In 2015, 3,027 Australians ended their own lives. That's 12.6 people for every 100,000, most of them men.

Nearly everyone feared that they were going to lose friends because of HIV/AIDS. Some of my friends had expressed their fears in the third person, afraid of saying goodbye. It was embarrassing for some to tell your friends that someone you loved had passed way from HIV/AIDS. These personal fears were explored openly at these personal growth weekends. Using the models of psychiatrist Dr Elizabeth Kubler Ross, described and discussed in her 1969 bestseller, *On Death and Dying*, we helped attendees through the five stages of coping with death: denial and isolation, anger, bargaining, depression, and acceptance. Our discussions were liberating for many of the attendees, who could finally come to terms with the pandemic and its personal consequences

Joe, the openly gay conscientious objector who I first met at Melbourne's largest anti-Vietnam War demonstration led by Jim Cairns in 1973, attended one of our weekends. This was the second time I met Joe (or Ken, as he was also known at the University Club). Even on this second occasion, he impressed me as a highly intelligent and sensitive man, and a great role model for me. (Although he had a bit of the larrikin streak in him. Then again, he came from Portland, Victoria, where the citizens are down-to-earth.) Joe questioned everything that we had planned for our personal growth weekend. He asked me "what kind of interpersonal bullshit" Bruce and I had planned for the weekend, all the while sporting a cheeky smile, which indicated that he was merely toying with us. In fact, he had been looking forward to the weekend retreat. Joe had confided in me that since his HIV infection, he found it difficult to maintain relationships or find a partner. I reassured him that he had come to the right place. Joe would become meek when I appeared serious, which indicated to me his love and respect for me.

Dirk had accepted my invitation to come along as well. He had recently been diagnosed with HIV, which came as a major shock to him as he had always practiced safe sex. (Although he did say that his sex was lively. I recall he once told me that "it's not just the missionary position: I do sexual acrobatics like an Olympian gymnast!") I told him that it only takes one prick in a condom for HIV to find its way into the bloodstream. I chastised Dirk that he ought to have known better. He confessed that his rationality would evaporate when he met an attractive person. I said he had mistaken lust for romance, but that I would always love him. Our Australian friends blushed at our typical Dutch straight talking.

Andrew, the figure skater, had made the big decision to come to a Porto Bello weekend. He responded well to the attention he received at the retreat, discovering for the first time in his 23 years feelings of beauty and tenderness, something that many of the gay boys did not get from home or school. He was now flourishing like the tulips of Amsterdam.

As people relaxed over the retreat weekend, they would begin to share some of the psychological wounds they had suffered up to that point in their lives. Many would self-sabotage and diminish the positives in their lives, such as Barry (his name being anonymised) who shared his story, which I recorded in my retreat journal:

> I freaked out. He told me he loved me. I could not understand how anyone could love me. My parents said I was not what I could be, and they made sure I suffered from plenty of guilt. Guilt is what they used to change my behaviour. I would not get Christmas presents from Santa because they'd tell him I'd been naughty. That's how it started from a toddler onward. And when I touched my penis as a toddler and later as a teenager I was slapped and told that was dirty, until I visited a florist shop, the rest is history. Now I am here with newfound friends, healing my wounds. Slowly, life is coming together, and as positive changes are made, I am getting a bit of my

self-respect back. I am exercising, drinking less. I have given up smoking and have peace of mind when I have safe sex and not exchanging any bodily fluids. I am liking being attracted to other men. It is very normal, not strange or sinful: I smiled and said that I could see that sexual satisfaction had washed every part of him clean.

The most profound therapy Bruce McNicol did with the attendees was mirror therapy. We would all sit around Barry or a few others who did not like some parts of themselves. They would sit in front of a mirror, repeating after Bruce lines such as "I love my hair", while at the same time stroking their hair. Then we would respond, saying, "Your hair looks good." Or the person would stroke their nose and say, "I love my nose," or biceps, eyes, hands, and so on. This was hard to say for some people, as they were not used to complimenting themselves. The mirror and group exercise reinforced positive self-expression, which was further promoted with hugging and genuine affirmations, such as, "I love your blond hair; it makes your lovely dark blue eyes stand out." These affirmations were not merely superficial compliments but genuinely heartfelt statements. Many tears were shed, and hugs given, during the mirror exercise.

Dirk, being the Greek scholar among us, said that this personal growth weekend was something the ancient Greeks were doing thousands of years ago, discussing much the same things we were then sharing. He regaled us with the tale of Plato's *Symposium*, in which seven notable Greeks got together in holiday attire and joined with Plato in social drinking. "Oh, and did they get *pissed*," Dirk emphasised. They would talk about their own loves at length, just like what we were doing that weekend. They talked about all types of love, too; from the Platonic ideal of love between friends, with no sex, to erotic love. In one of Plato's speeches, that of Aristophanes, we learned how Zeus created gay people, and Dirk quoted him at length:

Now the characters of men differ accordingly as they were derived from the original man–woman. Those who come from the man–woman are lascivious and adulterous; those

who are from woman form female attachments; those who
are a section of the male follow the male and embrace
him, and in him all their desires centre. The pair are
inseparable and live together in pure and manly affection.

These snippets of important gay history caused a flurry of positive
discussions in our groups, which lifted our spirits. It was quite something
for these young gay men to find inspiration from one of the world's
great philosophers, who also elevated same-sex relationships above straight
relationships.

I still remember two powerful questions being asked by several boys:
how can I survive or get rid of my dark negative emotions and the fear I
suddenly have when I am cold with fever all alone in bed at 4 a.m.? And,
how can I convert these momentary negative thoughts into strengths? I
would familiarise the boys with the writing of Victor Frankl, a Jewish
Holocaust survivor and author of the great work, *In Search of Meaning*.
Frankl was a psychiatrist who was forcibly moved to a Nazi concentration
camp and survived for three years, helping others at the camp to persevere
as well. The key, said Frankl, was to maintain hope in the future and not to
portray weakness in the moment. Weakness, of course, meant death at the
camp. Frankl also encouraged the camp prisoners to dream vividly of what
made them happy. For Frankl, it was reuniting with his wife and daughter,
who were interred at another camp. Each day, as the camp prisoners would
return to their barracks, they would hear a little bird nesting in front of a
circular window. It would whistle to its heart's content, lifting spirits and
giving hope for a different life. It was these weekends at Porto Bello that
likewise gave hope to so many men with AIDS.

As a Porto Bello weekend came to an end, it was a new beginning for
many, and many new friends were made by all. Perhaps we had not quite
got fully around the complex issues of love, eroticism, or attraction, but
we all knew that if we wanted to be loved, whether we had the physical
features we wanted or not, beauty remained in the eye of the beholder.
We had already planned follow up dinners, parties, bushwalks, and bicycle
trips. If attendees could not be physically active, we would push them
around in a wheelchair, like we had to do most of the time with Umberto.

Many of the boys knew they would shortly confront their destiny, which was not without hope. Many had finally found meaning, meaning through self-love and the love of others.

Those personal growth weekends at Porto Bello were indeed magical: they smashed negative attitudes and destructive self-images that attendees had inherited from their earlier lives. Here many learnt for the first time about their secret fetishes, good and bad, and their obsessive compulsions. Here we talked about everything important in life.

Chapter 20

An indefinable pleasure meeting and making friends

"There they come!" yelled Umberto. With sudden joyous shouting coming like a roar, we moved forward in unison. As I looked through my tears of joy, I saw the travellers all wore something of the rainbow flag. These young American men and women, our friends, were seeking a few weeks of reprieve from the battlefield of the San Francisco AIDS crisis for rest and recreation here in Victoria.

oday was also the first day of spring, September 1, 1985. Our Big Bunches crew came down to Melbourne International Airport to welcome our dear American friend, the Jewish Polish princess Gloria Jaworski, all the way from San Francisco, with her entourage of friends, for their well-earned rest Down Under. Her annual holiday depended on Big Bunches' takings. If they were sufficient, we could support her return flight. I felt it essential to see each other as often as possible, especially when we supporting each other in the fight for our friends' lives. Our daily lives consisted of shielding and helping others, there being no long-term effective treatment or cure for the disease. Lifting our spirits in each other's company was our weapon against the ceaseless onslaught of despair and darkness. Besides, these were the days long before Skype – we did what we could to sustain our friendship.

Although Umberto was wheelchair bound for distances longer than one hundred feet, and still sorrowful several weeks after the passing of his partner, Angelo, he insisted that he travel with me to the airport. Umberto wanted to reclaim his life to its fullest. Seeing Gloria and her friends would bring a semblance of normalcy back to his life. There was always a desire among my friends living with HIV/AIDS to return to what was wholesome: good health, good looks, love, and humour. Of course, I would always oblige, smiling as I exclaimed that hope doth live!

Umberto was uplifting company, and our regular, deep conversations helped embolden me, a chance for each of us to enjoy frank and honest conversations, relieving our pent-up emotions. We were determined to make a memorable day out of Gloria's arrival, and frame this memory for times when we needed joy.

Umberto was not only excited to see Gloria, but also Anthony, the English dancer from Bristol who had trained with me in San Francisco. Anthony brought another dancer with him from London, his friend Callum. Both boys had signed performance contracts with the *Rocky Horror Picture Show*, then being performed in Melbourne. A few other boys whom I vaguely knew from the Shanti Project had also travelled with Gloria. They were here to train some of our support group workers in Melbourne for the Uniting Church Care Group. (If there were only one denomination that sought to distance itself from the homophobia then rampant among the Christian churches, it was the Uniting Church. They, and the Catholic nuns from the Sisters of the Good Shepherd and the Sisters of Mercy, were fast becoming major protagonists for delivering care for the AIDS community.

Before our company's arrival, Umberto was fantasising about the Americans' personalities and what they would look like. He admired gay men living in San Francisco. They had the guts to fight for equality, he told me, and now they were dying by the hundreds. We were both interested in gay history and felt that it had too long been a marginalised subject. We figured that all of that was going to change with the rising strength in the gay community, to claim our rightful place in world history. I respected Umberto's mind and passion for human rights and justice. It was a good deal better than the political apathy surrounding us in the wider community. Thank God for the many gay boys and girls who were rattling the gates of the establishment! For my part, I was also interested in Gloria's updates on the latest ACT UP activities. ACT UP had been instrumental in shaking up the bureaucratic inertia around AIDS research and advocating for speedier drug approvals.

Melbourne put on its best spring weather that day. The horse racing Spring Carnival was on, and Melbourne's streets were visited by the throngs of ladies wearing their fantastic dresses and fashionable fasteners. Even Dorothy had taken to wearing a hat specially made for her by Paris, Melbourne's quintessential milliner, who often told us that he was regularly inspired by Big Bunches' beautiful flowers. Umberto revealed to me that Dorothy had made a deal with Paris in exchange for the hat: a fresh supply of flowers every week for the whole year!

Like little boys, our excitement knew no bounds; we were both flush with expectation. As I pushed Umberto in his wheelchair, he reminded me that we weren't competing in the Paralympics. I muttered some false agreement as I increased my speed even more: we were running late and Dutchmen are *never* late! Umberto quipped that as we were in Australia, we could run on "Aussie time"—that is, we could run late. "Yes and frequently missing the boat!" I laughed. Imagine what a shame it would be if our company had arrived and we were not there to greet them, I thought. How disappointed would they be at not meeting friendly, familiar faces like ours! I promised Umberto that we had a world-class Australian welcome in store for them. As it turned out, we were just in time. Their plane, a direct flight from Los Angeles, had already landed.

We waited in the Arrival Hall amid the masses of eccentric personalities that make up Australian society. Umberto and I both loved people watching, and we passed many a time as spectators, observing and picking on the crowds, a great source of amusement. Why are gay men and women so interested in noting people's idiosyncrasies, their dress and body language? Is it the excitement of guessing and surmising, perhaps wishful thinking that all the handsome men or women are gay? Some say they don't watch people, but of course, people watching is at the very least a subconscious activity; everybody does it. The most fun we had was sending up the suburban bogans (an Australian slang term for the unsophisticated). Robert joined us at the Arrival Hall wearing his splendid Ansett uniform. He must have been very happy, as both Umberto and I received a big hug and kiss on our cheeks. "Youse are a pack of poofters!" a pack of bogans yelled our way from a distance, but we weren't embarrassed at all. A public mocking only gave a public demonstration of their own bigotry. Terry arrived shortly thereafter as well and had seen the hugging and kissing. "I thought a ménage-à-trois was about to take place!" he said chuckling. He dismissed our nagging onlookers with a royal wave of his right hand.

We had managed to situate ourselves in a good spot at the railings, just in front of the huge double customs doors through which legions of tired travellers had to pass. When the doors briefly opened, I spotted Gloria in the distance, making her way in the long line. Every time someone walked out of the doors I would see her gradually approach the exit and announce her latest movements to Umberto, who couldn't see her from his wheelchair. I thanked Robert for organising a disability ticket so we had prime positions to park our car and to welcome our visitors. Our preparations had come together nicely: Jason and Dorothy joined us with bunches of flowers in hand, and Terry had asked Peter, his handsome (and gay) chauffeur, to divert to the airport to transport Princess Gloria and her coterie of darlings.

"There they come!" yelled Umberto. With sudden joyous shouting coming like a roar, we moved forward in unison. As I looked through my tears of joy, I saw the travellers all wore something of the rainbow flag. These young American men and women, our friends, were seeking a few weeks of reprieve from the battlefield of the San Francisco AIDS crisis for rest and recreation here in Victoria.

"Hello, darlings!" Gloria said, reaching out warmly to all of us. The group of us embraced in a giant hug. It was warm, genuine, an enthusiasm brimming with the positive energy that Americans seem to naturally carry, and it quickly boiled over to the rest of us. Gloria introduced us to five new women to the group. It instantly seemed as if we had known everyone for a long time. The additional five would stay at a Uniting Church manse on Punt Road in South Yarra, near my place and Big Bunches.

I thought Gloria was the best-looking woman in the airport. She was unconventionally stylish, and not gaudy in her tastes. Anthony looked stunning, too, as was his dancing colleague, Callum. And then there was Sandy, the gay sailor I had met several years ago. We had stayed in regular contact regularly and grew quite fond of each other. Sandy later rented one of Gloria's apartment, next to my old apartment in San Francisco. As so often happens, it was very happy serendipity that Gloria and Sandy met and knew me in common. Sandy had not changed one bit since he was hitchhiking from Los Angeles to San Diego. This time, he was a little coy, probably because he had not been to Australia before. Terry took a shine to him immediately and insisted that he would travel in his car to my place. We were also introduced to Randy, Peter, and Billy from the Shanti project in California.

Jason and Dorothy made sure that all of our guests received beautiful bunches of Boronia mixed with Victoria's state flower, the common but beautiful pink heath. The arrangement made the bouquets look like the rainbow flag. Dorothy added a small furry koala souvenir to each bouquet, together with a warm, welcoming message. Umberto smiled as if to say, "Isn't that a bit kitsch?" but I remarked that it was the thought and intentions that really counted.

Gloria and Marcy and Jane, who were AIDS nurses at San Francisco General Hospital whose airfare Terry had paid, came with Umberto and me in my car. Our travellers were all dog tired, as one expected of any international traveller to Melbourne. The plan was to get them home, showered, and asleep, which is what they wanted anyhow.

When we arrived at my place, Gloria told me that while she was upbeat, there was some bad news she wanted to relate to me later. "Sometimes the bad news sucks the oxygen out of you," she said. "But we must deal with reality. This is not the Last Supper. Every person bleeds red." With that, she retired for a quick sleep, a joint in hand.

Our guests were all asleep, and Umberto, too. Robert and another friend, John, also took a brief nap after our return from the airport. We had a dinner planned in about five hours' time. I had asked my friends in the support group to help in preparing vegetarian foods for the evening meal. Jason returned from his work down the road at the Alfred Hospital, and had collected Sandy from the manse. He was still talking about the energy and enthusiasm of our American friends.

Sandy, with his handsome American accent, brought me up to speed about his life. After he retired from the U.S. Navy, he pursued a degree in journalism and was now working for a San Francisco gay newspaper called *Have You Told Your Mother?* The gay community in San Francisco was being devastated daily by the onslaught of HIV/AIDS, Sandy told us, evidenced by the overflowing death notices in the papers. The crisis was not limited to the disease itself, but was worsened by the evils of misinformation and fear mongering, most of which came from fundamentalist and conservative forces. Even President Reagan refused to mention HIV or AIDS anywhere, at least in public. He would remain silent until 1987, far too late. Nor did the U.S. Congress promptly acknowledge the seriousness of the AIDS crisis. Yet notwithstanding the continuing devastation wrought by AIDS and having an unsupportive Republican government at home, Sandy, like all our guests, remained positive and hopeful about the future of the struggle and the gay community.

Chapter 21

There was a drought, our dancing boys, showered together

The bench sat beneath a century-old weeping willow, which filtered the sunlight through its young spring leaves. The boys fell asleep, their heads resting on the other's shoulders, legs overlapping, hair in each other's face.

After arriving home from the airport, our guests longed for warm showers and time to unwind. I made some herbal tea and put on relaxing sounds while they showered. I had three showers in my house on St Kilda Road, so no one had to wait too long and some, like our dancing boys, Anthony and Callum, showered together. Showering together saved time and water—or so they reasoned! Soon, these two pieces of sweet eye-candy were reclining on the inviting cushions of my Edwardian Marlborough bench, among the spring flowers basking in the warm sun. The bench sat beneath a century-old weeping willow, which filtered the sunlight through its young spring leaves. The boys fell asleep, their heads resting on the other's shoulders, legs overlapping, hair in each other's face. Our other American guests dozed off in comfy lounge chairs and hammocks. All was quiet but for the buzzing of flies. Even the birds rested that warm day.

Jason returned to work immediately after the airport trip, and Dorothy hurried back to Big Bunches. For my part, I had taken the day off and wasn't sleepy or tired. I sat on the veranda with Terry and another guest, John, reminiscing about that morning's events over a drink or two. John had arrived at my home earlier than expected, which would have normally irked me, but as we were all in high spirits, I didn't mind that day.

John had been a window dresser at Georges in the Jam Factory. He desperately wanted to fall in love again and I was forever, in his words, "vetting his love life." His Kaposi Sarcoma lesions had been successfully removed, but now the symptoms of toxoplasmosis began to show. John would forget things easily, mixing up sequences of events. Mercifully, he was not aware of his own confusion. In any event, we weren't going to constantly remind him: ignorance is bliss and life too short, especially in John's case. John had recently lost his job, which forced him to move houses for cheaper rent. Many of his friends were the usual fair-weather sort: like rats on a sinking ship, they left him once he fell ill. John increasingly felt deserted and lonely. He visited Big Bunches every day, sometimes twice a day. It was the best therapy he could manage.

Sitting on the veranda, John glanced at Terry and then me, looking perplexed. "How come people fall so quickly in and out of love?" he asked us. I tried to answer in a cheeky way. After all, it was far too early in the afternoon to entertain deeper thoughts, and everyone was still relaxing. I told John that, to a lover, every pimple is pretty, every unusual interest a badge of animated inquisitiveness. Each tickle in the throat is an excuse for wanton mollycoddling, but this kind of attention, or specialness, wears off after a while, doesn't it? The law of diminishing returns sets in; the routine of life makes it boring, and people don't take to boring things easily, so they move on to the next novelty. Love needs a lot of work; it doesn't magically happen, like in the movies.

Some of our friends from the VAC support groups arrived shortly thereafter to set up a barbecue for the evening. We also invited eleven friends who were unwell. There were many isolated people who felt they didn't belong anywhere. It was those kinds of people that the Big Bunches bunch sought to befriend, in the hope that they would join our extended family, just as the VAC support groups had. Besides, I was never much into only inviting celebrities or notables of the gay community, not that I ignored them. We were on friendly terms with everyone. (Whether people were on friendly terms with us was another matter. *C'est la vie!*) But our priority was the great number of Big Bunches friends who, in many cases, had no one else.

Later that afternoon, Gloria confided in me that nearly all the boys she had brought were exhibiting symptoms of HIV/AIDS, although none had been tested: that was done deliberately. In those early days, testing positive for HIV/AIDS could have devastating consequences for one's employment and health insurance, and many could no longer travel overseas. The Australian Government was considering such a ban at the time. The U.S. had already banned people who tested positive for HIV/AIDS from entering the country, but Gloria said the ban backfired when the Americans were refusing entry to some Dutch air force personnel, who they suspected had HIV/AIDS. Well, Gloria said, the Dutch Government threatened to cancel a multi-billion dollar order for the F115 Jet Fighter plane. The boys were promptly allowed into the U.S. I remarked to Gloria that the Dutch boys had probably intimidated their American male counterparts, with their handsome faces, blue eyes, commanding stature, well-endowed... Gloria chortled, and excused herself to prepare some of her infamous hash potato cakes.

Our other guests eventually awoke, feeling much refreshed, and joined us on the veranda. The warm spring morning had given way to a balmy afternoon. Our conversations came around to the life and death challenges we were all confronting. AIDS had now become a major catastrophe in the United States, in particular in San Francisco, with hundreds perishing each month. The word *death* was used rarely as we spoke; it was so final. Australia's tally of AIDS deaths was likewise climbing fast. One emotion impacted us greatly and Gloria had named it: *anger.* We felt a personal and collective anger, born of fear and anxiety. Anger was now the greatest challenge for people living with HIV/AIDS, besides survival and the race for a cure. We are so angry, almost to the point that we are self-destructing, Gloria said. She pointed out that the raw emotion was also motivating our community in a positive direction, too. "Anger gets things done," she opined. Its opposite, love, would ensure that our anger didn't overwhelm us. There was only one person that could say *love* with such feeling and authenticity, and that was Gloria.

Gloria recounted a medieval Jewish parable, which if memory serves me well (and this was a memorable moment), went something like this: A rabbi spoke with God about Heaven and Hell. I will show you Hell, God said, and they went into a room which had a large pot of pea soup in the middle. The aroma was delicious, but around the pot sat people who were famished and desperate. All were holding spoons. The spoons' outsized handles were longer than their arms, so it was impossible to get the pea soup into their mouths. Now, God said, I will show you Heaven, and they went into an identical room. There was a similar pot of pea soup in the middle, and the people had the same spoons as those in the previous room. But here, the people were well-nourished and happy. It's simple, God said, for you see, they have learned to feed one another. And that, Gloria explained, is how we are going to survive the AIDS crisis.

Terry and Gloria discussed the possibility of a hopeful future, when HIV/AIDS would no longer equate to a death sentence. They insisted that out of all of this horribleness, much good would come. I was likewise convinced, having seen the growing cooperation worldwide among the LGBT community. A new, high bar had been set for altruism, and the consequence of which would be victory over the AIDS crisis and, in important ways, over our community's enemies, the enemies of all good people. Robert, who had arrived in the middle of the conversation, added that I was going to do my part, writing a book about our struggle, which is this book here, written long after Robert's passing, his splendid Ansett uniform no longer adorning his beautiful frame.

Everything at the evening barbecue had to be fresh and healthy. Since the AIDS crisis hit, I had become more conscious of the role that nutrition played in boosting the immune system. I believed, and still largely do, that what one ate and drank walked and talked tomorrow. I had provided the shopping list myself – nothing was coming out of a packet! Dorothy even made the tomato sauce from fresh tomatoes, according to her grandmother's recipe. My mum Bets brought over two vegetarian casseroles, as well as homemade Thousand Island dressing, made from a recipe that I had brought back from Hawaii four years prior. Those four years had flown by: time moves fast when one lives in a crisis. Every day fighting for one's life, every day knowing it could be your, or a good friend's last. You tire easily.

We served only white meats – chicken, turkey, fish. There was no red meat in sight, nor any of that risky cured meats or sausages, stuffed with nitrates and other potential carcinogens. Those were for the carnivores "who murdered animals," Terry shouted as he tended a second grill for the vegans and vegetarians among us. The vegetarian smorgasbord consisted of vegie sausages, wheat gluten steaks, and tofu-and-cashew nut steaks, all neatly laid out and covered by cloth to keep away the flies. We had many types of lettuce to make your own salad: iceberg, butterhead, crisphead, celtuce, red coral, radicchio, as well as a variety of onions, tomatoes, radishes, capsicums, cucumbers, and several different preparations of pumpkin. In all, a delicious, gay cornucopia of colours. From past experience, I knew that meateaters gravitated to the herbivorous offerings: they'd tuck into it till there was nothing left for the vegetarians, and then they'd move on to their carnivores' banquet! My mum Bets, however, had ingrained into her children that good hosts always ensure there is plenty of food for all. Hospitality was the number one virtue for the Paulusse family. After all, Sodom and Gomorrah were destroyed for lack of hospitality, not sexuality, as the fundies would have you believe.

As the Tourist Commissioner for Victoria, Terry had brought some good donated wines and light beers. Anthony and Callum volunteered to serve drinks, including non-alcoholic beverages and our own concoctions of exotic fruit juices. Later on, the boys performed the "Time Warp" dance in their *Rocky Horror Picture Show* costumes. I sang a song from my teenage years, "The Impossible Dream," from the musical, *Man of La Mancha*, a song that was influential when I was forming my own identity all those years ago.

Picture; Boys from the VAC West Support Group. Some of our friends from the VAC support groups arrived shortly thereafter to set up a barbecue for the evening. We also invited eleven friends who were unwell. There were many isolated people who felt they didn't belong anywhere. It was those kinds of people that the Big Bunches bunch sought to befriend

Chapter 22

There is too much rubbish in my brain at times

It was a cold, wintry August night with a clear sky, almost a full moon, although my diary does not record the actual date. I parked the car at Fairfield Hospital's car park, as close to the ward where Angelo stayed. The three of us were hushed, the merlot long having done its work of relaxing us. I gathered my thoughts as much as I could. The other boys walked very close next to me; few words were exchanged. Perhaps they were contemplating their own demise.

"There is too much rubbish in my brain at times," Umberto blurted out in frustration at his partner Angelo, who had recently lost his mind to an AIDS-related dementia. There is no real silver lining to dementia except that oftentimes the sufferer is not aware of their own condition. Angelo remained a funny and sweet person. He just wanted to love everybody. Despite his deteriorating condition, he could still determine the difference between good-looking and homely. He wanted to kiss all the handsome men cruising around the Jam Factory and would call out "Free kisses!" as they passed by. (Sometimes he went too far and called out "Free kisses and free fucks when you buy big bunches of tulips!") It was around this time that it became necessary to accompany Angelo wherever he went, as he also required the use of a wheelchair. Angelo had his own care team by now, a good thing too as that relieved Umberto of the responsibility. Umberto wanted us to be his care team: Pearl, Suzanne, Jason, and me, his close friends.

At the same time, Umberto's absences from Big Bunches became more frequent. He was diminishing in health himself, and Dorothy and the girls now did most of his work. It was not the same when Umberto was gone; such was the nature of his outgoing and beautiful personality that if he was not at Big Bunches, even the plants and flowers seemed to mourn. Everything looked duller; things were dimmer. I had called his estranged father Mario, who lived in Italy, to inform him of Umberto's condition. Umberto had told me on my first visit to the University Club, in the lift, that his father had left his mother and eloped with a young nun. I took those stories with a pinch of salt at the time; just part of building up one's own sense of intrigue, I thought. Some people genuinely used bright colours when they described their lives, whereas others used shades of beige. I preferred the bright colours myself; they went well with effervescent personalities such as Umberto. The thought of losing Umberto soon bothered me and took a toll on me emotionally.

Unbeknownst to me or the others, Mario and his wife, Maria, arranged to come to Australia. They arrived at Melbourne International Airport and took a taxi straight to Big Bunches, appearing just as we were in the middle of unpacking a hefty consignment of West Australian dried flowers. We had hired an extra shop hand to assist with creating the display of vivid colours and unusually shaped flowers. Unexpectedly, after welcoming them and sharing coffees, Mario and Maria pitched in with the unpacking effort. It reminded me of our crazy world, full of everyday surprises. In the end, we welcomed surprises: all of us can suddenly be snuffed out at anytime and the world moves on, with our footprints upon history only temporarily remembered (unless, of course, they are footprints like this book, forever recorded in the U.S. Library of Congress).

We did not immediately take them to see Mario's son. Dorothy went out of her way to welcome Mario and Maria, and after she found out they were short of cash, invited them to stay at her place in Caulfield. Besides, Umberto and Angelo's pad was far too small to accommodate four people; it was full now of medical equipment, oxygen tanks and respirators, which filled a quarter of their living room. We affectionately called them our sweet M and M's.

I won't refer to Maria as the ex-nun, as Umberto had described her. She was no longer a woman of the cloth. She was, however, a delightfully clever and witty woman, well educated in the culture of Italy, and a smart dresser, too. I could see that she was being eyed by the Toorak set. Even Sheila Scotter, Melbourne's famous socialite with an acid tongue but kind heart, happened to drop in to Big Bunches one time and commented on Maria's travel outfit. Maria's English was what as you would expect an educated Italian woman to speak, like Sophia Loren spoke English. In fact, I was reminded of Sophia when I was with Maria. Her gesticulations were so quick and mostly with her hands; she seemed to be in a perpetual state of excitement. She simply loved life and it showed. Mario was an excitable personality, too, but had a more subdued manner than Maria. If he had a problem, he would make light of it and replaced it with a song. Both were sophisticated Italians, and did not have a negative word to say about Umberto's sexuality.

Dorothy asked me to call Umberto and calmly inform him that his father and Maria were in town. I told Umberto that they wanted to visit him and were currently staying at Dorothy's home. I knew that he would want a tidy apartment with a cosy and pleasant atmosphere before they would visit him there, although I have to admit that sometimes his place had the feeling of death about it. Thank goodness, however, for the VAC support group assigned to Umberto and Angelo: they were able to attend their flat almost immediately to clean the place thoroughly, as well as help shower and dress the boys. We delivered fresh flowers and provided dinner at their place that night.

Mario and Maria had absolutely no problems with their son being gay and that he had a male partner (in the 1980s we would call partners lovers, a term I prefer to this day as more affectionate and less ambiguous than the term "partner").In 1987, we had 26 Big Bunches friends who had been diagnosed with or displayed the symptoms of HIV/AIDS, and we knew most of the families. As these families knew that their mostly young sons would die soon, many had come to accept homosexuality and became protagonists in the cause for LGBT equality and health services. Some even formed PFLAG groups, parents of gay people; these were brave and loving parents and mighty allies. Not every one of these 26 friends died and some remain alive today, albeit not flourishing in excellent health, as even antiviral drugs took their toll on the body.

That evening I took Mario and Maria to Umberto and Angelo's pad. Unfortunately just then Angelo was admitted to the Fairfield Infectious Diseases Hospital for what seemed to be the umpteenth time. He was labouring for breath and I feared he was not long for this world. On the other hand, it was a blessing in disguise, I thought, as Umberto could then spend some intimate time with his parents. He asked me, however, to stay and support him; he found it difficult and awkward to be reunited with his parents. He was frightened that he had disappointed them, yet Mario and Maria were the exact opposite: they were proud of their son (despite not being his biological mother, Maria referred to Umberto as her son). Mario was equally proud of his son's ability, like father, to sing and dance. Umberto had always performed at weddings, especially ones where he also had made the floral arrangements. They were just the best weddings in Melbourne: his style of putting flowers in the brides' hair was so talked about that even Melbourne most famous florist, Kevin O'Neil, would ask him to do weddings for his clients.

The evening conversation was not awkward in the least, and even though Umberto was fading fast, his humour remained as lively as ever. He still liked to smoke cigars, the Dutch ones he said, although he did not really draw in the heavy cigar smoke; that was just a pretence. We all enjoyed the cigar aroma, which evoked memories for all of us. The aroma reminded me of comforting childhood years when all my uncles and granddads would sit together in those very cosy Dutch lounge rooms, drinking a "young one", as in, young Dutch gin. Mario reminisced similarly about the time he sang in Havana. He smoked cigars for comfort, to recall happier times. Sometimes we needed to escape to comforting times when we sensed something dark looming. Maria and I enjoyed much merlot that night as well. We did not serve too much rich food, as that would have made Umberto sick. He could not hold down most foods; only certain foods were appropriate and even then, his digestion was aided with some help from marijuana.

"I feel at peace with the world. I feel in love with the world, with people. I feel I belong and that I matter. So many people have shown genuine love to me," Umberto told us. It seemed that he was making a summation of his life, given these could be his last days. He said he felt sorry for Angelo, who did not have a family around him, and who, due to the onset of dementia, had lost his previous character and personality. He was like a different person but in the same body. Umberto said that that was the hardest thing to accept, but he comforted himself that Angelo seemed happy in his current state. he was not fearful he just did not realize what was going on he was still friendly and kind though. Maria encouraged Umberto to focus on the good times, and that in time, the bad memories would fade away. She compared it to childbirth: the love of a child overtakes any of the pains of morning sickness, the nine months of gestation, or labouring.

Umberto alertness and sensitivity had not faded as much as I had previously thought. He asked me to visit Angelo that night, even though it was 11 p.m. He felt that Angelo was sad and alone at the hospital. I called Fairfield and the night nurse said that Angelo was a bit agitated and that maybe it would do him well for someone to calm him down or just sit with him. I did not relay what the nurse said to me to Umberto, but I promised him that I would go and see Angelo. Dorothy came over to Umberto's after I left, to take Maria and Mario to her home while Jason, who was virtually living and sleeping at my place, volunteered to sleep over at Umberto's. This was the care for each other; love ruled.

Before I drove to Fairfield hospital I called Abby, a close friend of Angelo's, who himself was not yet diagnosed with AIDS although he showed all the symptoms (the debate as to whether to be tested or not was still raging. Personally, I encouraged testing for everyone; at least then one was able to access sickness benefits and use extra services.). Abby worked for the Victorian Opera Company, in their wardrobe department. He was very good stitching queen, as I jokingly and lovingly called him. It was odd to think that in a previous life, he had been a submarine sailor. He was a good-looking, masculine type, and I had first found it hard to see him needling and fitting all the delicate dancers at the opera. But I accepted that I was stereotyping him. Abby suggested that we pick up Greg, too, another of Angelo's close friends. Yet again, Greg was also diagnosed with this horrible virus. I wondered if it was a good idea for these friends to see their own demise in the presence of Angelo's current state. I did not have an answer at the time, thinking instead that I would leave it up to the love of God and reminded myself that"perfect love casts out fear."

"Bring your Walkman with speakers," Greg said, "together with Angelo's cassette tape of all the gay anthems he made for your birthday present. Maybe we can play these anthems." He also suggested that I should say a prayer. I knew Angelo used to be religious, Pentecostal, I think. But those holy rollers had shown him the door after he outed himself (those hypocrites forgot Jonathan and David of the Old Testament, whose love for each other surpassed the love of women) as so beautifully and erotically written in 2 Samuel 1:26 and in 1Samuel they kissed each other and cried together Johantan also took of his clothes in front of David 1 Samuel 18:3-4.

It was a cold, wintry August night with a clear sky, almost a full moon, although my diary does not record the actual date. I parked the car at Fairfield Hospital's car park, as close to the ward where Angelo stayed. The three of us were hushed, the merlot long having done its work of relaxing us. I gathered my thoughts as much as I could. The other boys walked very close next to me; few words were exchanged. Perhaps they were contemplating their own demise. Greg was suffering from the dreadful *Pneumoncystis carinii*and the cold air induced a horrible coughing fit which did not stop easily. The kind and attentive nurses had prepared a warm room for us, but first they settled down Greg while Abby and I quietly went into the room, one of the special palliative care rooms. That alone prepared one's mind for the moment.

"Hi Angelo, my dear," I said but I did not receive a response. Was he sleeping or in a merciful coma? Just then Greg walked in with hot cups of coffee. "Hi Angelo," Greg said in his soft manly voice, "I've brought you a soy latte." Greg's greeting roused him from his sleep. Angelo opened his eyes and smiled, but could not speak. The smile was enough. Abby connected the Walkman and quietly put on some Pet Shop Boys, which reminded me of the Bronski Beat. The music played quietly but enough to gently awaken Angelo. We sat around him on wooden chairs, and while he could no longer drink anything, he touched the warm mug of coffee and whispered "nice." The nurse had said we could dab the coffee on his lips as he could not swallow. Dabbing, holding hands, gently he faded, yet holding our hands firmly, there was no letting go yet; a squeeze was felt every time when the music changed to different song:"I am what I am","I will survive", Freddie Mercury's "Bohemian Rhapsody", Bach's "Jesu, joy of my desire". After Bach, all went quiet. I said a prayer. Angelo had passed, holding us, we embracing him, our faces touching his face, our arms over his shoulders. The first ray of Melbourne's winter sun penetrated his room, several rays shone on his resting face, a symbol of peace and love.

None of us were tired; that was reserved for later. That was how the body and mind functioned in a stressful moment: it always adjusted to physical and emotional circumstances, fight or flight. We were not that emotional in the moment, having had already cried plenty earlier. I escaped to the toilet where I sobbed into a soft cotton towel. Crying can be a wonderful, cathartic act: it relieves and takes the emotional load off one's mind. Abby and Gregg did likewise. Greg added, "I want to go like Angelo when my time comes," saying to both of us, "Can you be with me, too?"

The moment came as a great relief. Angelo was free, no longer tormented by the disease or cruel dementia. It was unfortunate that Angelo's parents were not there, their righteousness being a horrible barrier to loving their son unconditionally. They had yet to experience true love.

All three of us would rest for a while that day and later go to Umberto's to give him the news of Angelo's passing. We knew it would be a very sad moment, yet also a relief for Umberto, knowing that Angelo's pain had passed as well. Such was the contradictory duality of death in those early days.

We stopped by Queen Victoria Market to fetch some warm almond croissants on the way to Umberto's. Dorothy was already driving Mario and Maria to Umberto's pad, while Jason had tidied up the flat and ensured the coffee was percolating the Italian way. We all had a good breakfast, or at least pretended to enjoy the food. The moment was not about sharing food as much as it was about the togetherness in a bittersweet time. Umberto cried, laughed, saw what love could do. No one of the Big Bunches bunch would die alone.

Hundreds of Quilts were made so the world would not forget we made one for Angelo and this one is made for Ken Mclelland who I met during the anti Vietnam marches and later on at the University club in Chapter 2. We will never forget...then we had Vigil, Candelight Vigils:-

(Candlelight Vigil. c.June 1986, photograph by Jay Watchorn - C
courtesy of the Australian Lesbian and Gay Archives)

Chapter 23

The Asian Boyfriend

"Jim was smart; he read the sport pages of Melbourne's major tabloid paper, The Herald Sun, where AFL footballers are often in the news for dysfunctional behaviour. They were different creatures from the Big Bunches boys, whose smiles and wit distinguished them from many of the crass Aussies who Jim had come across during his time as a flight attendant."

The handsome Singapore Airlines crew were welcome money spending customers at the Fashionable Jam Factory where they frequently sauntered or may be cruised, sipped coffee, people watched, making eye contacts, smiling delightfully when picking up on funny Australian idiosyncrasies. They too especially loved our dried, lightweight native Australian flowers: my Asian customers, forever pragmatic, often preferred dried flowers, as fresh flowers did not last long. I, on the other hand, preferred the fragrance of fresh flowers.

I liked all the friendly Singapore Airlines boys, they charmed me for several reasons one of which was they spent a lot of money ordering gift boxes of dried flowers and native Australian gum nut Christmas wreaths, special and unique from Big Bunches. We shipped these wreaths all over Asia. The wreaths were made by several young men, including Robert, who were too unwell to maintain full-time work otherwise. They worked in our

Big Bunches workshop situated across from the storefront or from home, gluing and varnishing gum nuts on a circular Styrofoam base.

I encountered Jim a fashionable Singaporean at Big Bunches while he was browsing our exotic seashells and silently mimicking our pair of Peach Faced Parrots. Eight bright red Banksias sold to him by Jason 30 minutes earlier stuck out of his backpack; they initially drew my eye to him. I had seen him around before but we had never spoken, although I had wanted to. Jim had a quiet mystique about him that intrigued me. So, on this very hot December day, I threw him a friendly smile and cheekily asked if he was looking for "peace, love, and joy." He innocently evaded my question, instead, he nervously asked if I liked to play tennis with him, his timidity touched me, how I could not play tennis with Jim, me affirming with a positive 'yes' his eyes lit up joyously and a smile of happiness parted his lips when I said 'we will play tennis tomorrow, Sunday. One has to strike while the iron is hot, creating some excitement for myself. Jim's manner changed, his spirit was lifted I wondered if he really liked me or was it just Asian politeness, he was so handsome and energetic; he gave me a feeling of enchantment. Positive affirmations gives people confidence to be themselves it relaxes conversation, at this point he entered into our 'Big Bunches life', then out of the blue he asked if had heard of a drag show at a place called Pokeys at the Prince of Wales Hotel, and whether we might go there after tennis. I jokingly responded that I'd go "if you're shouting," which confused him. I had to explain that "shouting" meant if he were paying for me. Airline crews made much more money than flower shopkeepers, I added. He laughed, gaining confidence, beaming more smiles.

Jim carefully ventured into his next question, asking what I was doing after I shut up Big Bunches for the day. I said that I would be going to the gym. He volunteered to join, so we made plans for that afternoon. I had noticed his perfectly balanced body, indicating respect and being healthy, someone who took care and pride showing well-defined pecs, biceps and triceps, all stylishly packaged in a very tight white T-shirt, with body shaped denims and bare feet stuck into fashionable white Adidas gym shoes. His charm was even further enhanced when a discreetly placed on his firm neck showed a little devil tattoo .

On previous visits, Jim had coffees with the boys while they made the Christmas gumnut wreaths. I think he was more interested in the men who were making them, because he remarked once that he perceived the men to be gay. I asked why. "They are not like AFL footballers, are they?" he replied. Jim was smart; he read the sport pages of Melbourne's major tabloid paper *The Herald Sun*, where AFL footballers were often in the news for dysfunctional behaviour. They were different creatures from the Big Bunches boys, whose smiles and wit distinguished them from many of the crass Aussies who Jim had met during his time as a flight attendant. The Big Bunches boys had a higher social awareness and sensitivity. They were more in touch with themselves and others, which was evident in their creative decorating.

Jim and I became "friends with benefits," as the youth say nowadays, despite our being culturally divergent. He hailed from a conservative Chinese culture in Singapore, whereas I came from a liberal Dutch background where non-conformity was celebrated. We were both well-read loved literature and enjoyed philosophy and all types of music and questioned the status quo of things, enjoying each other's company.

During his annual leave he'd stayed at my place, playing many a game of tennis and gym workouts and we occasionally surfed at 13th Beach, near where my parents lived in Geelong; Jim was the better surfer by far. The only thing that bothered me about Jim was his secretiveness about being gay. No one should know that he preferred men: not his employer, not his parents, not the government and, most certainly, he told me, none of my friends. Is the Pope Catholic or does the Queen have corgis? I'd reply if my friends asked. Nevertheless, I respected his wishes, even though I knew there was a psychological price paid in the form of paranoia and living a culturally enforced fake life.

Once, Jim caught a venereal disease from a visit to Steamworks, one of Melbourne's men-only gay saunas, popular with closeted gay and bi-sexual men. Apparently a condom tore. He had felt slightly guilty going there and downed some courage at a pub with friends beforehand. Jim asked me to take him to the Melbourne STD Clinic, as he was too shy to go alone. I assured him that there was no shame attached having STDs its part of human the human condition; many people catch them like they do the flu, although they are a serious nuisance and should be treated promptly. The waiting room at the STD clinic was overcrowded, so we had to stand in the waiting room. The nurses were run off their feet and calling for patients, at times spelling out letter by letter unfamiliar surnames. Jim's embarrassment became obvious when he noticed four of his colleagues were also waiting. Their heads hung low, ignoring each other's presence. Jim later told me that most of the Singaporean flight attendants and other crew went to STD clinics overseas, in Amsterdam, Sydney, or Melbourne, as Singapore's health care professionals were ignorant and fearful of AIDS-related conditions. Homosexuality remained a criminal offence on the statute book in Singapore and people with HIV/AIDS were stigmatised badly. Jim explained that Singaporean gay men would not seek treatment promptly, choosing to wait to the last moment before seeing a medical doctor. They also feared the opprobrium and repercussions from a hostile justice system, or that a positive HIV/AIDS test result could have them reported as deviants to the police and their employers. Australia and Europe were safe in comparison because of their stricter patient confidentiality.

As soon as we had finished with the STD clinic and picked up Jim's prescription of penicillin from the chemist, we headed for another thought-provoking social luncheon at a St Kilda Beach hotel. Several of our Singaporean friends joined as well, along with Andrew, our Serbian-Australian friend. I started the conversation, suggesting how much should we respect cultures that violate the norms and values of another culture? Do cultures change? Stimulated by an article published in the morning papers Robert started the conversation about some conservative Moslem families in Brunswick practicing female circumcision thereby damaging or removing the clitoris. That is against our laws and our culture, but male circumcision is not, we all agreed and that is just as bad. In Australia more generally, nearly all boys are circumcised as a matter of course, without most parents even caring to question the morality of this cultural barbarianism. I mean if you believed that God created humans in his own image and therefore assuming our bodies to be perfect then why is there a need to cut this and the other. In the Northern European countries, male circumcision was largely considered unnecessary and cruel, and the practice was frowned upon, Jason being the satirist that he is quoted from the Bible; 1 Samuel 18:27, where (the bisexual) King David "took his men with him and went out and killed two hundred Philistines and brought back their foreskins." Proving that some cultures are absolutely obsessed with foreskins, we laughed. Like the ancient Hebrews, the old Aussies also loved cutting foreskins. Again we all chuckled.

Jim liked people watching it fed his curiosity, Westerners especially Southern Europeans he observed showed much physical affection hugs, kisses, a non sexual caress or two. He hated the emotional aloofness of Asian culture they do not kiss and hug even at home. Jim said his parents have never audibly said "I love you" or not giving a ruffle of the hair or a big heartfelt hug, even if he liked to tell his parents 'I love you' for him that would seems so unnatural, thank god this changed as soon as he landed in Australia he became as affectionate as any of us warmhearted gay boys. This is also the case as soon as Asian students land in Australia, they can't wait to experience personal freedom and mimic the body language and hand signs of the west and adapt to western mannerisms. Young Asians studying in Australia, especially students, experienced an entirely new freedom: now they could publicly hold hands, even cuddle and wear sexy clothes on Aussie streets. Many girls took to sporting Western haircuts with their waves, curls, and colour, but when they returned to China, Korea or Taiwan, the black straight hair returned. Age-old customs carried the day. In places like Singapore, expressions of nonconforming lifestyles were tightly controlled even in the mid-twentieth century. But now many young Asians hugged, kissed, and had as much sex as any young Westerner, which our visit to the Melbourne STD Clinic proved. There were as many Asians sitting there blushing as there were European Australians.

Many months later, I had not heard from Jim for a long while, which worried me. Then, after our usual Sunday morning Big Bunches breakfast, I noticed a middle-aged Asian couple hovering around the shop, pretending to admire the peach-faced parrots picking at the seeds of some Banksia nuts. I sensed a strange connection; maybe I had seen them before in a previous life, or was it déjà vu? The man gave me a shy smile and asked in a Singaporean English accent, "Are you Keith?" I replied yes and smiled back, reaching out my hand. They said they were Jim's parents, which momentarily stunned me. I asked how Jim was doing. That is when I learned the sad news of Jim's death, a sudden shock on that otherwise beautiful morning. While I was saddened by the news, I was not surprised. His parents had discovered my name and several pictures of Jim and me in his diary; there was a Big Bunches card in a dried flower arrangement as well. They had flown over specially to see me. I was, they said, the only living connection with their son that they could find. Jason said he would mind the shop while I took Jim's anxious parents to a nearby café for tea.

It was an awkward situation meeting with Jim's parents; they maintained their parental stoicism during our conversation. I interpreted this as a feeling of harshness on their part toward a wayward child. I momentarily felt anger at their cold attitude. I decided to break their icy stoicism, knowing they would not walk away. After all, they had travelled too far to see me. In exasperation, I asked if they loved Jim and whether they ever hugged or kissed him, held his hand, or patted him on the shoulder, telling him that they loved him dearly—or did they hope that cash was enough to show their love? I knew from Jim that they never said they loved him. I had learned from other Chinese friends that a reluctance to express personal feelings was not uncommon in their culture. My comments met with silence. Jim's parents wore their stoic expressions, until suddenly; Jim's mother erupted in anger, asking if I had given Jim HIV. She had read in his diary that Jim liked sleeping with me while he was in Melbourne. I was taken aback with her direct but honest question, albeit asked in a confrontational manner. I replied that sleeping with someone does not mean exchanging bodily fluids. I stressed that HIV could only be passed by exchanging bodily fluids, which was prevented by condom use, and I only used condoms with Jim. I had to explain what "bodily fluids" meant, giving Jim's mother an abridged crash course in talking openly about sex.

Jim's parents had been the only ones at his funeral. No one else was invited, as they did not want their friends or relatives to ask too many questions as to why, at the age of 29, a Singapore Airlines pilot had so suddenly died. When the question was raised, his parents told an untruth for face-saving reasons; they said Jim died of cancer. When asked what type of cancer, they would say leukemia. The more they fabricated their answers, they told me, the more awful and difficult the process became for them. They had largely withdrawn from all their friends and lived in solitude in their apartment. Worse yet, that the Singaporean Government wanted to dispose of Jim's body within 24 hours as he was considered a biohazard. His parents were not allowed to touch his body, and were only able to view him momentarily from a distance.

The ice was finally broken. We were now just ordinary people, no pretentions between us; the bottle of merlot we enjoyed together broke the nexus of awkwardness. Yet I was still calling them "Mr and Mrs Lee." They told me that Jim was not his real name, but like most young Chinese people, he had adopted a Western name. I smiled and asked for their Western names. As they had none, they asked me to choose ones for them. As quick as a flash, I blurted out Charlie and Joanne. Those names sound real Aussie, I explained to them; names we could all relate to. I invited them to let me introduce them to Jason, who had been minding Big Bunches for a couple of hours and others working that day. Everyone got along swimmingly and Jim's parents, newly christened Charlie and Joanne, invited everyone out to dinner that night. Jason, compassionate as ever, said that the Big Bunches crew were happy to become their new Australian sons and daughters.

Jim's parents were staying at a Melbourne hotel for the week following. I suggested that we go on road trips, picnics, walks around the parks and art centers, and visits to the places that Jim had frequented. I was always talking with them about the Jim I knew, which was more than they had known of their own son. I was able to reveal his true passions and charming character. Together, we looked at Jim's photographs and sorted through some of his personal things that he had left behind for me—a watch and some signed books with sweet messages, and a golden chain for me to wear. Joanne admired the long golden chain with its cross, something I never wore as a matter of personal style. It suited Joanne much better so I happily parted with it.

As we drove to Melbourne Airport on their way to Singapore, Charlie was curious about what kind of "gay lifestyle" Jim had lived. I said that there was no such thing as a gay lifestyle: that was an erroneous myth perpetuated by others. It was not like, say, choosing a vegan lifestyle, where one does not eat anything animal or derived from animals. Being gay was not a choice. One doesn't wake up one day and say, "I choose to be gay." It was what one was. Charlie and Joanne asked more questions but the greatest truth revealed in all of their interrogation was that Jim had been dearly loved by his friends. Joanne added that he died unexpectedly after catching a cold in Singapore. He was brought to an isolated ward for infectious diseases, fell asleep, and never woke up.

Today, Jim's parents are still experiencing the love of their son through their son's friends. Becoming close to his parents was consolation for my heart and theirs.

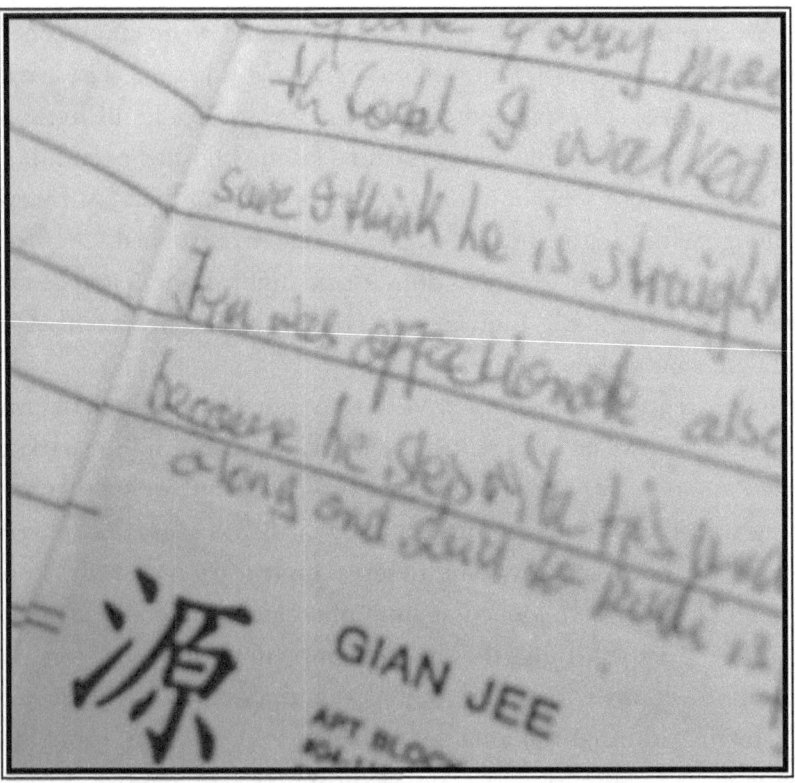

A few pages from my journals recalls good memories

Chapter 24

Will you march with my picture in the Parade

"virtually all the passengers on the plane were all going to Mardi Gras, as was evident by the enormous amount of clever camp humour and send ups circling the cabin. A lot of the clever satire and humour was directed against the enemies of the Gay Community".

Dorothy was dressed in her favourite yellow polka dot dress as she welcomed everybody to the monthly free *Big Bunches Bunch Breakfast*, which we called *4 B's* for short. It was an opportunity for all of us to sit around large attractively decorated circular tables to enjoy a Dutch- and Danish-style breakfast at the Danish Café and Bakery, also located in the Jam Factory and owned by one of my straight friends (and a supporter of our cause). The welcoming by Dorothy was saturated in warmth and her practice of greeting people by their name felt like a casual caress. Heart-warming banter was equally served with the almond croissants, hot freshly brewed coffee, several varieties of imported cheeses and seven types of freshly baked breads, and a choice of plant or cow's milk, a mixture of freshly cut and plucked fresh fruit and homemade yoghurts. These breakfast were different, not only because the food was unique and the best of quality but more importantly the unfeigned sociality reinforced love and always extirpated fear, yet the conversations always seem to move towards destiny, all our destinies.

The talk during this breakfast morning, so my dairy says, was about the Sydney Gay and Lesbian Mardi Gras, prompting Umberto to suggest that I take him and Robert to Sydney, as it would probably be their last Mardi Gras. I swallowed three times.

Everybody thought it was a great idea; I was hesitant, saying if you only want to go to a warehouse dance party you can go here in Melbourne. Robert tried to persuade me further when he made me aware that this year's Mardi Gras was almost cancelled by antagonists and enemies of the GLBTI community due to the rapid increase in AIDS diagnosis and their fear mongering that unsafe sex at Mardi Gras would increase infections, he quickly added that it was now going ahead and the theme for the 1985 parade was *Fighting for our Lives* . Fighting for our lives that's what they we're doing and wanted to be part of it. Robert made a profound observation when he mentioned that many people think we're just stereotypical gay party boys, without Robert completing his sentence, Umberto quickly prompted our memories that these party boys brought about the largest visible human rights peace movement for equality, the likes of which the world had not seen before; it is called Gay Pride" ; that was the first time I had heard this term Gay Pride.

Gay Pride marches around the world are now "Beacons" against discrimination, human right violations) not to mention bolstering confidence and self affirmation of the GLBTI community. And reminding rightwing authoritarian regimes and religious fundamentalists around the world that they will not get away with lies innuendo and stereotyping of the GLBTI community.

Mardi Gras was not just the Parade or the Dancing parties at Horden's Pavilion, the concerts, Queer Films, sports tournaments, important as they are, but in the end, for the boys it was the camaraderie and the feeling to belong to a vibrant visual Gay Community, especially this year when their community was under siege as never before. They viewed their attendance as their last stand so to speak Mardi gras was their contribution to Gay solidarity, a sort of symbiotic joining of the dancing with the social awareness and social justice movements.

I was in a quandary about going to the 1985 Mardi Gras and had not planned to look after three men one being high maintenance in care. At the time I had another young man living with me, Luke, a gay refugee, who was kicked out of home by his fundamentalist "Christian" family, if you could call such people a family. Luke was in a very poor state, not in mind, but in body: his head had swollen up to twice the size, from a sculptured face to balloon size that worried him much; he had asked me a question of when it would be his moment, as quick as a flash I said dearest Luke many people, the most only think about their death as the greatest happening in their lives, your moment is now not when you're dying or death that won't be your greatest moment, his tranquil honest yeas sparkled even more when we talked about when our greatest moments would be. He felt close to Robert and Umberto and the three boys were always, what to me sounded like made up stories, I though they all had an aptitude for gossip telling funny stories, making gay jokes keeping up each other's spirit, totally supporting each other. The only difference was that Luke cared more about his sandy-coloured Labrador named Flip than about his own circumstances. He could cope with his situation only because of the amazing amount of love, inclusion, care and cuddles he was receiving from everybody in his extended family, as well as the good affirmative conversations at my house and the breakfasts. Luke was much reassured not to worry about Flip because nearly all of his friends wanted Flip, I was not surprised as this beautiful dog reflected the love and character of his master, Flip reminded them of Luke and so it was after Luke's passing that a Lesbian couple adopted Flip as their own..

The VAC Support group had organised special tickets to the Mardi Gras dance party, and a balcony view of the parade at several gay-friendly hotels in Sydney's famous Oxford Street in Darlinghurst which from previous visits could easily be a Gay village not unlike The Jam Factory. Robert had organised half-priced airplane tickets provided by Ansett Airlines to people living with HIV/AIDS going to Mardi Gras. One needed to provide a medical certificate to qualify for the discounted tickets.

Yet I wasn't too sure about Mardi Gras itself, especially the dance parties often it was a lonely experience if one did not do alcohol or similar substances, yet I usually had a good time dancing and socialising, no doubt the metaphysical sweetness of wafting weed added to the expected excitement. And at 5:00am in the morning, I would still be dancing usually alone still full of energy, especially after eating fresh fruits and muesli provided as breakfast to dancers. But my friends were mostly too relaxed consequently not too social, enjoying their own comatose, floating states of mind. They knew that if they invited me out, it had to be fun and not involve being in a state of non-compos mentis, drunk or high enjoying their own ego centric world. Umberto and Robert fervently promised they would not ignore me, even though Dirk would supply them with pills of ecstasy, which had been certified safe and pure by Dutch laboratories.

While ecstasy is not legal in Nederland, its use is tolerated without prosecution for individual users. Unlike the homemade Australian stuff that was dangerous, laced with god knows what, several cases of death from ecstasy made headlines in Australia's sensationalist press,(in contrast to the thousands of deaths and diseases from alcohol abuse, on that score the news media of course was hush hush,) had led the authorities to punish users. I warned the boys that the Dutch ecstasy is smuggled into Australia. If they were caught, they were on their own. I did not want to be seen as their babysitter or guardian of morals.

Luke challenged me for being hypocritical, calling out my previous use of Amyl on the dance floor. I replied that Amyl, unlike ecstasy, was not an illicit substance, and besides I said, I only used it if I were dancing with the right person enhancing the pleasure of their presence

Umberto wanted some clarification asking whether by the right person I meant he would need to be HIV-negative. Not to put a too finer point to it I couldn't really care less, if a person were HIV positive or negative: I would still dance and may be do a bit of Amyl with them. Anyhow, my rule with everybody was safe sex. No exchange of bodily fluids and probably no one-night stands. My preference and modus operandi was that I preferred to build friendships first. My mum would say that for every jar a lid is made.

They persuaded me with some emotion that I should go to Mardi gras and was even more inclined to go when Jason agreed to come as well to support me in the care for the boys, as would Dirk from the Dutch consulate. We made our bookings shortly thereafter. The airline deal included accommodation on Oxford Street. The idea of being split up into different rooms did not appeal to us as we were going as a group of friends, so Dirk offered his large, three bedroom apartment at Bondi Beach, overlooking the iconic beach itself. That sounded good to us so we accepted Dirk's generous offer. The offer was contingent on my doing the majority of the cooking for the group, which was fine with me, as long as I did not have to do the dishes.

Over the five days of Mardi Gras, we attended many of the related activities, in addition to going to Sydney's many art galleries, classical and pop music performances, welcoming barbecues with people coming from all over the world. Tickets to the events were provided gratis to attendees with HIV/AIDS. One quickly learned of the awfulness of pneumocystis: the boys could barely walk a hundred meters without becoming out of breath. So we walked slowly. Umberto was the only one who could not make do without a wheelchair, morphine pumps, and an oxygen tank. Fortunately, we could swim at Bondi Beach only a couple hundred metres from Dirk's front door. In fact, Dirk measured the distance to the beach precisely to be 242 metres, having used a measuring tape, further proof that the Dutch are sticklers for time and precision.

We boarded the plane on what was a very hot day together with wheelchairs, morphine pumps and oxygen tanks. One of the airline stewards, Dennis, a well-known personality in Melbourne, welcomed our party of five, treating us like Queens—I mean like the Queen! We were all immediately upgraded to business class. Two weeks of preparation had paid of including extra work on our bodies at the gym but that started 8 weeks before, not to mention the pleasure of shopping for attractive and fashionable new clothes. We had got our haircuts at Avner's, a warm-hearted gay stylist at Prahran Central who knew what looked good for each man based on the shape of his face, and true to form, every time he cut our hair, our confidence rose significantly. We looked attractive and sexy: who does not want to look like that? The plane was almost full, packed with many gay men, including a whole team of marching boys also from Melbourne they sat in economy class but during the flight came forward to entertain us by sashaying down the aisle through the business class and lip syncing the chorus of Queen's "We are the Champions".

We are the champions, my friends,
And we keep on fighting till the end.
We are the champions.
No time for losers
'Cause we are the champions of the world.

One of the dancing queens did a very good impersonation of Freddy Mercury, of whom they said I was his doppelganger. I admitted that was true, but I was much taller and my eyes are blue, (obviously, however, I was not as talented as Freddy was in the musical stakes.) Prior to boarding the plane, I had quietly asked the attendants that no alcohol be offered to our boys, as they were taking a whole mixture of various prescription drugs and alcohol would fatigue if not kill them.

I realized that virtually all the passengers on the plane were all going to Mardi Gras, as was evident by the enormous amount of clever camp humour and send ups circling the cabin. A lot of the humour was directed against the enemies of the Gay Community. As usual, we read in the newspaper that Reverend Fred Nile and his "prayer warriors" were supplicating God for heavy rain to drown out the Mardi Gras festivities, praying, "Pour it out, Lord, show your vengeance on these Sodomites."

Luke was momentarily getting depressed, saying that he was embarrassed by his rounded face. I took his arm gently and sitting next to him, without being patronising, I asked him if people had been ignoring him. I knew that no one had ignored him, and he got as much loving attention as anybody else. He, too, was kissed and hugged, in fact many more times than I was! He agreed. I then asked why he thought he was receiving all the kisses and hugs, but he could not answer. I told him that he had an amazing personality, a beautiful character borne out of suffering when his family had kicked him out, which was why he was experiencing so much love. A big smile emerged, with his very white teeth, on his round red face, his blue eyes were sparkling again. The white teeth were thanks to my homemade virgin coconut cream, mixed with baking powder, which removed tea and coffee stains from yellow teeth. Luke joked that he would take anything virgin, and apologized for his temporary lapse into panic, saying, "I won't die alone, Keith, will I?" He wouldn't.

The very warm welcome at Sydney domestic airport was terrific, everybody got hugged and often kissed by the good-hearted friendly men from ACON (the AIDS Council of NSW). ACON had organised a bus to take us into town, a large bus as the marching boys from Melbourne were also riding with us, off to a motel on Oxford Street. There would be an informal reception once we got in, amusing us greatly. We talked about that reception for hours and days afterwards, it was so memorable: the drag queens were funny, warm and nicely rude as only they were tolerated in getting away with fantastic satire and sarcasm all encapsulated in their deliverance of witty barbs and insults without causing any offense but much hilarious laughing. Meeting other men who were probably consciously celebrating their last Mardi Gras, yet one could never know for sure. The camaraderie that Robert and Umberto had talked about was certainly evident at the reception and I might add spirits were raised with very little alcohol, yet bringing about such effervescent joy. I didn't think about their attendance at Mardri Gras was their last stand while we were all having a good time, although in quiet moments alone it was in the back of my mind. In thinking about it later, waves of sadness often overtook me, which were only assuaged by feeling expansive love and reminding myself that when my friends will have passed I would be left with good memories, and more so I would not feel any guilt for having been neglectful toward my friends in need. Too many times before, I had heard stories about regrets: if only I had done this or that. I was going to make sure that that was not going to happen to me.

After this almost royal reception we drove to Dirk's place at Bondi where a prepared dinner awaited us, much to our surprise Dirk had invited the Dutch Consul General and the Australian Manager of KLM, the national Dutch airline who were an advertising sponsor of Mardi Gras. They wanted to meet us even though the boys were dog tired, but we managed to muster enough strength to join them for dinner. I was asked to give an impromptu and entertaining talk about the history of the Sydney Gay and Lesbian Mardi Gras.

The was entitled; "Mardi Gras from deviancy to moral excellence " Realising that in the space of five year at first being described by the media as a march of deviants to become the largest Human Right demonstration and most economically profitable Community event in the Nation. The young men and women celebrating Mardi Gras were morally courageous at a time when under Australian law they were designated as criminals, now no longer criminals but tragically a thousand opening line of my talk or so Gay Australians are fighting for their very lives as are our friends here present Umberto, Robert and Luke lives not forgetting the fight for universal equal civil rights and social justice for all people. Homosexuality in New South Wales was shamefully still illegal in 1978. I knew a couple of my friends who joined the very first march back in June of 1978 my friend Laurence Hutchins who was having drinks at *Patches* a well know and popular Gay friendly pub told me that when several Gay people burst into *Patches* audibly encouraging all patrons out to join this Gay rights parade happening outside, Laurence told me that a hundred or so patrons all joined the parade and later only to be arrested because they were criminals, the law said so. Gay men were fair game for being stereotyped as limp wristed weak Nellies, of course the opposite was true, those men and women were being authentic to themselves, they had the courage of their convictions so much so that they were prepared the risks of sufferings such as humiliation, being expulsed from their families, jobs loss of friends ostracised from sporting clubs, churches Service Clubs, musical and cultural societies, much of it due to the printing of names outed by a low class tabloid media that was addicted to crisis, sensation and exaggeration all of this despite living in a supposedly civil society.

Mardi Gras therefore started off as a deviant civil rights march in 1978, in solidarity with the Stonewall riots of 1969 in New York. There was also San Francisco's Gay Freedom Day and its campaign against a Californian Government proposal to stop gay rights supporters from teaching in schools. These struggles resonated with Australian gay people. Some important things needed to be voiced and sitting on one's arse complaining about things was not going to solve anything. A small Sydney parade was organized on the 24 June 1978: one truck with a loudspeaker and several hundred people walking behind it, dancing and singing. The parade goers also promoted the National Homosexual Conference in Sydney, and protested against the Festival of Light, aka the Festival of Lies, organised by anti-gay campaigner Mary Whitehouse, a British Christian fundamentalist who happened to visit Sydney to promote her homophobic hate and misinformation campaign. The NSW Police stopped the march by blocking of streets and arresting the driver of the truck. A violent tussle ensued with the police arresting 53 men and women, gay and straight. Decent Australians were incensed by the police action and the NSW Government, to its credit, repealed the anti-gay provision of the *Summary Offenses Act*. In 1979 one year later, over 3,000 people marched for their civil rights without any incidents. Gay Aussies had finally stood up and fought for human rights. Soon, an avalanche of progressive change would rattle the halls of tradition and power for decades to come. I ended my little speech by saying that conservative fundamentalism would fight back with a vengeance but in the end their pathetic hate would not prevail, love, unconditional love always wins in the end. They gave applause, I smiled shyly.

Back in Sydney in 1985, we had taken our position on the balcony of an Oxford Street gay hotel, on the corner of Taylors Square, which afforded us a commanding view of the parade below. I was too overwhelmed by the majesty of the festivities to write much in my diary except for the solemn spectacle of a whole group of people walking in the parade, carrying large photographs of their friends, partners, brothers, sisters, mum, dads, who had died of AIDS, most of them so young. Luke asked if I would carry his photograph the following year. I looked at him sympathetically and just winked, saying nothing. He blew me a kiss, such a young 21-year-old. Some people could open the window to your soul; Luke was one of those people. I knew his time was very short yet he had already made an impact. My heart temporarily broke and I was torn up inside, just wanting to crawl into a foetal position and cry, pretending that none of this was happening. I was very good at hiding my feelings, and at times, it was wise to hide one's feelings.

Robert sensed my awkwardness, and being very caring and always able to read me like a book, broke the ice by reminding us that the Mardi Gras Parade looked more like Rio's Carnival, with all those skimpy costumes. More of a flesh show than commemorating civil rights, he said laughingly. I agreed in part but retorted that it was one's right to present one's body as beautiful, and for us all to admire it and be inspired to get fit and healthy and care for it. That was the only retort I could give. People were looking at us too, and I remarked that we were all dressed for show today as well. We were all participants, looking desirable and smart. Laughing, they quoted my mother in unison: "On every jar there fits a lid" meaning beauty is in the eye of the beholder.

Jason and I sat to the back of the boys, keeping an eye out like a pair of mother hens. We were also thankful that two doctors were present from Sydney's St Vincent Hospital, as Umberto, in his excitement, started having some breathing problems. The doctors took over his care and adjusted the oxygen and gave a morphine injection. He returned to a calm state. I feared Umberto was not long for this world, either. Down went another *Young One*, Dutch gin remember?, which Jason had also learnt to like. Now came the Dykes on Bikes, the roar, the cries, the colours.The extravaganza of the human spirit was on display and the cherished memory that Mardi Gras engraved on our minds for ever.

The VAC Support group had organised special tickets to the
Mardi Gras dance party, and a balcony view of the parade
at several gay-friendly hotels in Sydney's famous Oxford
Street in Darlinghurst which from previous visits could
easily be a Gay village not unlike The Jam Factory.

Chapter 25

The Wake; Yes, you're leaving dear she said, cupping his handsome face

He said that all of us were risking our livelihoods, and possibly our lives, in a society that was largely intolerant of gay people. On the bright side, he concluded that the risks also generated radical new possibilities

Our attention at the reception focused on Jason because it was his Dutch ex-boyfriend Wim, whose funeral we had been attending. Wim had contacted Jason and asked for help. He was one of the first people with AIDS who moved into the palliative care unit made available by the Good Shepherd Sisters, in a three-bedroom home near their convent in Abbotsford. The Sisters named the home *Gunya*, an Aboriginal word meaning "refuge". It was through the efforts of ordinary humble people like Geraldine Kirby, Peter Hayes and Vince Vergona that this palliative care centre was possible. They raised ample funds to renovate the place; it was these acts of kindness and practicality that raised all our spirits and confidence that we were not alone in fighting for our lives by our lonesome selves.

Many of us in the Big Bunches bunch had gathered around my mother Bets'Javanese Dutch teakwood coffee table, she had given the table to me because it was a work of art and doused with spiritual power and love. It was a large and intricately carved circular table that could fit the lot of us. We gave each other emotional support, and we talked about the philosophical matters that gave us a fresh perspective and inner strength.

Death brought many emotions and experiences to bear: the awkwardness, the mystery, the deep spiritual psyche that helped extraordinary people to comprehend death, to help humble and often nameless helpers rise above ordinariness. These gatherings gave us much needed resilience to carry on. We cultivated an ambience of *gezelligheid*, which is a Dutch word that does not translate easily to English. It means an atmosphere of cosiness, an atmosphere that encourages a sense of belonging. The atmosphere could not be *gezellig* if it were insensitive to the needs and emotions of those in attendance.

As usual, Mum Bets travelled down from Leopold after the funerals to make and serve freshly brewed coffee. She would roast the beans and grind them herself. Her Limburger girlfriend, Yetty, had baked several varieties of her famous *Limburgse Vlaai*, a circular cake that hails from the province of Limburg, traditionally served after funerals no doubt to cheer things up. The *vlaai* looked cheerful and mouth-watering, with its varied decorated fruits laid in a thick and creamy vanilla custard topping. They were similar to Australia's own very large bee sting cake, with every kind of freshly stewed fruit mixed in the vanilla custard, a delicacy only available in country bakeries where everything was freshly baked from locally grown ingredients. Bets and Yetty had made them especially for Robert. He loved the *vlaai*, or, for that matter, anything Dutch.

This time Yetty's *vlaai* had colourful fruits arranged to look like circular rainbow pride flags, which was, even as a small touch, uplifting for us. "Who else would even think of that beautiful gay affirmation," Gloria exclaimed. She was right: we needed strong affirmations, however big or small, in the time of the AIDS crisis.

Upon seeing my mother and Yetty, Robert said with great delight in his voice that he could smell real coffee and fresh homemade *vlaai*. Mum and Yetty, like many Dutch people from their generation, could meet adversity head on, all due to resilience and *gezelligheid*.

Not everybody was as cheerful as Robert. "What is reality, anyway?"

Ian said after we had attended Wim's funeral, picking up his large glass of *Troost* (a Dutch Port, its name means consolation). He drank the *Troost* before his coffee. I sensed sadness, grief and loss in his voice.

"I am next," Robert said. "It won't be long. I can feel it in me, this dying thing." His comments left us momentarily entranced in a deafening silence. "Yes, you're leaving, dear," Gloria said, while cupping his handsome face in her soft red finger nailed hands.

The Big Bunches Bunch was a diverse group of individuals. No one was superior in the way they gave others unconditional love. It made no difference if they were religious or secular, traditionalist or humanist. But none were right-wing or from a fundamentalist denomination; it seemed that those kinds of people did not have, or at least cultivate, the capacity to love unconditionally. Instead, they stood ready to judge others and moralize rather than help those in need.

We knew that around the world there were thousands dying every week, and yet a common question arose about falling in love when you know you don't have long to live. Love never stops, we concluded, even more so in the circumstances that AIDS created. In those nightmarish times, all love—physical, brotherly or platonic—had to prosper. We could not let fear govern our lives. Gloria agreed with me that it was the here and now that mattered.

Ian laughingly raising his glass, indicating that he too was comforted by his glass of Dutch *Troost*.

After every funeral for another victim of AIDS, Jason seemed more prone to falling into a melancholic state. His condition worsened with time, as the casualties of AIDS intensified. His fearful mood changed when he tapped into the abundance of positive love and energy streaming from his friends and supporters.

Ever since serving as a Shanti volunteer in San Francisco, I realised that we had to challenge the status quo, and its rules and regulations that were discriminatory and inhumane, racist and sexist, all at once. I was there amidst the gradual changing of the established paradigms, given how much our society's general assumptions and ways of thinking about sexuality have changed over the last forty years. Erroneous medical theories relating to homosexuals that had been commonly promoted after the Second World War by practitioners and academics alike could no longer be scientifically accepted. It was only ten years ago, in 1973, that homosexuality was declassified as a mental illness by the American Psychiatric Association. Being gay, the authorities had once said, was associated with loneliness, depression, guilt, shame, anxiety, and other negative mental health symptoms. But I thought that these mental health issues were common among all people, gay or otherwise, suffering from repressed desires. These false diagnoses suited U.S. Senator Joseph McCarthy and his conservative allies in their witch hunts against gays and Communists during the early years of the Cold War. This establishment orthodoxy affected us here in Australia, as well: whatever the U.S. did, we as a nation dutifully followed suit. As though we gays had no moral integrity of our own.

People like the Big Bunches bunch sitting around the circular coffee table were the change agents that challenged these established conditions and obligations. We had armed and fortified our minds with the research into homosexuality, the studies done by Kinsey and especially by Evelyn Hooker. Both of whom utilised empirical research as a foundation to debunk Western society's myths about sexuality at large, and that homosexuality was a mental illness. We also followed the works of Klassen, Williams and Levitt, which suggested that religious zealots harboured the most vehement homophobia. Someone had said that knowledge is power and for us caregivers that was true; to be ignorant was death by fear. If you did not meet society's conditions as a victim worthy of public assistance, the state and major social institutions offered little to no help. That was why so many people fell through the bureaucratic cracks and were left despondent, judged as unworthy and blamed for their own plight. It was the least of these that we befriended. AIDS was part of the struggle to birth a society that encouraged inclusion, equality before the law, and human rights for all, a society that opened hearts and minds. The magnitude of this catastrophic epidemic revealed not only the world of love, peace and serenity, but also the world of force, solidarity and power. It was with this in mind that the gay community was galvanised to be its own saviour.

Throughout the HIV/AIDS emergency I was continually exposed to gay men and women who were smart and funny and who possessed a very high degree of what we call today emotional intelligence. These were the people with a helpful and caring character, sensitive to beauty of oneness and genuine altruism, living for others. From the very beginning, since meeting Gloria in San Francisco, I started to ask myself who I was, who was my real self? It was through myself-discovery that my sensitivity became more acute, and new perspectives about me revealed themselves.

I began to see my needs and aspirations more clearly, and the roles and behaviour that society had expected of me were increasingly irrelevant. They didn't correspond with what I believed was needed, having been enlightened by reading and meeting open-minded people. The need for wholeness, authenticity and happiness became more immediate needs, and this is where good friends helped, those of like minds, who knew their inner selves.

Umberto told me that he used to suffer from depression. He realised that depression was a signal for a change of direction, and not a pathological state. For him, it was a sign that he needed to live on new plane of existence. AIDS catapulted all of us to this new plane of existence, in an urgent search for the self in all parts of life. Seeking a richer self through aesthetics, empathy, courage, and the ability to create joy through educating and nurturing gay men and women.

The second experience we all had in common was that we were the Baby Boomer generation. We had been involved in the great counterculture revolution that reshaped the Western world starting in the mid-twentieth century.

Ken had marched with me in the Anti-Vietnam War Movement, along with Jim Cairns and members of the Australian Labor Party. Ken was still not forgiving of the malleable Australian electorate who voted to send their boys to fight on the killing fields in a civil war that had nothing to do with Australia. Over 700 Australian boys had been killed. They were as young as our boys dying of AIDS—and had lost their lives for what? The lives of boys who died because of AIDS caused monumental and significant societal changes in terms of medical research and the struggle for human rights (now including marriage equality). There predicaments and positive action caused dramatic societal changes than what the lives of young Australian conscripts had been sacrificed for. I detail this in the last chapter of this book where I write about the legacy and contribution to the world left by people who died of HIV/AIDS. The United Nations would affirm the rights of LGBT on June 17 2011 and in the same year US Secretary of State Hilary Clinton speaking at the UN in Geneva declare that gay rights are human rights.

Then there was the birth of environmental movement, which for my friends and me started when with Rachel Carson's earth-shaking *Silent Spring*. I read Carson's work for my English Matriculation. The birth of the Women's liberation movement and the invention of the birth control pill changed forever the status of women in Western society, with ongoing ramifications worldwide. The counterculture had also birthed the gay liberation movement. Now we countercultural revolutionaries were gathering around tables, comforting each other and brainstorming ways of seeing our friends and community safely through the AIDS crisis. We had added another chapter to our lives and unwittingly become AIDS activists.

Terry had been quietly observing our conversation while enjoying his *Troost*. He said that all of us were risking our livelihoods, and possibly our lives, in a society that was largely intolerant of gay people. On the bright side, he concluded that the risks also generated radical new possibilities.

We all agreed that change, taking risk and mystery were the only constants in life, and that they brought with them uncertainty, continuing right throughout our lives. Risk, Terry continued, had a spiritual value, in that when we no longer feel secure, we discover who we truly are and are ready for truly loving. Terry quoted the Roman philosopher Seneca, who said: "Courage carries us to the stars; fear to death." Terry lauded the people who performed acts of courage, such as the volunteers and leaders of AIDS organisations, who were fearlessly making life more open for gay people. Freeing them from being locked into conformity and immobility.

Jason, who was not only a medical researcher but also an avid reader of philosophy, shared his favourite Gandhi quote: "Fearlessness is the first requisite of spirituality. Cowards can never be moral."

At times, Robert said there were so many voices speaking in his mind that he found it difficult to listen to or distinguish his own voice. Many of the voices in his mind were arguing, being destructive, and confusing.

Robert admitted that his inner voices were the not always positive voices of his family: aunts, grandmothers, his father and mother, lovers.

Terry counselled him by reflecting on how we had learned to ignore the voices of the neurotic tabloid media, which had mocked and condemned gay people. So the destructive voices in our mind must be dismissed, he said. We needed to re focus on the enlightening thought that we were loved unconditionally by our friends and community.

And we must do the same with the voices of doubt, Gloria offered. With hundreds of anxious questions assailing us, we should dismiss questions of doubt because we are fearless and we are loving. The inner voices of peace laid alongside the destructive thoughts of war, anxiety and hopelessness. Sometimes they short circuited, taking away the inner voices of peace and calm. We needed to evoke the memories of past, voices of loved ones or friends; their voices had become our inner voices.

Andrew, our champion figure skater and who had recently come out of the closet, had also been quiet until now. He empathised with Robert, saying that before he could hear his own inner voice, he had to exclude all other voices, getting rid of those threats, fears and doubt. By removing all the negativity in his mind and replacing it with positivity, he still realised that he could be reinforcing his own prejudices, comforting himself with what he wanted to hear. We had to continue cultivating our real inner voice. He thanked all of us for our shared conversations. Conversations that positively helped him to survive his daily struggles with negative thoughts.

Now it was time to actually eat our *vlaai* and have a bit of fun and entertainment. Umberto was about to play "Iam what I am" on the piano and I would accompany him with singing. The subjects were heavy but necessary, which made our time for play.

Picture; At times, Robert said there were so many voices
speaking in his mind that he found it difficult to listen
to or distinguish his own voice. Many of the voices in his
mind were arguing, being destructive, and confusing.

Chapter 26

Things not talked about, Euthanasia or Assisted Suicide

Dirk explained that he was thinking about doctor-assisted suicide, or what is called euthanasia. He said that he was having serious bouts of depression and mental anguish over the state of his bodily deterioration, although he was in no physical pain.

Umberto had called our dried flower suppliers in Western Australia to order thirty six-red banksias: not red roses, but banksias. They were for me to take on a quick and unexpected flight to Amsterdam. Dirk had moved back to Nederland because his health had deteriorated at lightning speed. He had telephoned me earlier that he had decided to have "Tot Ziens" party, which was Dutch for "See you later." It was just as well that the Dutch airline KLM departed from Melbourne faithfully every week. Their jumbo-jets were always full and I was fortunate to get a seat. Terry had organised a business class seat for the price of economy class because he was a frequent traveler with KLM, the oldest airline in the world. He also knew I hated to travel cattle class on long distances! Nevertheless, it was still a grueling 25-hour flight to Amsterdam. It seemed strange to me that the flying time had not improved since I first flew to Europe in 1967, aboard a DC-8. It was 25 hours then as well.

This flight would be one of sweet sorrow and deep contemplation. But first, I needed to clarify exactly what Dirk meant, as I would not hop on the plane for anything frivolous: a return ticket was still an odd $3,000 dollars even 30 years ago. Dirk explained that he was thinking about doctor-assisted suicide, or what is called euthanasia. He said that he was having serious bouts of depression and mental anguish over the state of his bodily deterioration, although he was in no physical pain. He did suffer from chronic stomach discomfort due to the number of antiviral medications he had to take every day, and his breathing was becoming labored. He also felt that he had become a burden on his family, especially his mother, who wanted to care for him but was physically unable. Dirk's father pretended that his own son was not even ill and ignored his predicament, acting as though everything were normal. I hasten to add that notwithstanding how he treated his son, Dirk's father loved him and made sure he was financially and materially comfortable.

Dirk had always enjoyed my company—a mutual feeling—and implored me to spend the last week of his life by his side. I could not think quickly enough but I gave him an affirmative answer. While I felt I needed to think about this decision, I said yes mainly to ease his state of mind. I promised to come but said that I needed to call him back to confirm. I harboured a few serious questions about his intended euthanasia, which I admit was due to my ignorance at the time.

Euthanasia was illegal in the 1980s (as it remains today at the time of writing in 2017). Social enlightenment moves at a snail's pace in the land of Oz. It was also a taboo subject, rarely discussed in most circles until the AIDS crisis impacted thousands of loved ones. It was then that several of my Australian friends asked if I could take them to Nederland to live for a while before they would choose euthanasia. I had felt uncomfortable with this sudden snuffing life out by choice and wondered what would drive a person to take such a drastic measure. Dirk indirectly answered some of my questions, but I needed to dig a bit deeper into his state of mind. He had mentioned that he was lonely, that he thought of himself as a burden on others, and he was shocked daily when he looked into the mirror, only to see how quickly his handsome face and once toned body had degenerated.

Drs Vaughan and Peter, who were frequent visitors to our Big Bunches discussions, had shed some light on the reality of euthanasia in the wake of AIDS. I was amazed by the many requests from their young AIDS patients to assist them in ending their lives. Many of those with HIV/AIDS suffered from a hopelessness that brought on depression, physical and mental pain, and fear of an ignoble and lonely death. There was a high rate of self-harm and suicide among gay men in Melbourne, although this was only discussed in whispering tones and almost left unspoken. Only yesterday we made a flower arrangement for the coffin of a very popular twenty-four-year-old gay man, who drove to Melbourne's Westgate Bridge, parked his car alongside the bridge's rail guard, and jumped, to his death. Peter and Vaughan said that, in the San Francisco Bay area, many doctors were providing euthanasia services to their HIV/AIDS patients. Physician-assisted suicide was, after all, much less harrowing than hanging oneself in the wardrobe, slashing veins, or carbon monoxide poisoning in a car parked in a suburban garage or along a remote bush track, as was so often the case in Australia.

The questions that I planned to ask Dirk were: did his doctors say nothing more could be done for him? Did anybody offer him genuine hope? Is the caring service adequate in his home so his family does not have to carry the whole burden? Was he still visiting friends? Do they visit him? If his depression were lifted, would he feel any different? If I came and stayed with him, would he carry on, or was the mental anguish too unbearable? I hated asking these questions, but I had seen so much hope restored in men living with HIV/AIDS, especially when they encountered genuine love and care. Perhaps then they could look forward to living a longer life, albeit one day at a time.

I called Dirk back and we spoke at length. I began to ask my questions until he told me his psychological distress had been so great that the doctor had sedated him with drugs. In the same breath, he said that was no life either. He felt like the walking dead under heavy sedation. He had also lost control of his bowels, the indignity of which humiliated him. The one positive result of my asking questions was that we had revealed further physical and mental health issues that neither Dirk nor I had been aware of. This was a good thing in itself, as blissful ignorance is not always beneficial, and silence not always golden.

I had already called a psychiatrist friend of mine living in Haarlem, in Nederland, who was by now specialising in HIV/AIDS-related depression. I saw fit to enquire with him as not all medical doctors knew how to relate to the new and, in our time, unprecedented health crisis. Many had become desensitised by the sheer number of HIV/AIDS cases that overwhelmed the medical institutions.

One doctor friend of mine in Melbourne, also gay, had already committed suicide, as he could not cope with his Orthodox Jewish family's rejection, nor the onslaught of his own AIDS patients dying. Reading his suicide note, it was clear that he could not deal with the heavy matters of mind and heart. His boyfriend, Dennis, an American Air Force officer and another friend of mine, had died of AIDS-related causes in the U.S. a few weeks prior to my friend's suicide. My friend's grief over his partner's death only compounded his personal misery.

Dirk shared that he could talk to his psychiatrist about a range of topics, from death to personal integrity, spirituality and hopelessness. Fortunately, Dirk did not see anything meaningless in confronting his AIDS diagnosis. He understood the positive legacy of his and others' imminent deaths, which would benefit humankind at large with the forging of gay solidarity and community. We had also discussed his death for some time, which helped prepare Dirk psychologically and emotionally for the event.

The thirty-six banksias were symbolic: one for each year of Dirk's life. They had arrived from Western Australia before I boarded the jet to Amsterdam, holding the dried, bright red banksias wrapped in clear cellophane. The flowers were a head-turner. As I was about to put the bouquet in the overhead luggage compartment, the steward said that the flowers were so beautiful that once the plane was in flight and the passengers settled, he would display them for all to admire. He was also worried that they would be ruined if they stayed in the luggage compartment too long. My fellow passengers did indeed enjoy the flowers, as well as the poem I had handwritten for Dirk on a card attached to the bouquet. Passengers stopped by to read the card; many shed a tear.

I spent several days comforting Dirk with unlimited love and beauty. They were some of our best days together. I could finally see and understand

and respect fully his decision to die. And seemingly in no time at all, the moment for Dirk's *Tot Ziens* party had arrived.

On a misty Friday evening in the Dutch autumn, about thirty friends turned up at Dirk's parents' house in Wassenaar. It was no ordinary house; it was a large villa surrounded by old elm trees that had survived the cataclysm of World War Two. I was familiar with the process of dying. Most deaths were quite the same and not at all sensational like the American evangelical Billy Graham's grandmother, who apparently exclaimed in her final moments that she had seen Jesus at the end of her bed, coming to escort her to heaven. That may have been a feverish, delusional dream, but it was comforting to her family, and probably to Graham's believers, but I had not experienced anything like this. Yet I was apprehensive as to what to expect from Dirk's farewell party. There were always surprises in Dutch culture. Since 1982, I had been with friends who had died, and each occasion was a beautiful and peaceful experience. Not dramatic, not even sad, especially at the moment of release, at the loved one's last slow breath, when all of their cares, worries, pains and physical degradation came to an end.

At the end, friends and loved ones usually held hands, often holding each other's head close to each other as they gently embrace. Then the sudden loss hits, the sadness, tears, torn hearts: once another friend had gone, the grieving began. Memories were forged in motion, tears dried, hearts mended. Yet there was also peace. Dirk had told me a few days beforehand that he had meticulously planned his exit from this world. Many people, he said, died suddenly or un-expectantly, not even to have the chance to say goodbye. It was undoubtedly tragic.

In a euthanasia ceremony, the lethal injection was administered by a medical doctor in such a way that no one would notice. Other preparatory processes had already been administered hours before the guests arrived. Dirk was lying in a comfortable chair, looking relaxed as he sipped his Dutch Gin. One friend was smoking a Willem Two, a famous Dutch cigar brand. Dirk could not smoke himself as he could hardly breathe, but he always liked the aroma of cigars. It evoked *gezelligheid*, security and, dare I say, manhood and sophistication. Gentle music was played in the background, while several handsome waiters, picked personally by

Dirk, served refreshments and petit fours to the guests. They were very polite in what could have otherwise been an awkward and tense situation. I cannot recall what was being played on the piano but it was beautiful. Dirk's mother sang a Dutch melody. I knew there would be no speeches, as Dirk did not want any melodramatic fuss, such as everyone saying their farewells, standing all around the bed. Dirk smiled at me and thanked me for coming and for the red banksias and the accompanying poem. The radiant flowers now adorned the main table in the home, the centre of attention and a talking point that touched on Dirk's time in Australia. He asked me if I was enjoying the party. I said it was a lovely party and only wished it were for a birthday, not a final parting. He told me to think of it as a transition party. I smiled and kissed him on the forehead. It was to be my last kiss for Dirk. In all honesty, I was not enjoying the occasion, although after a few gins, I managed to become somewhat more comfortable.

Dirk fell quietly asleep with a big smile on his face. He looked so peaceful. His glasses were raised and the wheelchair in which he was resting rolled away behind a curtain. We all knew the moment had come and passed; all had ended well. Dirk's mother used to be an opera singer, something I did not know until I heard her sing *Panis Angelicus*, "Bread for the Angels," which in itself was slightly dramatic. She was accompanied by a piano, cello and violin. We raised our glasses to toast Dirk's life and memory; many tears rolled down our cheeks. We lingered awhile and socialised for the rest of the evening.

Another of Dirk's friends handed me a small envelope with my name written on it. I recognised Dirk's distinct cursive Dutch writing. The envelope was sealed, but it had instructions written on the back that I was to open it immediately. I was to read it by myself under the *lees lamp* (a beautiful art deco reading lamp) near a large potted palm by where Dirk kept all of the books. I was intrigued and touched at the same time. The card within the envelope was a simple announcement of Dirk van Sant's birth and death, and gave thanks to each person by name who had been present at his transition. He also wrote that Toby van Sant, his cousin and one of the waiters that night, would make very good husband material for me. The note continued by saying that Toby would have served me one

Advocaat with cream and one without cream (Advocaat being an alcoholic drink akin to egg nog). If I were interested in him, I was to approach him and ask for *Zwarte Kip*, a popular brand of thick yellow *Advocaat met slagroom* (Advocaat with cream), a sign that one was interested in friendship.

The polite waiters stayed on for delightful conversation and continued to pour *borrels*, another Dutch word that struggles to find an equivalent word in English. Borrels were small glasses of spirits. I learnt much later that the waiters were all social psychology students at the major Dutch AIDS foundation. One waiter was Toby van Sant, with jet black hair, dark blue eyes, and a grasp of Dutch that would melt a thousand hearts. I ordered a Zwarte Kip. Toby innocently asked me if I would also like to try "a farmer's boy." I blushed, which he noticed. He then called the drink by its proper name, *Boeren jongens*, a popular drink traditionally consumed at funerals, birthdays and holidays. It was actually a dish of raisins soaked in brandy with a few other secret herbs. It did indeed make one very happy.

Dirk would later be cremated and his ashes planted beneath a Dutch elm sapling tree. His majestic tree still shades part of miniature park Madurodam, a popular tourist attraction in the The Hague,

Picture; They were rarely superficial conversations, especially
when talking about consciousness and destiny, yet most
conversations with Dirk were about destiny,, and he
decided his own destiny he was in control no one else.

Chapter 27

Queen Street Massacre

"In the end he plunged to his death, would it have been different if penises and vaginas and sexuality were openly discussed? Would Frank have been relieved to know that in more civilised, socially advanced countries, baby boys do not get circumcised and that, in fact, he was a normal, healthy boy?"

I eventually sold Big Bunches to a Chilean family, who were also observant Roman Catholics. The shop was renamed Thymes and transformed, in my opinion, into mediocrity and a straight conventional environment. Nevertheless, the Big Bunches legacy lived on through the personalities, alive and dead, that defined the shop and the era.

Umberto and Robert had passed away and dear Dorothy had suddenly succumbed to breast cancer that she never told us about. Just as well, as we had loved her every day and whenever there was a cross word between us, we always made amends quickly. She was sixty-four. Dorothy died a widow, her husband having passed away many years prior. We always found it odd that she never talked about him very much. I was the sole executor of her estate. She was laid in her coffin wearing her favourite yellow polka dot dress; Jason had emptied a whole bottle of Chanel No. 5 perfume over her resting body. I say resting because that's what Dorothy believed: death was merely a deep sleep, until Jesus would come again and she, along with the other faithful, would be resurrected. She once told me that when she was resurrected, she would have the most stunning body, even better than her transgender girlfriends. So we said "Dorothy is sleeping". Even as her coffin was carried down the aisle, all the pallbearers being "her boys, one could smell Chanel No. 5 flooding the church, complementing the hundreds of Frangipanes displayed on her silver coffin. Her work was done her functions fulfilled she will be missed but it is not the end of her story. As I gazed upon her moving coffin, thinking that it is only in the absence of memory that she won't be missed, but her bubbly, slightly neurotic openness and kindness are stored in millions of memory nodules and neurons. There is no absence of memory about Dorothy, farewell, rest in peace dear, see you in the morning.

There are days that are forever etched in my mind. These days are akin to when one first falls in love, first experiences of a break up, or a death of friends holding them in their last minutes of life before their conscious leaves them. Then the Cuban Missile Crisis, in 1962, when the world was poised for a nuclear war or President Kennedy's assassination in 1963. For me, there was soon to be another date I would never forget.On this fateful, blistering hot Tuesday 8 December 1987 I was attending a conference at Australia Post's Victorian headquarters at 191 Queen Street in Melbourne's Central Business District. The conference dealt with HIV/AIDS in the workplace, as Australia Post had problems with needles being deposited in street letter boxes, as well as having over 24 of its young male employees diagnosed with HIV/AIDS. Brian attended with me, as did Jim Nagle, a work colleague and future Vice President of the Victorian AIDS Council.

We had morning tea with a Dutch friend of mine who wanted to become a volunteer with the Victorian AIDS Council. She worked in Australia Post's finance department. After the conference, we planned to work out and relax with a sauna and massage at the City Baths or Steam Works, followed by some finger food and cocktails at the Collins Tower Sofitel's cocktail bar. We were celebrating several birthdays that day, including Jason's it was a sort of reunion, too. We had many reunions, about once a month or more frequently HIV-AIDS was claiming many lives sadly often it was someone's last reunion we only needed the slightest excuse or cause to celebrate—say a promotion or new boyfriend, a new house, and so on. The whole crew would join us tonight: Terry, Jason, and Gloria, who was over from the U.S my friend Anthony, over from London, the Salsa dancer who had a part in the touring production of *Rocky Horror Picture Show*.

Yet with all these celebrations there was something not right about this day. May be I was nervous about my HIV-AIDS presentation, as all of senior management were going to be at this meeting, or may be AIDS was then always a sort of "apocalyptic topic", four employees had already died of it. No matter how I tried rationalising this ominous feeling in my mind it would not go away, even though I was going to be together with all my mates. I often have these intuitive and "déjà Vu" feelings and I am affright they are rarely wrong.

After afternoon tea had been served, shortly before 4:30 pm, in the Australia Post headquarters, we heard the loud piercing of fire trucks and ambulance sirens, as well as the Gestapo-like wail of the Victorian Police car sirens. (The Jewish community of Melbourne had earlier complained about these police sirens sounding like those from the Gestapo raids.) These sounds were not unusual in a city as large as Melbourne, yet Brian looked at me and nodded, as if to say *this does not sound normal*. He was trying to calm a young woman called Miriam, who seemed extremely frightened by the sudden events. An Australia Post manager, appearing very nervous and white as a bed sheet, entered the room. She told us in a high pitched, gravelly voice that she was closing the window curtains and that it was better not to look outside to what was happening on the street. She added that "We should be concentrating on the tasks at hand." Then informed us that all exterior doors were to be locked going into the foyers and that toilets were not available. There was no longer any concentration on the tasks at hand, the intensity of real live drama was unfolding as the conflagrations above and below us increased.

We tried to telephone the news service but all the phones were dead: not a good sign, I thought. There were no mobile phones in 1987 and later found out that the lines had been deliberately cut off by the police, as they thought the Queen Street terrorist might use them. We had converted paper bins with plastic lining to use as makeshift toilets for those who needed to urinate, while encouraging others to hold on. Obviously something serious was unfolding outside and it was impossible to focus on anything else. We collectively decided to reopen the curtains and look to see what was going on below at the corner of Queen and Little Bourke Streets. It was not pretty. Hundreds of people stood watching on the curb side, waiting patiently with extreme, perhaps morbid, curiosity. Many television cameras were present.

On occasions like this I go very quiet. I was very quiet. Brian was, too as it is best not to say anything that you're not sure of, I was sure to keep my mouth shut. Others in my group, obviously motivated by fear, were audibly relieved when police in jet black attire appeared on the streets below. They were dressed like some sort of ninjas, bearing large automatic weapons. We were informed that the authorities were sure the terrorist, yet to be identified, had entered 191 Queen Street, where we were. We all feared the worst. Consequently, the makeshift toilets were being filled quickly by the fifteen people in the training room. We heard rapid gunfire then the sound of glass panes shattering on the pavement below. I thought that the situation was becoming serious and both Brian and I began to plot how we could escape or protect ourselves. The thick, heavy solid wooden table tops were one possibility of shielding ourselves.

Suddenly, as we were all standing by the large windows, in a blink of an eye, a body fell from above, followed by a loud thud from the street. I looked at my watch: it was 4:28 pm. A burst of noise immediately drew our attention to the foyer of the eighth floor. The police, looking like Ninjas had arrived with their large black automatic weapons. Their faces seemed to be painted or camouflaged. They oddly seemed to be enjoying doing their job, judging by their body language. Brian commented that he overheard them say that they thought we were being invaded by several "Rambos". They told us to stay put. We had already figured out as much given the loud shooting going on the eleventh and twelfth floors.

The training room TV set was locked away in the room's cupboards. We broke the locks and connected the TV set to the power. The news we heard shocked us. None of us could believe our eyes: eight people were shot dead on the eleventh floor, five more were seriously wounded. On the TV, we saw the drama that was unfolding outside. Even after the terrorist had jumped to his death, the authorities did not allow us to leave the building around 10:00pm, when we made our way to the blood stained lifts to our journey home.

My mum Bests and dad Piet had watched this horror on television and knew that I was in the building for a conference. They immediately drove the 90-minute journey from their country home in Leopold, just out of Geelong, to downtown Melbourne. They waited for me at the curb, alongside many other parents anxiously awaiting their own children's safe passage out of the tower. Terry, who was the then Tourist Commissioner of Victoria, had cancelled a speech he was due to give that day and instead called all our friends that were going to the birthday party that night. Here was the gay brigade assembled: Terry, Gloria, Anthony (who had just finished dancing the time warp), Jason, and Bram (the manager of the Maling Road Coffee shop where I had met Dale and his homophobic father in chapter six) all standing at the curb waiting silently, witnessing the steady parade of sober, distressed but relieved faces trudging out of the building one by one. I walked out with Brian. Sadness engulfed me as I learned that my Dutch friend, who wanted to join my VAC support group and with whom we had morning tea that day, had been mercilessly shot dead. Another friend, Michael, a father of three boys, who eight hours earlier had greeted me and told me that it was his youngest son's fifth birthday I heard that he pleaded for his life to no avail. He, too, was mercilessly shot dead.

My parents together with all my other friends including nearly the whole of the VAC support group and hundreds of other families and their friends had stood quietly with stoical expressions devoid of any hysteria waiting silently for hours even after the ambulances had carried away the dead and wounded, the waiting at the curb side continued. The moment of waiting was now over; we hugged silently, very silently. These were hugs of sadness and of reassurance and love. Nothing much could be or was said, no silly questions asked of us as to what happened. It was far too obvious, the trauma all too present. We drove to my new house on The Esplanade in Port Melbourne for what seemed an all-night wake. Everyone slept over. The VAC support group came over the next morning to make breakfast and to emotionally support me Brian and Jim. I felt good being reassured by the people I loved, grateful too that we all had worked so hard to build our strong extended family all part of being on an AIDS war footing for the last five years. We were prepared.

Melbourne's cheap common tabloids went haywire the day after the Queen Street Massacre, just as they did during the early days of the AIDS crisis. There was always a quick buck to be made in going sensational with half-truths and gossip. The murderer was Frank Vitkovic, a twenty-two-year-old Roman Catholic and dropout from Melbourne Law School. Frank's parents were from conservative Italian and Croatian heritages. He attended a Catholic Primary school that is where as a young boy' Frank's problems began. When Victoria Police first visited his devastated parents, they confiscated Frank's diary. In his diary Frank confessed to sexual frustrations stemming from a young age. He suffered from fears borne out of experiences at Catholic School, where he was teased by other boys, about his uncircumcised penis. He began to express violent intentions, going so far as to address portions of his diary entries to his family members

Fast forward to December 2017

'T was a splendid first day of summer. Clear blue skies, warm sun gently kissing and caressing our skin, me still wearing my "James Dean" look alike clip-on tortoise shell sunglasses the ones I bought in the U.S 35 years ago. Brian and I had bicycled down from Leopold to Queenscliff amongst blossoming fields of flowers, being entertained by colorful Rosellas, pink grey Galahs, yellow crested Cockatoos and many Magpies flitting about in large eucalyptus and banksias trees along the route: today was Australia at its best. The bicycle ride took 90-minutes via the famous *Bellarine Bike trail*; we rode fast on purpose, as we were meeting other friends from Melbourne who had taken the Sorrento to Queenscliff ferry crossing Port Phillip Bay at its narrowest point to meet up with us. Now older, but very fit, with not too many grey hairs between us, still both having flat stomachs and not having reached the stage of melancholic memories, we're still too young firmly believing that age is an attitude of mind.

We ate at our favourite restaurant along the picturesque Queenscliff

Yacht club pier, noting the carefree friendliness of the people around us enhanced our mood even further. The purpose for our lunch was one of celebration as we had reached a climax in our human rights activities and chat about how much progress has been made since HIV/AIDS first reared its ugly head in 1983. An extra bottle of Moet Champagne was opened and enjoyed (so much so I could not safely ride my bicycle for several hours) toasting the momentous events happening in Australia, buoying our spirits and restoring our confidence in Australian society because Same *Sex Marriage* was voted upon in favour by the vast majority of decent Australians. We laughed and almost cried when recalling that gay citizens of Australia had to ask their straight neigbours for permission to get married because it was not a democratic parliamentary vote but only a voluntary Postal vote. The other event was, that we had always surmised that religious conservatives had been creating hell on earth, this had now been borne out by no less than 17 volumes of damning reports of *The Royal Commission into Institutional Child abuse* taking five years to complete, interviewing 1.200 witness accounts and more than 8000 private sessions with survivors grossly detailing religious child abuse, lies and atrocities all laying bare their manipulations and spiritual blackmail. I reflected that if hell had its religious branch on earth where was heaven? The abusers held positions of power, leadership and authority and most were religious and male the very people who oppose enlightened sex education programs in Australian schools.

A brewing issue of sex education in particular the Safe School program was a great concern to us because LGBTI young people have a six times higher suicide rate then their heterosexual peers, and a recent study found that 61% reported verbal homophobic abuse, 69% reported other types of discrimination, including exclusion and rumours. The nerve and audacity shown by conservatives, even after their disastrous defeat in the Same Sex Marriage Postal Vote and the "17 Volumes of their shame" showed moral bankruptcy. The Australian Christian Lobby, together with the Roman Catholic Church and fundamentalist sects, still had the gall to pressure the cancelation of government funding of the voluntary Safe Schools Coalition, an anti-bullying program designed to educate young people about LGBTI issues and to nurture safe spaces for LGBTI youth. These reactionaries want to replace this vital program with, well, nothing.

We seriously asked ourselves repeatedly if Frank Vitkovic had the opportunity to attend sex education classes at his Catholic school would it have made a difference to his relationship with women later on in life, we shall never know. In the end he plunged to his death. Sadly Frank was bullied at his Catholic school for his uncircumcised small penis. There was tragically no outlet to address children's anxieties and fears about their sexuality. Would it have been different if penises and vaginas and sexuality were openly discussed? Would Frank have been relieved to know that in more civilised, socially advanced countries, baby boys do not get circumcised and that, in fact, he was a normal, healthy boy?

Instead, there were no discussions then as there are few discussions now, except for what is provided by vital programs such as the Safe Schools program. Ignorance and dismissive, or worse negative, conversations about sex gave religious priests ministers, and religious teachers unearned clout over young minds, warping many and, in the worst cases, leading to horrendous acts of sexual and mental abuse. If the uses and abuses of penises and vaginas were discussed as a normal subjects, say like the weather, beginning at a very young age, then children would have greater knowledge of right and wrong—not only in relation to their own conduct, but also the conduct of their peers and superiors. Yes and there might not have ever been the seventeen volumes detailing sexual abuse by primarily religious organisations. Sadly, their self righteousness and certitude knows no bounds, everything remains shabby and grubby as they fight tooth and nail to stop enlightened sex education, including all forms of sexual orientations.

We felt that everything we had fought for and suspected had come through and karma favoured us the Gay community and dammed the religious fundamentalists.

It was time to bicycle home again before darkness set in, but we delighted even more when we heard that the Synod of the Uniting Church of Australian had accepted Same Sex Marriage and has requested the Australian Government not to give religious institution special rights to discriminate against the GLBTI community in terms of employment, renting property and the right to refuse gay student in their schools. There should be no exemptions the Uniting Church argues all citizen and organizations of any kind should be equally treated before the law and there should never be religious exemption in a secular society where Church and State must separate. Let's toast to the Uniting Church of Australia said Brian. And that we did.

Picture; Sadness engulfed me as I learned that my Dutch friend, who wanted to join my VAC support group and with whom we had morning tea that day, had been mercilessly shot dead.

Chapter 28

Friends died too soon, funerals chilling to the bone

Monty was suffering badly from AIDS-related complications until we obtained cannabis oil, which is extracted from marijuana and was illegal at the time in Australia. He stopped vomiting and consequently put on weight and continued to live relatively well for several more years,

Suzanne, one of our favourite Big Bunches customers, owned a popular hairdressing salon. I would visit her every fortnight to have my haircut and eyebrows trimmed (but not yet any hair removed from my ears or nose; that came much later!). I also had my haircut at Avner's, another great stylist. He was openly gay and referred to himself as "the Queen of Queens". Later, he would get a physical heart transplant and told me that he had had a change of heart and wondered if we could become an item. His sense of humour was inimitable. Dorothy and all the Big Bunches staff would have their hair done by Suzanne or Avner.

Suzanne's salon was located a few blocks away from my gym. I remember the day as clear as a morning sunrise over Lake Connewarre where I live now. It was the day that she would do my flat-top cut, her specialty. Sitting where I was, I could see from her body language and smudged mascara that something was wrong. I hesitated to ask what was wrong; she knew me well enough to confide almost anything in me, as she often did about her boyfriend's behaviour. While she finished shampooing my hair, she quietly asked if I knew her brother, Stewart, simultaneously pointing to a picture on the right-hand side bottom of her mirror. The photograph was of a handsome young man, who I did recognise. I confessed that I had only heard of him and that he had reputation in the gay community as a hot commodity. Plus, he was one of those men with intimidatingly good looks. Many younger gay men hesitated to approach Stewart.

Suzanne continued whispering in my ear, although she did not need to whisper, as we were the only people in the salon. Stewart was recently admitted as a patient at the Fairfield Infectious Diseases Hospital, Suzanne told me. She did not know what to tell their mother, who knew nothing about Stewart's condition or sexuality. Their mother was 73, and their 89-year-old father had died the previous year. Their mother did not cope well with that bad news. Suzanne feared an equally poor response to Stewart's condition. I was not shocked by the news but I played dumb and asked Suzanne why her brother admitted to hospital. At that time in 1984, Fairfield had an excellent reputation of looking after people with HIV/AIDS, but there were other patients with infectious diseases. Suzanne did not answer me directly, saying instead that she should not have to tell me. I told her that I was not going to assume anything and that she would have to verbalise what was happening to Stewart. She then quickly said that Stewart had developed AIDS, "the type with the blue patches", she said. Suzanne said that it was a tragedy because Stewart was angry with himself and the world and, due to his volatile temperament, had no friends. She asked if I would see him, which I agreed to do.

The day I saw Stewart was also the opening day of the Tesselaar Tulip Festival and Big Bunches was full of colourful tulips. I thought to take a bunch of tulips in a stylish vase as a gift for Stewart. I did not announce I was visiting beforehand. I was confident that Stewart would recognise my face, if not my name.

I knocked softly on Stewart's door. A languid "Welcome" from within the room encouraged me to enter. I wore as big a smile as I could muster. It was not a fake smile, however, as I genuinely wanted to become better acquainted with Stewart. I hoped to give Stewart some relief from his recent difficulties. I figured that a big smile was as good as sunshine, triggering feelings of warmth and cheerfulness.

I began to introduce myself when Stewart interrupted me ecstatically. "You're Keith from Big Bunches!" he said. "My sister is always raving on about you." I was relieved by the warm reception. We talked at length, including about the Art Deco-style vase carrying the tulips. A good conversation piece, I thought. I had heard from others that Stewart was somewhat of a style queen. That broke the ice and we settled into a comfortable conversation over a couple café lattes I had brought with me. Dutch *Gezelligheid* had weaved its magic once again.

Our conversation steered towards the subject of being loved. Suddenly, Stewart asked if I had ever been in love. It was also a warning to me that his mood had changed. I said yes and in return asked Stewart if he had ever been in love. Stewart became tense and abruptly said no. He continued with a sort of self-analysis, stating that he was "not in love but only in lust," intimating that this was why he was in his health predicament. He felt that he was loved for his body and for nothing more. He confessed as well that he never spent much time getting to know his casual hook-ups. He said he was only interested in conquering the most handsome men for a one-night stand. Then it was back on the hunt. "I was addicted to sex," he said.

Stewart asked me to explain what love was. He said he was afraid he didn't know how to find it, which caused him grief. "I want to experience true love," he said, before he "kicked the bucket." Stewart stressed to me that he did not want a simple answer. I replied that love was the most important part of being a gay person. I explained to him the three types of love, according to Plato: *eros* (erotic love), *philos* (brotherly love) and *agape* (unconditional love). All three types of love were equally important in sharing with one's partner. I also referred to the Old Testament Bible, where it is written that two bodies shall be joined together to make one (Genesis 2:24). Romantic love was only in part about giving one's partner deep physical and psychological pleasure. Love was equally about religion, art and philosophy, as well as in deep conversations, sharing good food, discussing politics. Sharing each other's dreams, joys, fears, successes and failures.

We spent three hours together. Before I left, Stewart said that, for the first time in his adult life, he found commonality with someone he did not want to bed. He said he valued developing a friendship more than having sex. He asked if I could tell his mother about his sexuality and condition, and more poignantly, that he did not have long to live. I agreed to talk to his family. I reassured him that it would be a conversation centred on hope and unconditional love. His folks were not religious, so I also assured him that it would not be a religious talk. I said, however, that I would try to make it a spiritually uplifting experience for his mother. It was difficult news to convey, let alone receive.

I met with Stewart's mother sometime later. As I had expected, she had no difficulty with accepting her son as being gay, but she was worried that he would die so soon. Stewart lived for another twelve months. During that time, he and his small family made new friends through the VAC Support Group. Stewart also regularly attended our Big Bunches Friday night discussion group, where he found true love before he died.

Rest in peace, Stewart.

Peter was one of my regular customers who spent a considerable amount of money every week to purchase flowers for his home and office. I did not know him very well but we were on friendly terms. I would see him frequently at Pokey's, the gay cabaret show held every Sunday night at The Prince of Wales Hotel in St Kilda. Peter occasionally assisted in dressing the performers. I noticed that when I did see him at Pokey's he always looked smart. He wore expensive leather vestments. I discovered that his day job was as a high-paying computer consultant, a career that necessitated frequent travel to the United States and Nederland. He loved the Dutch and the freedom that Amsterdam afforded men like him. He did not have to lead a fake life there. Gay men could be their real selves in Dutch society, living openly, even at work.

Peter called me out of the blue one day and asked if I wanted to go cycling with him. He sounded very excited because he had just purchased a 10-gear Malvern Star bicycle and wanted to cycle around the Yarra River. There was only one problem, he said: I would have to teach him how to cycle "the Dutch way." We agreed to have our first lesson on a Sunday morning, have lunch, and then go on a six-kilometre ride for starters, depending on his confidence. He turned out to be a quick learner. I told

Peter that the secret was to keep your balance and to keep going. "Life is like that," he said.

It was a happy Sunday. The following day, he called to inform me that he had a very sore derriere and could hardly walk. It was a very different pain to what he was used to, he said.

We went cycling again the following Saturday. I had told Peter not to be overly confident, as he really liked going fast and overtaking me. Some people just are a lot more competitive, I thought. Unfortunately, while riding along Swanston Street, someone suddenly opened the door of a parked car and hit Peter in the mouth. The sharp end of the top right of the door did much damage. Peter had fallen unconscious onto the roadside and was bleeding profusely from the mouth. He was breathing irregularly and murmuring in pain. I wrapped my exercise towel around his mouth to stopping the bleeding while cradling his head. The ambulance came quickly. Other kind passers-by encouraged Peter with softly spoken reassurances: "She'll be right, mate" and "Hang in there." I was livid at the careless driver for opening the door and angry at myself for not riding beside Peter at the time. I thought I could have avoided the door as I was a proactive rider, always prepared for the dangerous but improbable. My bicycle was parked against a parking meter where I had forgotten it when the ambulance came. It had been stolen when I returned. Some weeks later, a leather cap was passed around the Laird Hotel in Collingwood and consequently I received a new bike.

Peter was now in the emergency room at the Royal Melbourne Hospital. The bleeding had stopped but his face was so swollen that I barely recognised him. He had gone from a highly confident computer executive, with the world at his disposal, to a frightened man.

The attending nurse asked for his next of kin. Peter still could not speak but he pointed to me. She then asked me what relationship I had with Peter, asking if I were his brother or cousin. I had to think very quickly. I recalled the medical difficulties that gay men in San Francisco had if they had not a designated next of kin. I answered confidently, saying that I was his "other half." She did not understand that concept until I made it much clearer. I said I was his lover. Only then did the nurse understand.

She then asked Peter who should make medical decisions for him if he were unable. Again, Peter pointed to me. The nurse wrote down my name on the power of attorney form and Peter was able to sign with his right hand. Peter then wrote me a little note to say he was HIV-positive. He was concerned that I might have come into contact with his blood while I was trying to stop his bleeding. I reassured him that I was not in any danger.

Some friends later asked whether I had been untruthful in designating myself as Peter's next of kin. While Peter was not my lover in the erotic sense, I loved him as a friend. And I knew that Peter was estranged from his Pentecostalist family in Queensland and that he needed the emotional support and a good listener.

Peter was subsequently admitted to Fairfield Infectious Diseases Hospital, where our friendship would continue to blossom, until... In those early days of the AIDS crisis, there was always a conclusion.

Picture of Peter and moi. Peter called me out of the blue
one day and asked if I wanted to go cycling with him. He
sounded very excited because he had just purchased a 10-
gear Malvern Star bicycle and wanted to cycle around the
Yarra River. There was only one problem, he said: I would
have to teach him how to cycle "the Dutch way."

In Chapter 17, I introduced Monty van Doren and his mother, Irene, at the Big Bunches flower shop. Monty was suffering badly from AIDS-related complications until we obtained cannabis oil, which is extracted from marijuana and was illegal at the time in Australia. He stopped vomiting and consequently put on weight and continued to live relatively well for several more years, certainly longer than what would have otherwise been the case.

During a visit to Nederland as part of my AIDS studies, I was fortunate enough to meet up with Monty and Irene at a barbecue thrown in my honour at Arjen Broekhuizen's home. There I was introduced to a colleague of Arjen's, a journalist named Fred Bakker, although he went by Edwin. He explained that he was friends with a girl called Wilma in primary school. The two of them were, of course, Fred and Wilma, after the Flintstones. So Fred called himself Edwin for the longest time, but reverted back to Fred when he attended journalism school in Nederland.

Fred was also a friend of Monty and Irene's; the world was indeed a small place. Our first chat was about Dame Edna Everage, the Australian comedian Barry Humphreys' star drag performance, forever sending up Australian housewives. I said that Humphreys was a clever satirist. Fred had met Dame Edna at a book-signing for Dame Edna's recently published memoir, *My Gorgeous Life*. He was a real devotee, as many thousands of Duchies were.

Fred's charm captivated me and I enjoyed his intrepid reporting on the human tragedy that was the AIDS crisis. He made a documentary called "Edwin". There was nothing superficial about him. I, with 120,000 other readers, eagerly read his popular serial columns about a man called Rick, who had been diagnosed with HIV/AIDS (then called "GRID") in 1982. Rick struggled daily with his health and staying alive and the column detailed his interactions with doctors, pharmacies and alternative medicine. All of it was intriguing, confronting and encouraging. Everyone fell in love with Rick because his story was quintessentially Dutch: nothing was hidden and there were no euphemisms.

During a conversation with Fred and Monty, Fred told me that the column was actually about himself. He had chosen Rick for the column because, as a 20-year-old travelling in the United States, he met a gay man in Atlanta called Rick who worked at Coca-Cola's headquarters. They fell in lust and did "everything God forbade," Fred said, words that reflected the Calvinist streak in mainstream Dutch culture. Even Dutch atheists had Calvinist norms and values.

He was tickled pink when I told him that I had translated Rick's columns into English, especially the ones about the controversial Kenyan antiviral medication called Kemron, which Rick had taken for ten months with some results, but not enough. Rick went back on AZT. The Dutch were somewhat more adventurous when it came to experimenting with new drugs and the Dutch Government approved new drugs quickly when there was a glimmer of hope in the drug's ability to halt the virus.

I also knew Fred published a weekly entertainment page for Radio Veronica. Whenever possible, he would highlight news and performances for the Dutch gay community. Everyone in the media was charmed by this celebrated journalist.

In the end, when Fred's time was up, he told me how lucky and fortunate he was to have Laurens Schuurkamp, his beloved partner who ensured that his quality of life endured till the end. Despite his being worn down by the virus, Fred said there was one battle yet to be won. In Nederland at the time, pictures were not included in bereavement notices. Fred used his enormous charm to convince Dutch newspaper editors, except for *De Volks Krant*, to carry his picture with his bereavement notice. He wanted to give AIDS a face and public recognition of the reality that it was primarily young men who were dying prematurely.

Fred died in 1993.

Friends reported that his funeral was no ordinary run of the mill service. For the many in attendance, it became a life-impacting event. Around 400 people attended Fred's funeral and Fred had asked that each attendee bring a white rose and place it on his casket. I smiled at the thought that queens never do anything thing by half measures. People had brought more than single flowers and Fred's coffin was inundated with bunches and bunches of white roses. Henk Krol, the publisher of *De Gay Krant* and Fred's employer, spoke highly of Fred's full and purposeful life. Fred had also asked that his coffin be carried by his colleagues at *De Gay Krant*. His final resting place was alongside a forest the mist moved in at four pm in the late afternoon, out in the forest a lone saxophonist played "Baker Street" by Gerry Rafferty. The music began soft and gentle, my friends said, and seemed to float out of the forest and envelope the gravesite all around. Goosebumps, **chilling to the bone**, Baker Street engraved forever on my mind and heart...

Rest in peace, dear Dutch Fred.
3 November 1961 – 13 July 1993

...

Fred Bakker was a colleague of Arjen Broekhuizen's. Arjen has been featured throughout the pages of this book as my friend and educator. I have asked another dear friend of Arjen, Don Baxter, the former President of the ACON-AIDS Council of NSW from 1988 – 1989, to share his eulogy:

Arjen Broekhuizen – Memorial Service Eulogy for Arjen

Don Baxter, Sydney, Australia, 13 April 2004

Dear friends in mourning – and in celebration – of Arjen's life:

My name is Don Baxter and I live in Sydney – nearly 20,000 kilometres away from Den Bosch.

I met Arjen in 1988 – at the Stockholm International AIDS Conference – and have seen him every year since, sometimes at occasional AIDS Conferences but more usually at his annual expedition to Sydney for the Gay & Lesbian Mardi Gras.

My partner Rob and I have an attic built into the roof-space of our house. Arjen named it – of course – the "Anne Frank Room", and he stayed there many times, with Arno or whoever he was traveling with that year. He had a permanent reservation for the Anne Frank Room, much to the chagrin of our New York friends. Only in the last three years did the two sets of stairs become too much for him.

Over those 16 years Arjen and I came to share many of our mutual passions: Dutch politics, Australian politics, European and world politics, AIDS politics. We became soul-mates about these issues – and couldn't understand why others did not feel the same passion.

We both looked forward to our annual meetings and discussing "the Future of the World" – though I do have to say we very seldom talked about "the Meaning of Life". Whether we liked to recognise it or not, we were both too Protestant for that: life is for hard work, and that is life's reward.

What I admired most in Arjen was the intellectual rigour mixed with passion, the incisive analysis, the intimidating explanation. Whether it was how soon the euro would banish the dollar, how long the Purple Coalition government would last or whether Glaxo's new HIV drug was going to be effective – his analysis and opinions were both challenging and entertaining.

However, rigour combined with passion can often make people seem rigid, inflexible. And Arjen asserted his ideas and opinions forcefully – as all of you know and suffered from at times.

But what I valued about Arjen was that he was also capable of independent thought and good judgment – usually. It just didn't sound like that when he launched into a formidable tirade about a particular issue. You had to fight back – even if you didn't feel like it – and only then would you see him begin to take on board what you were saying.

It's what made him an excellent journalist, why SBS Radio in Australia had him prepare the Dutch news for all those years. Why he was such a formidable negotiator for the European AIDS Treatments Group with the pharmaceutical companies. Many people can be passionate and thump the table. Far fewer have done all the homework and have the judgment to know when to compromise – or when to get up and walk out the door.

But life with Arjen could be exhausting, I could see. Living 20,000 kilometres away was perhaps a luxury for me that none of you had – I saw Arjen for only short periods of time – when he was on holidays, when he was bright, relaxed, even playful.

I said earlier that Arjen came to Australia for Mardi Gras – but that is not really accurate. He first came here with Martin Golding, his partner in the 1980s, and a friend of mine from Australia. After the Stockholm AIDS Conference, I came to Holland to stay with them at Best. It was a beautiful summer and they were so happy. I remember so clearly the bright sunny day we drove across to the Australian embassy in Den Haag, where Martin worked, to pick up a kitten from the Ambassador. It was a magic day.

But Martin had HIV and in those years there were no effective treatments. Arjen regularly visited Australia with Martin but things were often not easy. Arjen and Martin's mother, Joan, were people with much more similar temperaments than either of them would like to recognise.

The visits did lead to Arjen's love affair with Australia. And it was a love affair that never ended – carrying on for all the years since Martin's death. Arjen creatively organised the contract with SBS Radio – or perhaps I should say cunningly organised it – and his intimate understanding of the tax laws of both Holland and Australia ensured that the contract funded the annual pilgrimage south of the equator to escape the Dutch winter.

Arjen loved Sydney's sparkling harbour and glittering Mardi Gras but his real obsession, what brought him back every Australian summer, was exploring remote and outback Australia – the endless red desert of Central Australia, the drama of Kakadu National Park, the magic of the Great Barrier Reef, the lushness of tropical Far North Queensland and its endless, magnificent – and deserted – beaches.

He could never get enough of it – even if rained every day in the wet season and the leeches extracted his blood, or the wind blew his camper-van head-over-heels off the hill miles from anywhere near Uluru.

Actually, I expect many of you know of this passion for Australia all too well, having been forced to sit through thousands of photos and far too many hours of home video. And for me it meant that Arjen has seen far more of Australia than I have in my 50 years here.

In December 2003 I flew to Bangkok to see Arjen; the additional 9 hours trip to Australia from Bangkok had become just too long for him to do and he was staying in Bangkok with his great friend John Griffin.

Arjen and I said our "final good-byes" – not an easy thing for two "stitched-up ex-Protestants" to do – but we did eventually get to talk about our feelings for one another and what a wonderful friendship it had been.

And we both cried a lot. And sat silently together for long periods. We had never done either of these before.

At one point on that visit Arjen was expressing sorrow that many of his friends had, in his words, "disappointed him" over the last few years. It was a difficult conversation but I did get to say that I thought perhaps his style, the very things I liked about him – that forthright assertiveness, that intimidating intellect, those high expectations – might have driven many other people away. With some reluctance, he agreed that this could have been the case, and, I think, he reached a point of peace about it.

Of course, that month in Bangkok was wonderful for him. John and Pete's spacious and spectacular apartment, Sylvie there looking after him, staff to prepare all the food, the swimming pool entirely to himself. And most of all – the hot weather: never below 28 degrees [Celsius] (and that was at midnight!).

As it happened, I was able to be in Bangkok again last month, in March, just before Arjen was making that long flight back to Holland for what we both knew would definitely be the last time.

We agreed we'd done our farewells last December – so, of course, we launched into the politics making news at the time: the Madrid bombings, which had only just happened. Arjen, lucid to the last, was asserting that the Spanish government would be defeated in that weekend's election if it kept saying that ETA was responsible. And of course, he was right again. The Embassy car drove us to the airport at midnight and I put him on the plane at 2 a.m., just as it was becoming clear that Islamic terrorists had done the Madrid bombings.

Well, he won't be staying in the Anne Frank Room again – but in a sense he will always be there – in the walls, in the bed-frame (which was too short for him, as he constantly reminded me) – or coming down the stairs in the morning, already spouting forth about the latest news.

Arjen, my life has been so much the richer for knowing you all these years – you will always remain in my heart.

Tot ziens,

Don Baxter

Sydney

13 April 2004

From left to right Arjen, Don and Robert

Chapter 29

The first aging HIV generation

I want to start on a happier note it began in 1990 when I needed some respite of HIV-AIDS it had almost psychologically consumed me, I had started to act and think as though I myself was dying of HIV -AIDS. I thought the break would invigorate and restore my clarity of life; AIDS had fogged up some of the clear mirrors of my life.

It is a tragedy to think your time is almost over, but assuming that your life did not make any difference to anyone, that is an even greater tragedy. Some long term HIV people feel themselves being edged out of life through fear because they think their life has become meaningless. A recent tragic event in Leopold the Australian country town where I live, a long time survivor friend living with HIV surprisingly committed suicide. His untimely death caused me to write this chapter about the oft forgotten long term HIV survivors; at *Big Bunches* we valued life with all its meaningful foibles and that is why we fought for it.

All epidemics such as HIV- AIDS like an operation leaves scar tissue, not only for the long term survivors but for people like myself that survived the killing fields that was AIDS, it confounds me to realise that the friends and lovers we lost during the 80s, 90s are comparable with those young Australian soldiers who fought and died in the First World war at the western front battle fields.

I will come back to the suicide of my friend in a few paragraphs, I want to start on a happier note, beginning in 1990 when I needed some respite of HIV-AIDS because it had almost psychologically consumed me, I had started to act and think as though I myself was dying of HIV -AIDS. I thought the break would invigorate and restore my clarity of life; HIV-AIDS had fogged up some of the clear mirrors of my life.

I felt emotionally burned out after ten years of being a volunteer with VAC, I had to get out and escape to a heaven or something like it. I decided that heaven was to visit my "bromance" Ewen who lived in the hills between Byron Bay and Nimbin the infamous Australian Hippy town.

I first saw Ewen in 1976 when he worked at *Café Paradiso* in Lygon Street Carlton, in fact many of my friends whom I later met at *The University Club* worked there, most of the staff of 12 were young gay males usually university students. I noticed them because they were different in the way of self presentation their delightful quirky personalities stirred me, the geniality and efficient manner, clean well groomed and their body language had an attractive male sensuality and a sexy sparkle all at once. My straight male work colleagues at Australia Post had many lunches at *Café Paradiso* and often commented and wished they had such gay magnetism and panache to attract women, alas they did not. But it was Ewen who caught my special attention every time he smiled shyly at me making a Latte it was like bliss and I am sure it released great amounts of the infatuation hormone chemicals "Oxytocin and Serotonin", and that was only thinking about "bromance bliss", imagine what a gentle caress would have done.

Traveling by road coach to Byron Bay took all of 24 hours and an eighty dollar return bus fee: the bus journey was nonstop night and day except for frequent comfort stops. The ride gave the opportunity to see the country side and to meet all sorts of interesting people especially on the bus. Sitting next to an older Australian, friendly enough obviously not well read, slightly insular having a range of popular and mythical views. I switched on my new Walkman when I needed privacy and quiet, and had also taken "Memoirs of Hadrian" written by *Marguerite Yourcenar* a well known French Belgian writer who won the *Erasmus Prize* for exceptional contributions to culture literature and the social sciences, Marguerite was also the first woman to be a member of *Academie Francaise,* her partner of

40 years was *Grace Frick* they were of course Lesbian. Ewen had introduced me to her writings and on my Walkman I was listening to a cassette also given to me by Ewen about the Art Deco era crooner Al Bowlly so I was in the mood and well prepared for a joyous journey. It was on this trip that I learned from Jack Norris the all knowing passenger sitting next to me that, "poofters got it coming to them with this AIDS business" he kept telling me that they could only blame themselves, "they a acquired it you know they are not innocent," repeating it too many times sputtered with moral righteousness emphasizing the words "Acquired Immune Disease". Jack had previously told me that he was visiting his 34 year old daughter who was sadly diagnosed with cervical cancer and he himself had a heart disease. After his comments about "poofters acquiring" I gave him one of my contemptuous expressions and that shut him up, so much so that he said,"sorry mate no offense". It was beneath my dignity to tell him that he acquired his heart disease because of his lifestyle seeing he was a boozer, a smoker not to mention a Bible basher too, and his daughter well, she acquired the Human Papilloma Virus probably from sleeping around I thought, but did not say. I suddenly realised how pervasive HIV- AIDS had entered into the psyche of Australian society I could not get away from it; of course once Jack saw the title of my book he made some very homophobic comments about the ancient Romans and Greeks asking me in a half joking manner if I was doing it the Greek way, it was not the moment to get prickly with Jack as I realized I had to endure another 13 hours sitting next to him. I then understood that Jack Norris epitomises the ignorant type of "larrikin". But he did like Al Bowlly, poor bastard he said when the Luftwaffe dropped a parachute mine outside his house and it killed him at only 43 years of age.

Nevertheless Jack was not that bad he offered to shared his sandwiches with me including a tinny of warm VB Beer, this gesture showed that he actually liked me, and wanted to show Australian mateship especially after I told him I was a "poofter'; half jokingly I asked, "you're not bias Jack are you ? because small biases repeated over time can have large consequences". I think my comment flew over his head, what can one say about a man who told me firmly that James Cook had discovered Australia and the Dutch were completely irrelevant, did I say he was ignorant?

I have always objected to the name *Acquired Immune Deficiency Syndrome,* acquired is such a judgmental term. People living with AIDS already felt themselves being edged out of life through stigmatisation and being ostracised from the living healthy. HIV is now its proper name and that is what I will call it.

Now that I am in a much happier state of mind having buoyed myself up by reliving my pleasant memories being stoked on my way to see Ewen on the coach to Byron Bay. I will forward again to 2018 and the recent tragic events causing me to write this additional chapter about my friends, the long term. HIV survivors;

Seeing Ewen my "bromance" relieved me of being
stressed out by the HIV-AIDS syndromes

Suicide of an HIV Elder evokes powerful after effects.

Bill's suicide note said he was lonely felt isolated and lost all meaning, he felt that people like him had faded from public consciousness and he believed that he no longer had a useful function in life and that society had side lined him. I felt guilty, he lived near me and I should have visited more often instead of once per week, I am sorry that I never asked him what his life was like while he was ill, he did tell me once that he wanted to leave behind specific messages about himself, I neglected to pick up on this and I regret it now when it's too late. I could always sense his excitement whenever he got a visit, he seemed happy or perhaps he was just pretending, several of his acquaintances who tried hard to create a bond with long term HIV survivors depending on each other for emotional and economic support. During the times we talked together he always presented someone else's opinions and I felt his life was a mimicry having some mind demons from which he could not escape, yet he had such a handsome face that for most of the time carried a gloomy expression, now I realise that he kept most things to himself, there was no outlet to express his emotions. Bill had no relatives they had all died and depended on us, his extended family. I had also suggested he moved to the city to be near the support systems especially for People living with HIV etc, but high accommodation rents and other costs made that impossible. Bill suffered from depression the crux and the crucible of his demon, which at times made it difficult to visit, but thank goodness we persisted even though he could be brusque and was astoundingly fastidious about insignificant little things such as which side of his coffee I would have to place the tea spoon for stirring, or only ring the bell once when calling on him. We had contacted *Beyond Blue* the organisation with the slogan "R U OK" seeking advice on what could be done for Bill, they encourage people to talk freely about their depression without attaching any stigma to mental health issues.

Lunches and coffees with Laurence Hutchins

Our luncheons were never the superficial type, instead they were always loaded with funny illuminating, humorous and authentic talk, mixed with good gossip, not much small talk if any . We're having these lunches, at iconic Melbourne Cake shops, restaurants and Cafes, wandering into old book shops. I am eager to capture as much as possible of Laurence's memory because both of us are of the generation that lived through and still lives with the AIDS experience. Each time we meet up it's like performing the past, a replay of the theatre of the memory.

"The spectrum of HIV never leaves you; it stays with you everyday even after 36 years, the residue of HIV eventually catches up" said my friend Laurence Hutchins after he was diagnosed with pancreatic cancer in April 2018. Laurence appeared not too upset rationalising that he had received 36 bonus years after doctors told him in 1983 that he only had six months to live, "therefore to say my days are numbered signifies nothing: they always were", and so it is for all of us. Laurence then sold his house and most of his possessions embarking on a last hooray whirlwind world tour before his time ran out. But as he said in so many words, the emotional world of preparing himself to let go, had to be reversed when life was given back to him and he needed to take up life's cudgels again, that was all difficult, considering Laurence had outlived two partners who died of HIV complications and recently lost his 18 year old companion *Arky* his pet dog; suffering can be a very long moment only if you surrender to it, Laurence tries not to but it is still tough, softened only by caring friends, good memories a cigarette, a Latte together with a French Vanilla slice. Ironically, his last partner was Martin who baked the first cake for our VAC support group about 38 years ago at his mothers' cake shop in Acland Street St Kilda. Only then Martin was called by his Jewish name Mordecai.

During our coffee times we do get moments of melancholia when we remember hundreds of the friends we've known and who died too soon at the very prime of their lives. I call that 'friendship sadness'. But in reality they are not really dead are they? Because they are not forgotten, it reminds me of this song from my Fair Lady;-

"I have often walked down this street before "Just to know somehow they are near. The overpowering feeling that any second they may suddenly appear."

No they are not forgotten! when Laurence tells me he was volunteering with the *VAC Quilt Memory* group how he would feel two emotions all at once, sad and happy, sad because too many Gay men died alone even shunned by their own mothers or families, and often they died without obituaries let alone a grave marker, such was the stigma of AIDS; the other emotion of happy occurred when a mother, father brother or sister came in to display or sought assistance from Laurence with making their AIDS memorial Quilts that always caused great joy and warmth. The Quilt for a loved one was and is the conscience of the HIV epidemic a resonant way to remember friends to challenge prejudice, and at the time during the eighties a handmade "social media" all people connected to this patchwork of fabric. I thought that may be one day the AIDS Quilt will have its own Smartphone app to find lost lives of our friends. Then there were the drug trials, Laurence said he was part of a group that trialed new HIV drugs, musing and wondered how any people were saved and benefited by these trials.

Laurence became friends with Vaughan's mum
through the placement of this touching Quilt
placed by the parents of this young man.

Remembrance is good therapy

As we habitually talk about the past we galvanised the ties that binds us together by recalling we gain and activate additional memory traces renewing or reconnecting in our own minds, by reliving and refashioning we are positively sustained by good feelings. We often laugh at our sense of nostalgia when we were sitting in the *Monarch Cake Shop* in Acland street straight out of the 1950's everything is the same, old worn threadbare chairs handwritten notifications, period cup and saucers some chipped, all original old pictorial magazines books from the 60's 70's 80's stacks of them and usually playing popular Gay Anthems a feast of nostalgia. We sense our loss of friends through nostalgia and the passing of time, the poignancy of it of frequently leads us to idealise and depart completely from reality the world of HIV AIDS we left behind, but I don't think that is such a bad thing, throughout history we gays had to depart from reality just to survive. Fantasy, imagination, creativity and our dreams, but never reflectors of things boring or other peoples thoughts; our survival function and contribution to civilization thrived on the unreal until we made it real, all of it.

Sometimes we tried to play a game of one upmanship for the fun of it, about the celebrities we had personally met. I mentioned Peter Allen (Australian singer –songwriter who died from a HIV related disease on 18 June 1992) meeting him on the beat, sorry I meant beach and several other celebrities I have mentioned elsewhere, but I have to say Laurence topped the lot when he had dinner with Richard Burton and Elizabeth Taylor at their home in Acapulco Mexico, that's when Laurence was in the US working as a representative for *Qantas* the Australian National Airline.

Every time we met for coffee and cakes or chatted over the phone we generated shared memory and the collective history of our parents. Laurence's parents Alfred, aka Chum his nickname, and Nancy his mum, were like my parents, enlightened people who totally accepted and loved their sons just the way we were. His dad Chum was training as an Australian Air force Pilot in Britain in 1941 part of *NO 457 an RAAF fighter Squadron* of World War II. At the beginning of the war learning how to fly Spitfires and fought the *Luftwaffe* then later they sailed back to

Australia on the *MV Stirling Castle* but the Spitfires were flown modified for the long flight back to Australia. During the fiftieth Anniversary of the battle of Britain Chum and all the other Spitfires pilots that were alive then were invited to Buckingham Palace unfortunately Chum was unable to attend due to health reasons but Nancy attended the celebrations after Queen Elizabeth II especially invited her to represent her husband and to accept the "thank you" to Australia's contribution to the defense of Britain. Laurence regretfully did not meet the Queen and had to make do seeing his mum sitting on the dais with the Queen taking the Spitfire fly by Salute. Before Nancy took her place on the dais she met the Queen Mother who appeared that morning at Nancy's breakfast table in her dressing gown, all these intriguing stories created a live theatre of memories. Then there were the stories of Joan Golding's friendship with Nancy both women cared for families struck by the curse of HIV-AIDS.

Long time HIV Survivor Laurence and his best friend for 18 years Arky
RIP Laurence died on Friday 6 July 2018.

Eddie an old *Big Bunches Customer* survived all these years, until.

Only yesterday we were discussing with his other friends the design of a memorial HIV-AIDS Quilt for Eddie (Edward) he too survived for thirty odd years but had many health problems, may be caused by the early HIV antiviral cocktails of tablets and capsules including the AZT drug with its too many side effects. I know that in his life he had done too much grieving and like Laurence lost a lot of friends and lovers. In the end he had withdraw keeping mostly to himself he was far too proud, and could no longer look at himself in the mirror, as he felt the loss of not being desirable to himself and others, as a result he became lonely especially at night when he could not sleep and he suffered from Aids survivor syndrome a sort of Post Traumatic Stress Disorder (PTSD). Yet when we did come together for cakes and coffee in Acland Street, Sundays lunches at the Queenscliff Yacht club, he put up a front as though the devil may care seemingly relaxed, yet I knew that he was like a butterfly that fluttered more then it flew. We had began work on restoring his feeling of being desirable again, and together had gone shopping for some designer clothes made possible because he had received almost 600 dollars worth of Birthday gift vouchers from all his friends for clothes, we both loathed the conforming styles and sameness of design and colour of mass produced clothing manufacturing. Eddie had also joined the gym another birthday gift membership that was useful (especially when your income is very limited) he came with me three times per week considering me as his personal trainer, we talked much or were silent he was one of those rare sweet man with whom it was nice to be silent with as well as to talk. Three days before he died he told me that he was getting firmer erections and said that must be because I can look at myself in the mirror again and thinking about all the eye candy at the gym: then he suddenly died. Now the memorial Quilt; we will stitch include his jacket from *Scotch and Soda* a Dutch male fashion house, he loved good design and smartness. I will make sure this is reflected by sowing his jacket onto the Quilt.

After his death last week, talking to Eddie's doctor, who told us that People living with HIV are experiencing a range of non AIDS related co morbidities (co morbidity, the presence of two diseases) are at a higher risk as they age for developing chronic non AIDS conditions such as heart diseases and cancer and they may do so at a younger age, Eddie suffered from Kidney impairment and bone loss - osteoporosis and a heart condition which eventually killed him he was 62 years. He had kept his new medical conditions a secret yet we could see his gradual deterioration, but not serious enough for us to think he was not long for this world, death was never the most important thing in our circle of friends living and loving, that was the function and purpose of our lives.

Finally the Bus Coach arrived at Byron Bay where much to my excitement Ewen was waiting for me in his vintage 1953 FJ Holden Ute, hopefully as happy to see me as I was him. I need not to have worried the first glances conveyed emotion and love. The ride up to the hamlet of *Rosebank* in *The Night Cap Mountain Ranges* is initially a fantasy experience because the area is still revealing its mystery and intrigue being the most ancient forest refugia in Australia from the Gondwanic period some 200 million years ago. Steep winding unsealed narrow roads with nail baiting hairpin bends rugged yet gentle, having many types of multi stemmed Eucalyptus trees spreading their green canopies of scented leaves as welcoming arches hanging over the roads and the abundant road side ferns waving, not to mention the senses being bedazzled by the many other plant and shrub varieties including the imported Camphor trees spreading like noxious weeds among the lush semi tropical native vegetation.

After a one hour's drive windows half open for fresh air and much evocative talking recalling memories we suddenly stopped at what seemed to me a slow flowing river, a faded old name plate said *Coopers Creek,* instead it was a low water ford crossing, the entrance to Ewen's and Bradley's property. My watch showed 11 am, time for my mood and sociability enhancer, hinting at a coffee, desiring the ones Ewen used to make at *Café Paradiso;* the cool humidity positively affected my temperament and with coffee it would even get better. I could hardly believe my eyes what beauty they saw, everything instantly felt romantic even more so when I got out of the 'ute' I was delightfully confronted with a magnificent paradise, a garden of Eden but better, Ewen had designed his garden to flow with the surroundings of the forest in opposition to it being strictly symmetrical. I felt an immediate liberating force, nature for me is a source of sensual pleasure and spiritual insights, the 'mysterious stimuli' I called it. The way of inner beauty, was reflected in his garden. Coopers Creek, I had no doubt, was the river Pishon running through the garden of Eden and later in edenic style we would have nude swims together with the biggest dragon Goanna's I had ever seen. Like Eden fruit trees abounded, guava trees, fig, orange, macadamia, plum, nectarine mango and a smothering of very large old Eucalyptus trees and large Morton Bay Fig Trees planted by the previous owner Mrs. Tickle 70 years ago.

Their 1920's large wooden Edwardian style house painted pale green featured impressive Art Novae timber fret work, inside it was mostly Art Deco style furniture and fittings and Deco wool woven Frieze hangings with themes reflecting elegant lines and curves of human and botanical forms, exciting shapes. I don't find it strange that I always gravitate to men that adored Art Deco and those who delighted in it. I recall Ewen saying the search for beauty is the real secret of a happy fulfilling life, that philosophy was clearly demonstrated here in his paradise. These were interesting handsome, intelligent hard working men yet deep down there was something, and sadly I knew what it was, despairing for the moment because my premonitions and intuitions are always spot on. I was determined to enjoy my stay for the moment. The abode was shared with Bradley and Julian both of whom I knew were HIV positive, interesting men with a great Australian sense of humor and a polite deprecation of themselves, down to earth with no obnoxious pretences that were obvious; yet I still have to meet a gay man with absolutely no pretences. I mostly see pretentiousness as a sign of a curious mind, a driving force in the art because it entails risks to be different, some people take pretentiousness out of context and foolishly use it as a term of judgment; they read books, were artistically and scientifically inclined, great conversationalist, listening to them always resulted in the expansion of my consciousness, and not the least they were cafe latte drinkers and occasional weed smokers, these type of men showed me that intimacy did not rest on only drinking champagne.

Ewen and Bradley had earlier been part of what could be called a Gay self sustainable farm named Eungella after a nearby town. The farm was created by seven gay urban boys from Melbourne : Ewen, Martin Jeffrey Rodney Tony Robert and Bradley who all had a desires of going back to the land, its main mentor and facilitator was Jeffrey Hill whom I occasionally met in Melbourne, he had a certain intellectual clarity in which he analysed things, he told me once that the idea of Gay men starting a sort of a commune farm for him stemmed from a certain social emptiness that gay men felt before Gay law reform and his disillusionment with the daily slog of his work in Melbourne. I was well aware of many gay men moving up to the North West of NSW in the early 1970, I met Johnny Allen one of the organizer and gay activist he invited me then to the 1973 *Nibbim Aquarius Festival* that was Australia's Woodstock thousands attended, including Gay men and women forging connections and networks albeit in an almost clandestine way, from that moment on many took the "great trek" escaping from the oppression, marginalisation and persecutions they were experiencing in not being allowed to be authentic and express their real selves including sexuality, because being Gay was yet a criminal offence in Australia, not unlike the Dutch - Afrikaner Boers "trekking' and establishing their own areas and nation states, escaping from their English oppressors.

Chapter 30

Eugenella a Gay Household of seven wiped out by HIV-AIDS

The Lesbian recipes intrigued us immensely as we had never eaten Lesbian food yes and I have to admit that the food served that afternoon by the boys was a kind of extended orgasm of taste and art and style.

The land from Nimbin to Jeffrey's place was situated on the ancient remains of a gigantic volcano plateau evident by huge pieces from the volcanic ring still standing raised like peaks in the forms of giant stalagmites. Ancient rocks looking down on us mortals hundreds of feet below, feeling connected with this beautiful earth, for me this was not a little emotional thing, spirituality is not always emotional, it is much more, a tree does something to most humans it calms, it evokes thoughts, I want to touch, kiss and hug it. No, it was not something initiated by my mind, the stimulation of my thoughts came from the trees, rocks sky and fresh air, thoughts and more thoughts of peace and calm, overcome with tranquil beauty, this continued as we chugged along in the FJ Holden ute.

The beauty of Eugenella and the hospitality we received was unequalled anywhere I had experienced up till then, like Ewen's place, Jeffrey and Rodney were also living in a paradise garden and abode which I equated with heaven on earth.

We were lead to the kitchen for fresh drinks bitter lime and lemons on ice, home made from fresh lemons and limes, then the books : 'de-Javue' there in a flash before me I saw the great Gay and Lesbian writers those who changed and enhanced the thinking of the civilized world, coincidently I had with me the book *The Counterfeiter* the story of homosexuality in pre WarII Paris by Andre Gide, then there was Rainer Maria Milke, Patrick White, Gertrude Stein, Marguerite Youcenar, Jean Cocteau, Christopher Isherwood,Oscar Wilde, and Dutch Gay writer Gerard Reve no doubt left by Martin who was fluent in the Dutch language . Now was not the time to talk about books but I knew I was with kindred spirits, not the usual thing one would expect in an Australian country kitchen but that's not where it ended. These men delighted in art they painted and sketched evident by the warm colored and unassuming pieces conspicuously hung everywhere even the dunney seemed a mini art gallery, unassuming I said, except for one small *David Hockney* a painting of a child and a number, minimalist I thought, not being an art specialist, which Jeffrey said he picked up in the early 1960s I asked, how much? he gave me a slow gentle smile, his discipline of prudence said enough.

The boys had really prepared for our visit, fresh large banana leaves and palm leaves were strategically placed in the vine covered 1920s pergola to provide extra cooling shade from the hot piercing sun. Jeffrey put on some old 75 Bakelite records featuring Al Bowlly then to my surprise he showed me his *Alice B Toklas Cookbook* containing her superb but robust Lesbian recipes they had prepared and were going to be cooked on their BBQ built from volcanic rocks gathered from around the property it was lit even on this hot and humid day. The Lesbian recipes intrigued us immensely as we had never eaten Lesbian food yes and I have to admit that the food served that afternoon by the boys was a kind of extended orgasm of taste and art and style. The topics of conversations besides the garden, planting seasons, donkeys chooks and geese, was about the fact that gay men were much more then handsomeness and having sexy bodies, Patrick White Australia only ever Nobel Prize winner for literature and his bitchy type of humour were talked about and the time he came down to their farm: before Jeffrey could continue telling the story the telephone rang, softly speaking, while everyone was quietly pretending not to eavesdrop, a message came to hand that Julian a very close friend of theirs and Ewen, had died from HIV –AIDS complications; the boys faces changed from joyous animation of a nano second ago to gloomy frowns of vexations dawning on their handsome faces. Our own vulnerability was once again presented by the death of another, the continued devastation of the HIV –AIDS seemed to continue unabated with no let up yet, little did I realise that there would not be a let up, the residue of long term HIV survivors would be with us it seems forever and that's a long time.

After a while of reminiscing about Julian and coming to terms with his death, Rodney with his tranquil honest eyes would tell me that he would plant a tree for Julian I asked him if there were other trees in memory of friends that have passed away Oh yes he said a whole forest he mentioned a Greame Humphries from Geelong did I know him? Then I mention Martin Golding he smiled saying that Martin has a whole forest planted to memorize him although it need some cleaning and weeding especially when Joan, his mother would come shortly to pay a visit.

They were great hosts, I was enchanted by their genuine curiosity, intelligence and humour; I folded them into my heart and memory for ever. All of the boys died with the exception of Ewen, the forest of memory is dense and the quilts are many.

A quilt was made and a tree planted

Chapter 31

Their legacy

This last chapter is written as a journal entry to the boys who died as though they were still alive today. I am telling them that they did not die for nothing, their deaths and struggles cumulated in a "legacy of good things" they're no longer languishing, their suffering is done, of course I would rather they were alive today just the same.

Dear Boys,

I am writing this entry with radiant emotions as though your blood were pulsing through every word on these pages of our book.

Finally done! My promise fulfilled to you, Robert, Dirk, Angelo and Jason representing as it were the thousands of gay men who died of this virus, memorialized forever, you're collectively deeply imprinted and imbedded in the consciousness of the world, your footsteps of achievements will not fade or peter out in the twilight of HIV-AIDS now that it is no longer a death sentence.

Every day of my life I remember those times when you were all physically still walking or dancing around on planet Earth. Despite living in a constant state of uncertainty you kept singing your songs, painting your pictures, writing your poetry, prose and books, directing your movies, creating fashion and conducting your orchestras, designing your buildings. Together we read aloud, shared thoughts and memories, looked at photos, played board games and piano, watched movies, went on bush hikes, and made steaming cups of coffee and soothing soups – especially my warm *snert* (Dutch pea soup). We cuddled or hugged when that was necessary, had very quiet moments and abundant deep, serious and jovial uplifting conversations.

History elucidates that you made the magic happen because of your insatiable exploratory drive in fighting for survival, with an energy that shook up the unbending bureaucratic systems that no longer adequately coped or understood that you were fighting for your lives. You showed courage and resilience by breaking the yoke and chains of conventionalism and all of its distortions and myths, especially as there was no epic in recent history that could console you except our friendships. It was through these trails that all of us were connected to something much bigger then ourselves, it was "empathy" a mysterious process of you entering our minds and hearts like a symbiosis becoming part of another, almost like sex becoming "one" an "altruism" a self transcending experience that longed to enter a virtual symbiotic joining with you, for me this was an expansion of my consciousness, a feeling of oneness and solidarity with your vulnerability. The AIDS crisis demonstrated that altruism clearly was practiced, that generosity was sustainable and that our kindness was more authentic than what most organised religions only preach. Altruism in the gay community was our survival instinct because, especially in those early days of the crisis, no one else cared about us.

All of you expressed your inquisitiveness as though I had a crystal ball, wanting to know what being gay would be like in 35 years' time. You all seem to be curious whether your young lives had made any positive difference and what the longer impact of HIV-AIDS had been on the world at large.

Since your deaths, the Gay world has changed almost beyond recognition from what it was prior to 1993. Now every Gay man and woman in the world can be connected together through the "Internet" all of us are now only a few nano seconds away from each other no matter where we are on planet earth. The internet has changed our thought processes, the way we think and act and it has altered our relationships especially our mating strategies, we now have access to millions of potential Gay partners instantly! It is both a blessing and a curse, a curse because we have become a culture where there is no respite from blame and complaint 24/7 and corporate charity has taken over from personal empathy and altruism we have collectively been desensitised. If there is a problem to be solved the "Smart-phone" has the answers and Google will give all sorts of information including disinformation, a fact and a counter fact, an experts opinion and a counter experts opinion all in a nano flash of time, and our thought processes if any are often reflecting the thoughts of another. The blessings have been that the tyranny of distances have vanished, we can talk face to face through "skype" with loved ones knowledge is shared quickly For the record I use the internet in a active positive way rather then in a reactive negative.

The younger gay *Millennials* rarely know anybody who died because of HIV/AIDS. To me these *Millennials,* are from another planet and that is not a bad thing. I rather like aliens; they intrigue me. They have different norms and values compared to us "Gay baby boomers", counterculture people and early Gay liberationists. They now all have cell phones the new social prostheses together with their plastic water bottles a virtual brain implant often outsourcing their own minds. Seemingly for some, Gay norms and values have changed primarily due to technology. The new smart phone-based applications, such as *Grindr* or *Scruff,* for Gay males *Her* for women and *Tinder* for straights have enabled people to meet virtually. The electronic meat market: here you are impersonally dealt with, as if a disposable commodity, with little or no face-to-face communication. Definitely no empathy let alone altruism! One look and touch of a screen and you are judged, deleted, conned or dismissed if your image is not sexually desirable. People put up tasteless messages on their profiles, such as "No fems" or Asians, fats, blacks or old creeps. No wonder many gay men feel anxious because they think they are not handsome or well-endowed enough. Because of these dating apps, psychiatrists have reported an increase in body dysmorphia in Gay men. Umberto's dictum of "a standing cock has no conscience" is spot on in the case of these new apps. I have recently discovered a new word to describe these new apps: "solipsism" meaning an extreme preoccupation with one's own ego.

Sadly hundreds of Gay venues and businesses have closed, including the demise of many stylish gay cafes, clothes and bookshops and other places of "rendezvous" depriving younger people of safe meeting places. You probably remember your first kiss, dance or heart break in a Gay bar, they were safe places where you could try out being your real self. The Gay world is changing as it finds its equilibrium in a world were we are now treated "equally" under the law: recently Melbourne's *Grey Hound Hotel* and Sydney's ultimate gay icon the *Midnight Shift* shut their doors for good mainly through lack of patronage and high rents.

May be the closing down of so many Gay places and neighbourhoods is the cumulative effect of these electronic Apps providing alternative "virtual" dating pick up places: or may be many GLBTI people are settling into marital bliss and monogamy since gay marriage is now available to 23 civilised countries in the western word covering 1.2 billion people. As an aside, I have to tell you boys that I have been to eight same sex marriages already since it legally took effect in Australia on the 11 January 2018. You know our friends Henk and Patrick were one of first ssm cab of the rank for me when they tied the knot on the 11th January 2018 after being together for 30 years, it was actually thanks to your advocacy efforts 35 odd years ago that same sex marriage came about, thank you.

Attending Henk's and Patrick's, marriage, my first same sex marriage on the very day it was made legal on 11 January 2018

I can hear you say in my mind how sad it is that there are no longer the golden gay miles as they once were in the Castro streets, Commercial Roads or Oxford Streets or London's Gay Soho were 151 Gay bars shut down in a four year period, sadly once bright creative Gay Mecca's of the world are boarded up returning the expensive neighborhoods to blandness, boring middleclass gentrifications pushing the bright, creative innovative GLBTI people out because of exorbitant high rents. Oh but there is good news too remember when we visited the oldest continuously run gay bar in the world 't Mandje established in 1927 at Zeedijk 63, Amsterdam. 't Mandje brings me back to 1990, when I visited there with Arjen and Dirk how could I ever forget it because I was attacked outside the venue by some backward-thinking Nederlanders, who unfortunately drew their bigotry from their religion's intolerance toward gay sexuality. There are still many gay dance clubs in Amsterdam.

Yes, and yet it was a big surprise when U.S. Supreme Court, legalised same-sex marriage in 2015 and another, albeit expected surprise when it finally also became law in Australia on 11 January 2018, but not through a parliamentary vote, no! We were denied direct access to Australia's representative democracy, instead many were traumatised as we were all humiliated as GLBTI citizens in having our equal rights put through a voluntary postal vote, and for four months it was open slather for hate vilification and misinformation by the likes of the Australian Christian Lobby and their cohorts including Sydney's Anglican diocese who contributed 1 Million Australian Dollars to the "No Gay marriage campaign" it was despicable shameful donation. Jesus wept.

The good news was that we won the voluntary postal vote with more than 12.7 million Australians voting, a huge turnout of 79% registered voters of whom 61. 6% voted "Yes" and 38.4% voted "No"; a decisive victory, an incredible show of support. Yes love won in the end as we knew it always would and will. I have placed a front page news paper picture of our mutual friend Phil *Carswell* showing the moment in Australia when the results of the Postal vote were read out, you'll remember him being the first President of the VAC. But there is a bright side to the story: the churches' hold on society is now greatly loosened and they further lost all moral authority when at about the same time *The Royal Commission into*

Institutional Responses to Sexual Abuse came out in 17 Volumes detailing the sordid criminal activities of moralistic religious conservatives.

Picture courtesy: Courier Mail Brisbane. See our
erstwhile Phil Carswell hands on head overwhelmed,
like we all were on 17November 2017

Thanks to you, everything you sowed is bearing fruit, our well developed activists and advocacy skills practiced during the counterculture years of the 1960's and the early AIDS years of the late 1970's and early 1980's were passed on by us old battle axes to the new Gay *Millennial* generation, they stood on our shoulders and finished the job.

Our dearest Jason, our in-house medical AIDS researcher and long-term HIV/AIDS survivor from Monash University passed away in early 2017. Just a few months before he died talking about this book he posed a question, no doubt to encourage me to continue writing, saying "what do the HIV/AIDS crises of 30 years ago matter for us today, and what would be the portrait of a society that emerged".

Well Jason you being a medical AIDS researcher together with Gay activists changed the way Medicine was done, the patient became empowered and the pharmaceutical drug companies held accountable for subsidised research cost and manufacture, not the least in the production of cheaper cost effective generic drugs, the world's poorer nations are benefitting from these today.

We have come a long way since the cards were stacked against beginning from day one, when the first person with GRID (later called HIV/AIDS) was diagnosed. Things immediately went from bad to worse never forgetting the early days that in hospitals in cities like San Francisco and Melbourne, we had to wear protective clothing and masks to serve your food or even to visit you. But we refused to wear those white protective chemical overalls and the breathing masks, and protested against the bio hazard signs placed on the doors of your hospital room, they were signs of fear, ignorance and prejudice.

Many of you were guinea pigs in trying new potential antiviral drugs and alternative medicine. Most of these treatments did not ultimately work, giving you false hope. But you figured anything was worth a try as it was better than nothing, although many of the drugs tested on you were good for treating other diseases. You taught us how to question doctors about drugs and treatments giving you the ability to choose and manage your own medical treatment, forever changing doctor-patient relationships. We're all indebted to this legacy, all people with AIDS and those with other illnesses or diseases who are now living longer, thanks in no small part to your pioneering HIV/AIDS treatments.

Your legacy took gay culture out of the closet and placed it on the world stage. Before HIV/AIDS hit in Australia and elsewhere in the West, gay people were isolated in society, so we developed our own underground cultures where we could belong. We formed our own tribe in opposition not dissimilar then to the *Sacred Band of Thebes*, an army of 300 male soldiers and their boyfriends, all couples. They were a special Greek military force defeating every intruder, including the fearless Spartans at Tegyra in 375 BCE, lasting for forty years, not only as a military power but also as catalyst for cultural enlightenment. They were the most potent military force in all of Thebes. To think that the gays totally obliterated much bigger and powerful "straight" armies, so much for the stereotype of being sissies! I believe that all the gay men that died between the 1980 and 1995 were like the *Sacred Band of Thebes*: courageous, resilient, just, authentic and honest. The ancients' legacy is still being discussed centuries later and yours, my dears, will be, too. You opened the eyes of the world to recognize an open and inclusive gay culture.

Gay culture restored true human values. Everything to do with the AIDS phenomenon caused our lives to be thrown out into the open for all to see. We knew that authenticity and social justice, respect and empathy for all people would win the day and would forever liberate us from the prisons of an underground Gay culture. Straight suburban culture prior to 1980s had diminished us with lies and innuendos until AIDS reared its ugly head and mainstream society could no longer pretend that we did not exist. The gay community had long been designated as criminal so we created our own values. We formed those values through our search for objective truths because society's values, as far as gay issues were concerned, were hypocritical and false. Values that also considered women as less valued than men. Other gay values included equality, wholeness, authenticity, civil rights and freedom of thoughts in all things and equality before the law for everybody, not just for millionaires and billionaires, as is now the case. You showed us that a famous footballer is no more esteemed than a harpsichord player or drag queen. Gay people generally value and celebrate what is unique like no other.

Your collective suffering unfolded our Gay Identity. Every human being wants to mould their own identity. Young Australians want to have an Australian identity. That is why thousands travel each year to the shores of Gallipoli, in Turkey, where their great-grandfathers died as young men. So, every year on Anzac Day, 25 April, many Australians attend the ritual of a long night vigil at *Lone Pine* in Turkey, virtually sitting on the blood and bone of their ancestors, searching for meaning and identity. So it was with your battle with AIDS: your identity changed from the moment you became a person living with the HIV virus. Instead of visiting Gallipoli for our identity, we found ours in the hundreds of Pride Marches and Parades worldwide, we felt connected by listening to any of the great Gay composers, singing the Gay anthems: *I will Survive, I am What I am, You make me feel mighty real, Go west* all anthems of our identity. Then, further we see and feel our identity in reading the books of most famous Gay literacy geniuses and we resonated with identity symbols of Gay solidarity: *the pink triangle* as well as new symbols of hope, such as the *Red Ribbon* and the waving and sounds of the fluttering *Rainbow Pride Flags* around the world. Then there was the largest moving memorial the world had ever seen the AIDS quilt weighing and estimated 54 tons, it is the largest piece of community folk art in the world nothing of the sort has surpassed it. The AIDS Quilt started off as one panel measuring 90 by 80 centimeters made by the highly respected gay activist and author *Cleve Jones* in 1987, to honour the memory of his partner, Marvin Feldman. We followed Cleve's example in Australia and as you know we made all of you and everyone mentioned in this book a memorial Quilt, truly a gay cultural phenomenon and a touching memorialisation of human hardship, perseverance in love. The quilt project was nominated for the 1989 Nobel Peace Prize.

Some say gay identity is a social construction and this may be true, but then every identity is likewise a construction. We are gay (or bisexual) because we are sexually attracted to the same sex; that is our common identity. This has been so since the Neanderthals and Homo Erectus wandered the earth. Of course, sex is not the only aspect of our identity; "who" we are is much more important. Hopefully, dears, the last 29 chapters have been about who we are, not who we have sex with! The gay identity is not about stereotypical clones, such as being camp, feminine, butch, muscular, bear or brawn or whatever else. Gay identity is such that we can pick out a GLTBI person from the crowd as though we have a sixth sense bordering on EGSP, (Extra Gay Sensory Perception) It takes one to know one. I found our identity is really in our genes when reading a book by Harvard professor emeritus Edward O Wilson the world's preeminent biologist and naturalist. His studies led him to conclude that:

[A] low dose of homosexual-tending genes may give competitive advantages to a practicing heterosexual. Or, homosexuality may give advantages to a group by special talents, unusual qualities of personality, and to specialized roles and professions it generates. There is abundant evidence that such is the case in both preliterate and modern societies. Either way, societies are mistaken to disapprove of homosexuality because gays have different sexual preferences and reproduce less. Their presence should be valued for what they contribute

constructively to human diversity. A society that condemns homosexuality harms itself".[1]

This is not the final word; your legacies continue to bring benefits to society. You would agree that our fight was never a single issue. We were not only fighting the AIDS epidemic; that alone would not have won the battle. Our battle was as much about social justice, equality before the law for all people, and, perhaps hardest of all fights, acceptance in the broader community. It was against poverty as well. So many times, our boys and girls lost their homes or their jobs because they suddenly became sick or were bullied because they were gay. More serious still, some of our gay brothers and sisters lost their lives through hopelessness and committed suicide. The issues were life or death for thousands and your legacy demonstrates that, even in death, you fought to bring dignity to millions of lives, then, now and into the future.

Yet in many ways the differences between gays and straights have diminished. Generally, we are much more accepted, although there are segments of the population that remain antagonistic, ignorant or homophobic, and want special exemptions under law to discriminate against us and I am sorry to say most Christian Churches are guilty of all of these, with the exception of the *Uniting Church in Australia* its governing body accepting Same Sex Marriage completely and has publically stated that it wants no exemption and special treatment under Australian Law; that is the ability to discriminate against same sex families, gay students at religious schools, not employing GLBTI people and an ability to sack them at will and refusing housing rental, these are issues about which we need to be continuously vigilant. In Melbourne, the Labor State Government has invested A$15 million in the upcoming *Victorian Pride Centre* in St Kilda. We have come a very long way, indeed. As a sign of this hopeful future, I have chosen the last picture for this book, a picture of a same-sex family, Oliver and David and their three happy children. Family and love and acceptance: that is our shared future.

---

[1] E.O. Wilson, *The Social Conquest of Earth* page 254 Liveright Publishing Corporations.

I have chosen the last picture for this book, a picture of a same-sex family, Oliver and David and their three happy children. Family, love and acceptance: that is our shared future.

www.ingramcontent.com/pod-product-compliance
Lightning Source LLC
Chambersburg PA
CBHW030409130626
46549CB00004B/1689